Curriculum, Culture, and Art Education

SUNY series, Innovations in Curriculum

Kerry Freedman, editor

Edited by
KERRY FREEDMAN
FERNANDO HERNÁNDEZ

Curriculum, Culture and Art Education

Comparative Perspectives

STATE UNIVERSITY OF NEW YORK PRESS

Published by
State University of New York Press, Albany

© 1998 State University of New York

For information, address State University of New York Press,
State University Plaza, Albany, NY 12246

Production design by David Ford and M. R. Mulholland
Marketing by Fran Keneston

Library of Congress Cataloging-in-Publication Data

Curriculum, culture, and art education : comparative perspectives /
    edited by Kerry Freedman, Fernando Hernández.
        p.   cm. — (SUNY series, innovations in curriculum)
    Includes bibliographical references and index.
    ISBN 0-7914-3773-6 (alk. paper). — ISBN 0-7914-3774-4 (pbk. :
alk. paper)
    1. Art—Study and teaching—Case studies. I. Freedman, Kerry J.
II. Hernández y Hernández, Fernando. III. Series.
N85.C87 1998
707—dc21   97-47444
                                                                                         CIP

10   9   8   7   6   5   4   3   2   1

Contents

Acknowledgments

Contributions from many people go into any edited book. The most apparent, of course, are the chapter authors. We thank the authors who graciously allowed us to include their work in this book.

The editors would also like to thank Arthur Norberg, David Thistlewood, Paul Duncum, and four anonymous reviewers for their helpful comments about various chapters. We greatly appreciated the support we have received from Priscilla Ross and the other people at State University of New York Press. Thanks to Elisa Barros, for her help with translation in São Paulo, to Karen Olsen Beran for her help with the index, and to Cathy Zemke for her help with formatting. We are grateful to the McKnight Arts and Humanities Fund for International Travel and the Institute of International Studies and Programs at the University of Minnesota for helping to defray travel costs. Finally, warm regards go to David, Rosalyn, and Debra Thistlewood, who very kindly hosted a meeting in their home between the editors.

Kerry Freedman
Fernando Hernández

Introduction

Cultural Histories of a School Subject

International comparisons of education are useful on several levels. They can help us to understand our location in the world as part of a professional community and provide a vehicle for examining what we have in common across national borders. They can illustrate the vital differences of culture that have been a basis for distinctions between nation states and the formation of national identities. Comparative studies can reflect educational conditions at the macro level, such as the influence of "modernization" and centralization on policy, and at the micro level of regional and local practice (Altbach, Arnove, & Kelly, 1982).

In the past, the idea of separating macro and micro levels of investigation has been an important underlying influence in the shaping of comparative educational research. Recently, however, researchers in the field of international education have called for a marriage of these levels of study for an analysis of how structural factors, such as social class relations or the degree of centralization of political authority and control of the state over education, and international factors, such as importation of textbooks and curricula, affect who learns what from whom with what effects (Altbach et al., 1982).

These structural factors shape education and are dependent upon conditions of culture. The international factors are also influenced by culture, not only in their formation, but in their transferal and implementation because when curriculum is moved from one location to another, it is

1

transformed through reinterpretation in the new context.

In part, it is because such transformations occur, that an analysis of curriculum in its relation to national, cultural contexts must be done if we are to understand education from an international perspective. Culture is not a unified whole (Clifford, 1988). Even the culture within national boundaries exists as fragments loosely connected through experience and geography. Through the process of identity construction, people consciously and unconsciously select and move the fragments to new conceptual and physical locations, resulting in shifts in the cultural landscape. These shifts often involve the recycling of cultural ideas and practices that may give the appearance of stasis, but are continually changing as new combinations of social life are juxtaposed one with another by individuals and groups.

It is because culture is not static that cultural analyses of curriculum must include considerations of the past. Historical studies cannot help us predict the future. Events in the past will never be precisely repeated and we have no way of knowing which of the many trends of the past will continue on. However, history can help us to understand the present and the range of possibilities for its interpretation.

A great deal of theoretical work has been done in recent decades concerning the relationship of general conceptions of culture and the interests of various social groups to curriculum. Yet, few studies have focused in depth on the ways in which these interests have been played out in a particular school subject. Analyses of historical cases of a school subject provide deep looks at a particular past that influenced, or is representational of, ideas, beliefs, and practices within a professional community. Case studies that combine aspects of the macro and micro level of study can inform us about the many sociopolitical influences that have resulted in the creation of curriculum, and when considered in combination, such studies provide a way of revealing national and international commonalties and differences.

This book consists of international case studies of art education that illustrate the translation of cultural knowledge as part of the process of curriculum conceptualization, development, and implementation. Each of the authors has contributed a chapter that focuses on historical and cultural influences on art education in a particular country. These chapters include discussions of ideas that have emerged in, or been transported to, a particular country and transformed in the new context.

Problems of Method

The case studies in these chapters were written using critical and historical methods. Some draw on empirical data and include philosophical inquiry. A critical perspective requires attention to certain sociological and anthropological forms of analyses. It involves consideration of hidden assumptions and contextual influences on art education, such as those of national politics, economy, and religion. For example, several of the chapters wrestle with conflicting definitions of art and aesthetics, internal contradictions of schooling, and incongruities between theory and practice. The social and cultural institutions in which art education has been played out are also given attention.

The methods applied here are somewhat new to educational history. American history of education has until recently been guided by a millennial sense of progress, including the assumption that education continually moves forward and improves the nation over time. Also, educational history has largely been made up of biographies, intellectual histories, and institutional histories. As a result, much of the history of education has focused on policy and the important men (and a few women) who have influenced policy. Such histories are often studies of large-scale educational reforms, such as progressive education, the ideas associated with them, and the people associated with the ideas. As a result of these foci, certain other topics have been left unattended. Although some notable exceptions exist, social and cultural histories of education and histories of classroom practice have been given little consideration. Also, a general neglect of the histories of school subjects has pervaded the field.

Since the 1980s, however, the conditions of educational history have changed. Research on curriculum has become more popular and a sociocultural perspective has developed among some educational historians. As part of the growing interest in history of curriculum, several texts of historical studies of school subjects have been published that focus on or include chapters about art education (e.g. Efland, 1990; Korzenik, 1985; Popkewitz, 1987; Soucy & Stankiewicz, 1990; Thistlewood, 1992). International conferences on history of art education have been held, for example, at Penn State University and the University of Barcelona (Hernández & Trafí, 1994; Hernández & Planella, 1996).

In recent discussions of general historical methods, the boundaries between history and other disciplines are talked about as having broken down to the extent that sociological and anthropological studies are considered cultural histories, and philosophers, such as Michel Foucault, are referenced in historical texts (e.g. Hunt, 1989; Karsten & Modell, 1993). The combination of historical methods with cultural critique involves drawing on fields of social science, such as anthropology and sociology. In doing so, the new history is not traditional in the sense that it does not necessarily focus on the people and events that influence the professional field. It may instead, for example, focus on people who have been influenced or that represent a general condition. Cultural history involves the study of rites and rituals, products and artifacts, and mentalities. The new per-spective of cultural history includes a critical interpretation of texts writ-ten in and about the past involving an examination of social contradictions and discontinuities. For example, the application of feminist theory to American history illustrates the dynamics of exclusion in a democracy (Burke, 1991; Foner, 1990). To critique the past from the present has its dangers because what is possible to see at present may not have been within the horizon of vision in the past. As a result, the new history is con-troversial and the appropriateness of its topics, methods, and analyses are in debate.

A common concern of scholars writing the new history is the shift in focus from the surface behaviors of people to deeper linguistic constructs. For example, Foucault (1970) focuses attention away from the idea that social change is a natural process and a generalizable condition toward the transformation of a particular, cultural and historical context that main-tains its structure, but shifts certain aspects of social life. Although dis-course maintains structure, promoting constancy, power arrangements shift and new social patterns emerge through discursive conflicts. Groups are excluded or included through discourse and those with little power are given new legitimacy by adopting legitimate language.

Because cultural historians ask different questions than other types of historians and are interested in new topics, such as cultural identity, what constitutes data is often redefined. Important documents are no longer only those that are public or private. That is, information is not only thought of as located in published documents or the personal papers of "important" people. Rather, the most useful documents may be located in the space in between, created and used by relatively small groups of people or people traditionally written out of history. For example, in the case of education, documents such as those produced and used by public school teachers with students could be essential.

Understanding the educational past in the context of national culture requires an external view of history. An internal history of education is one that focuses on the workings of a discipline from the inside; that is, it is about influences of change and stability that appear to be initiated by forces within the professional community. In contrast, an external history attends to larger social and cultural influences on the ways in which teach-ing and learning are conceptualized. The methods used to write external history involve sources that, at first sight, may have little to do with edu-cation. However, education is a notoriously public enterprise that is dis-cussed and enacted in a public forum. The way people think about education is dependent upon a wide range of social knowledge.

Such a history of education also depends on a particular view of time and space. Instead of being imagined as linear, the past is represented as a conceptual space in which things occur in an interactive manner, referring back to earlier times. A conceptual space is helpful in thinking about history in part, because various histories exist concurrently in the same past; for example, different cultures have histories that do not "fit" on one timeline. Also, in a sense, the past continues to exist in the present. Time and place make up a structural space in which only some things are possible and certain consciousness can exist as a result of directions taken in the past (Braudel, 1980). When the history is relatively short (as it is with much educational history), and the structure is the same for both the content and creation of history, critique becomes most important because the perspectival distance afforded by long views of the past are not possible and conflicts that may in the distant future be resolved or forgotten because they are inconsequential in the long run, have not yet been laid to rest.

Different problems are chosen by new historians than those by traditional historians. The linguistic focus of their analysis has influenced the character of research questions in educational history, and opened up new possibilities for research in art education. For example, educational mottoes and shifts in the meaning of discourse that are relied upon to justify educational practice require further study. The focus of problems may be different even when considering the same historical event. Consider the example of the Owatonna Project in Minnesota. This project has been written about by several historians of art education, including one of the editors of this volume. It was a project that was to bring art into the daily lives of the residents of Owatonna, Minnesota, a town about sixty miles south of Minneapolis. The project was the brainchild of the dean of the University of Minnesota School of Education at the time and funded by the Carnegie philanthropic foundations. Often the Owatonna Project has been studied as an example of a successful art education program. Studied from a critical perspective, it can also be looked at as an example of the ways in which funding by philanthropic organizations control educational experiences and values (Freedman, 1989b).

Although the new history might be defined as being on the fringe of the discipline of history, and bridging history with sociology, anthropology, and philosophy, such definitions may defeat its purpose. Many critical perspectives fall under the rubric of critical theory in education, the roots of which include neo-Marxism, French semiotic and poststructural analysis, as well as feminist and cultural theory. Perhaps the greatest common ground among critical theorists of education is their skepticism about historical positivism and progressivism. However, to marginalize critical perspectives gives the appearance that other perspectives are central and, therefore, more authoritative representations of the past. Good history is inherently critical in that it addresses underlying assumptions, interests, and effects, as well as surface behaviors. In a sense, critical perspectives are now located at the center of the discipline of history, and push outward to influence the field.

The discussion of methodology links together some new directions in art history (e.g., Preziosi, 1989; Rees & Borzello, 1986), educational history, and history of art education. For example, the new cultural history includes an interest in information connected to forms of production other than written text, such as painting, architecture, and film (e.g., Frisch, 1993; Starn, 1989). Certainly, pictures have long been used as a source of historical information. However, alternative sources and interpretations are necessary for writing history of art education. For example, an analysis of the art made by Franz Cizek's Austrian students in the 1910s and 1920s has provided valuable insights into educational practices of the past. For decades, the discourse about these practices has led educators to represent Cizek as a vital influence in the international shift in art education toward the promotion of free self-expression in children. Since the turn of the century, Cizek's efforts to eliminate adult influences from his student's work have been documented. However, when the words are compared to the pictures, an incongruity is apparent. The student work is highly stylized, technically proficient, and remarkably similar. Although Cizek apparently did not teach by showing students adult examples of art in class, the children's work closely resembles a popular adult style of the period, which they reproduced in class and which was praised by their teacher (Duncum, 1982).

The incongruity between pictures and words in the case of Cizek's students' work and the discourse about it illustrates several important aspects of understanding international curriculum history. For example, the meanings of words change over time and as they are used in new places. What was conceptualized as free self-expression in Europe in the 1910s and 1920s is not the same as the notion of free self-expression that has permeated art education in post-Abstract Expressionist America. The work of Cizek's students was, in fact, a great step away from the previous common art education practice of copying adult drawings to learn drafting and rendering techniques. The drawings, paintings, and prints by Cizek's students are seductive in their beauty and joyfulness, which is one reason why educators who saw them displayed in the great art museums of England, the United States, and Canada, wanted their students to be able to achieve a similar visual competency and apparent freedom. However, the historical and cultural analysis illustrates psychological and sociological aspects of the relationship of child art to a range of adult imagery, the importance of context to educational practice, and the dynamics of the construction of educational discourse.

Problems of Content

The chapters in this book reflect historical debates that continue to influence the field. Curriculum development in general typically reflects the agreed-upon knowledge of a particular culture. Rarely do educators construct curriculum deliberately focusing on knowledge that is fundamentally conflicting and rooted in disagreement (Graff, 1987). Yet, all the chapters here illustrate underlying differences of opinion about what knowledge is most important for students, the ways in which knowledge should be presented to students, and what is to be gained by students as a result of educational experience.

The development of art in public schooling is a common thread throughout the studies. In each country, public schooling has played a hegemonic role in the political and cultural life of the nation through the mass education of large populations. At the same time, several of the countries have political agendas that involve interpretations of education as a means of promoting individualism and difference. Public school art education has often been given this particular role and been influenced by the vital contradictions the role suggests.

In each of the chapters, historical periods are laid out. The structure of history organized in terms of periods sometimes constrains ideas about the past and may suggest that things are radically different outside any given period. However, the periods reflect continuities of stasis as well as disjunctions of change, and as a result, help us to understand relationships between stories about art education in different places at the same time.

Although the focus of historical writing is often on what Foucault calls sites of contestation, which signify points of change, the case studies illustrate ways in which the new becomes institutionalized, such as in the case of girls' art education to prepare for marriage and motherhood and the long-standing focus on industrial drawing at the expense of other art activities. Once institutionalized, these practices resisted change and seemed to provide continuity, often at the same time that new ideas were providing problems and possibilities.

As well as historical periods shaping the case studies, topical structures are at work. Each of the chapters has a particular emphasis, such as influences of multiculturalism, the notion of self-expression, or conceptions of artistic development. These topics are revisited throughout the book, but contextualized differently in each case. The analysis of the field in relation to these example themes demonstrates that art education has a relationship with power; it is not neutral or innocent. Sociopolitical conflicts and national and international ideological struggles have helped to shape the field.

At least three general topics have directed research in public school art education. First, the field has focused on the developmental aspects of learning art knowledge. Research in this area has ranged from studies of children's artistic production (e.g., Lowenfeld 1947, 1957; Lowenfeld & Brittain, 1964; Wilson & Wilson, 1977) to those concerning an understanding of visual art based on viewing behaviors and cognition (e.g., Gardner, Winner, & Kircher, 1975; Parsons, 1987). Most of the work concerning artistic production has been based on a psychological approach to development. However some, such as the work of Brent and Marjorie Wilson, have understood development as heavily influenced by sociological conditions.

The second topic of research in art education has focused on curriculum theory and design, including definitions of purpose for art education, the selection of appropriate information for students, and the organization of that information. This theme includes the creation of curriculum materials and the representation of art knowledge in curriculum. Debates concerning the relative influence of professional fine art disciplines are important to this theme.

Third, practices of teaching art have been investigated. This research has focused on instructional aspects of art education, such as teaching methods, student assessment, classroom management, and program implementation and evaluation (e.g., Boughton, Eisner, & Ligtvoet, 1996; Eisner, 1985). These studies have included debates about professionalism in practice, such as whether art educators should embrace the notion of accountability as based on student testing.

In the United States, the study of these topics in relation to sociopolitics of art education is increasingly becoming a part of mainstream art education. These studies make debatable what is deeply embedded and taken for granted, such as the institutional aspects of public schooling (e.g., May, 1994), influences of national and local politics on educational reform (e.g., Blandy, 1987; Freedman, 1987b; Stuhr, 1994), and social issues, such as the relationship of gender to art education (e.g., Collins, 1987; Collins & Sandell, 1984; Freedman, 1994). Debates about the relationship between art and education are included, for example, concerning economic and cultural elitism in fine art and the democratizing vision of some school communities.

These topics characterize common interests in the professional field and are reflected in the following chapters. However, the ways in which the topics are played out in different national contexts reveal important cultural distinctions. In the United States, for example, the topics are conceptualized as somewhat discrete, and sociocultural perspectives are often considered a separate topic or other "level" of investigation. In South America, such boundaries tend to be more blurred. Also, the varied uses of primary and secondary sources in the chapters illustrates that more work has been previously done in some areas than others. The stylistic differences in writing reflect cultural differences in the ways in which scholarship is reported. Of course, we would have liked to include more country chapters in this book, and in fact, not all of the invited scholars were able to contribute work; however, the collection as it is introduces a broad range of school issues.

The similarities and differences between art educational theories and practices in different countries can be seen in three major influences on the field: (a) state regulation, (b) professionalization, and (c) cultural ideals. These influences are enmeshed and interact in ways that are illustrated in each of the chapters. They are conceptualized as different themes here in the sense that they involve somewhat different social collectivities, such as institutions, organizations, and communities. It is the study of these collectivities that can aid our understanding of the relationship between agency and social structure (Giddens, 1987) and can help us to understand what about our work is reproductive and how and what we may produce that is new.

The final chapter of the book is an analysis of international aspects of cultural knowledge translation in curriculum and includes theorizing about the messages that can be learned from the example of art education. It contains a comparative, sociological framework for curriculum based on issues discussed throughout the text. It includes a discussion of the importance of historical context in understanding the relationship of curriculum to culture. Few large-scale cultural analyses of any type have been written about art education, or any other school subject. This book contributes to such an analysis of curriculum.

I

State Regulation

Interest and Influence across Social Boundaries

One of the major influences on art education has been national politics. The influence is channeled through general sociopolitical agendas as well as policy that directly affects schooling. The chapters in this section reflect political influences that have had roots in colonialism and other cross-cultural conditions, including those brought about by governmental agencies as they appropriate ideas and practices from outside their country. Political power has been used to make art education a tool for enculturation.

Yasuhiko Isozaki's chapter focuses on these influences on Japanese art education from the sixteenth century to the publication of the first art education textbook in 1871. Painting and painting education had been closely tied to religious, political, and socioeconomic structures within Japanese culture. However, influences from outside the country, particularly Dutch and Chinese, were important to the development of educational practice. The first textbook on art, *Teaching of Western Painting*, was produced by Western-style painters of the Tokugawa shogunate based on the idea of rationality in art. It was a result of an educational policy, established by the national government of the period, that promoted the European enlightenment idea of rationalism. Later, governmental structures renounced such outside influences.

Doug Boughton's chapter reviews the cultural origins of peoples in Australia and sketches the early history of ideas about art education derived from European sources and transformed in the Australian context. The review provides a framework for his discussion of the contemporary crisis for visual arts education that has resulted in the development of a national curriculum. The process of this development illustrates tensions between sociocultural needs (with a particular focus on Aboriginal Peoples), and the incompatibility of governmental policy and the national curriculum initiative.

In Graeme Chalmers's chapter, the teaching of drawing in nineteenth-century Canadian schools is viewed against a backdrop of discomfort about the formation of a nation based on an uneasy federation of former British colonies and a newly conquered French Quebec. A rigid system of instruction in drawing was transported from Britain and widely implemented by Canadian education and religious leaders. In addition to serving a God that abhorred worldly pleasures, these educators supported political and industrial purposes and saw education as a means for social control and to create an obedient and dependent workforce.

Fernando Hernández explains the general picture of art education in Spain in two main phases: (a) art education as a strategy to create a working-class culture of reproduction in the late nineteenth century; and (b) handicraft as a school subject and the creation of kitsch taste under the influence of fascism throughout the 1940s and 1950s. The author defines these phases through the connections between the dominant trends in art education ideology and practices and the significant political, artistic, and social events that have influenced them.

1

Yasuhiko Isozaki

Artistic, Cultural, and Political Structures Determining the Educational Direction of the First Japanese Schoolbook on Art in 1871

The Japanese Renaissance began in the late sixteenth century, nearly corresponding to the High Renaissance in Europe. In Japan, this time was a comparatively peaceful age, a political and social emergence from the chaotic conditions of the preceding century. During this modern age, especially the Edo period (1603–1867), Confucianism was the important way of thought, imposing restrictions not only on one's ethical and political conduct but also on one's philosophical and educational ideas.

As Confucianism enjoyed the official recognition of Tokugawa shogunate during the Edo Period, the successive shoguns of the Tokugawa shogunate employed many scholars as Confucian advisers. Confucianism was divided into many schools, among which the Shushigalu school gained official recognition as the central teaching of the shogunate. Shushigalu traced Confucian learning established by the Chinese philosopher Zhu Xi (1130–1200) to its origin. Zhu Xi's Confucianism had the RI and KI dualism as its basic concept. RI is the principle basic to all that exists in heaven and earth. Because RI has no shape, it can become a concrete existence only in conjunction with KI. Being can be produced by the cooperation of the RI and KI combination. In 1790, Shushigaku was recognized as the orthodox learning of the Tokugawa Shogunate.

With Confucianism for a background, the world of painting in the Edo period was mainly dominated by the Japanese Kano school of Chinese painting. The Kano school exerted a stylistic and thematic effect on the other painting schools. Because the artists of the Kano school were educated according to Confucianism, they willingly selected traditional Chinese subjects: eight Chinese views of Hsiao and Hisiang; retreat among streams and bridges as landscapes; Confucius, Zhong-kuf, Hau-shan as portraits; plum trees, bamboo, orchids as plants; dragons and tigers as animals, the Seven Wise Men in the bamboo grove; and Xiama and Tieguai as fables.

Professional artists of the Kano school increased in number during the early Edo period. Their hereditary leaders were the painters of the inner shogunal quarters who had shogunal patronage. Their students became the painters of the outer shogunal quarters and spread the artistic power of the Kano school. Consequently, the Kano school rose gradually to power in the early Edo period, but was unable to maintain its power from around the middle years of the Edo period. Because the painters of the Kano school strove only to copy the various depictions in the painting books, they adhered strictly to their teachers' instructions and created nothing new. Their reproductions were lifeless: the Kano school, which held the highest position in the world of painting during the first Edo period, fell into mannerism.

In addition to the Kano school, a wholly new school of painting arose: the Western-style painting school, connected with Dutch learning. The study of Western art and science by the Japanese during the Edo period, the so-called Rangaku, effectively meant Dutch learning. Western art and science were introduced to Japan by the Portuguese, the Spanish, and the Dutch. The Portuguese were the first Europeans with whom the Japanese came into contact. Portuguese missionaries and tradesmen brought many things to Japan: the Bible and books on Catholicism, firearms, world maps, precious stones, clocks, curious animals and birds of Africa and South Asia, glassware, printing machines, oil painting, engravings, and so on. They symbolized Western material culture for Japanese. Japanese referred to them as the Southern Barbarians and they learned from the Southern Barbarians. For example, they not only sketched the structures of firearms, they also imitated their manufacture.

But the Tokugawa shogunate established a policy of eliminating Christianity from Japan, aiming to strengthen its own authority. The main purposes of national seclusion were the exclusion of Catholic missionaries and most tradesman from Japan. A series of national seclusion edicts were issued by the Tokugawa shogunate during the 1630s. Portuguese ships would no longer be allowed to come to Japan. Any ship disobeying these edicts was to be destroyed. Portuguese and Spanish material culture disappeared with the demise of Christianity.

However, Chinese and Dutch traders who were engaged in business, not missionary works, were allowed to carry on their trade according to the strictly limited regulations of the Tokugawa shogunate. The Chinese and the Dutch traders were permitted to enter one port, Nagasaki. In 1641, the Dutch were transferred to the artificial island of Dejima, constructed in Nagasaki harbor. Dejima had been the residence of the Portuguese. In short, it was the only place where Europeans were allowed to reside in Japan, and it remained a point of contact between Japan and the West during the period of national seclusion.

The Import of Western Books in the Edo Period

Under the policy of national seclusion, imports of Western books were rigorously restricted by Tokugawa shogunate. In particular, the import of books concerned with Christianity was absolutely forbidden. One important figure who realized the necessity of Western studies was Tokugawa Yoshimune (1684–1751). Yoshimune was eighth shogun of Tokugawa shogunate. He decided to partly relax the ban on Western books in 1720. The imported books were mainly Western in Chinese translation.

While partially relaxing the ban, Yoshimune and successive shoguns agreed to accept Western novelties presented by the Opperhooft, the trading company director of Dejima. Among those novelties there was a famous Dutch book, *Nauekeurige Beschrijving van de Natuur Vier-voetige Dieren, Vissen en Bloedlooze Water-Dieren, Vogelen, Kronkel-Dieren, Slangen en Draken*, which was presented to the Shogun Ietsuna by the Opperhooft Heindrich Indijck in 1663. It was known as an illustrated animal book in Japan. *Nauekeurige Beschrijving van de Natuur* was compiled by Jan Jonston, a well-traveled writer on natural history, who was born in Poland in 1603 and traveled in England, Holland, and Germany. This zoological book was full of pictures of a large number of creatures, both real and imaginary. Perhaps Yoshimune had assumed that all of them were real, existing creatures, owing to the realistic and elaborate illustrations. He must have regarded *Nauekeurige Beschrijving van de Natuur* as a practical book, which would be of use to the progress of industry. He decided to have this book translated into Japanese and ordered Aoki Konyo (1698–1769) and Noro Genjo to study the Dutch language in 1740.

Nauekeurige Beschrijving van de Natuur:
A Treasure House of Artistic Inspirations
to Japanese Painters

During the national seclusion, foreign travel by Japanese was strictly prohibited by the Tokugawa shogunate. Consequently, Japanese could not see curiosities and strange animals living in unknown lands. It was Jan Jonston's zoological book that introduced creatures to the Japanese public that they had never seen before. The book also provided fanciful inspirations to Japanese painters, who often copied the exotic animals, giving rein to their own imaginations. Lions were copied by So Shiseki (1715–1786), Odano Naotake (1749–1780), Shiba Kohan (1738–1818) and others (see figure 1.1a–b), European dogs by Aodo Denzen (1748–1822), a rhinoceros by Tani Buncho (1763–1840), and elephants and horses by Watanabe Kazan (1793–1841).

Japanese painters in the Edo period, who had never seen strange animals from foreign countries were introduced to the rhinoceros in Jonston's book and painted it full of amazement. Jonston's rhinoceros, which is explained as "De naam Rhinoceros, is hem van der hoorn, die hem op den neus wascht, gegeven," covers a full page. In reality his rhinoceros was plagiarized from Gonrad Gerner's woodcut of a rhinoceros, which was based in turn on that of Albrecht Dürer (Isozaki, 1979a, p. 60).

Dürer sketched a rhinoceros sent from Cambodia to Lisbon, which met with an untimely death.[1] But he never traveled to Lisbon. He happened to see a rough sketch of the animal enclosed in a letter at a friend's house in Nürnberg. The letter was sent by a typographer, Ferdinand, living in Lisbon to his friend in Nürnberg. Ferdinand enclosed not only the rough drawing sketched by an obscure painter of Lisbon, but also a simple explanatory note about the Indian rhinoceros. Dürer drew it in ink in 1515 when he also executed a woodcut from the drawing, adding an explanation as follows: "It is armed with a thick skin like armor and is very lively and in good condition. The animal is called *Rhinocero* in Greek and Latin and *Gomda* in Indian."

Dürer's rhinoceros is somewhat exaggerated and fanciful, because in fact he never saw it. For example, it has a small twisted horn besides the

FIGURE 1.1

a. Morishima Churyo. Leeuw *(above)*. Illustration from "Komo zatsuwa." Woodcut, 1787.

b. Jan Jonston. Lions *(below)*. Illustration from *Nauekerurige Beschrijving van de Natuur*. Etching, 1660.

large horn, but the Indian rhinoceros does not have two horns. Dürer had probably confused the rhinoceros with the imaginary unicorn. Moreover, the thick skin patterned with circles, ovals, and scaly shapes seems like armor. Those conventional patterns would be expressed not on the strength of his observation, but on the basis of the description written in his friend's letter (Isozaki, 1979a). But the concept of the rhinoceros was clearly outlined in the European public by Dürer.

It was the German artist, Hans Burgmair, who first copied Dürer's Rhinoceros. Then, the Zurich naturalist, Conrad Gesner (1516–1565), made Dürer's Rhinoceros widely known, placing it in his monumental work, *Historia Animalium*, which was one of the greatest publishing achievements of the mid-sixteenth century. The rhinoceros in Gesner's *Historia* is facing the opposite direction to that of Dürer's, but both are the same iconographically. In 1660, Jan Jonston published *Nauekeurige Beschrijving van de Natuur* in which Gesner's rhinoceros was copied. Not long after Jonston published the illustrated zoological book, his rhinoceros landed in Japan.

Tani Buncho (1764–1841) was an artist to the senior councilor Matsudaire Sadanobu and a representative of the Edo Nanga school. Nanga (Southern painting) was Japanese literari painting of the eighteenth and nineteenth centuries. Japanese literari painters were mainly influenced by the landscape styles of the Chinese literari. Tani Buncho studied not only the painting of the Nanga school, but also the painting of the Kano school and Western-style painting. Buncho, seeing Jonston's *Nauekeurige Beschrijving van de Natuur*, owned by either the Tokugawa shogunate or a certain scholar of Dutch learning, carefully copied the rhinoceros in light brown and black ink. Thus, the rhinoceros, which was sent from India to Europe, landed again in Japan. Jonston's book was an educational treasury for Confucianism-bred Japanese artists, because lions, giraffes, and rhinoceros were quite different from the traditional Chinese animals they knew from Confucian mythology.

Akita School as a Pioneer of Western-Style Painting

Japanese scholars studying Western art and science were known as "Rangakusha" meaning Hollandologists. Dutch learning (Rangaku), the source of research by Ragakusha, extended to a wide range of science and art: medicine, geography, geometry, surveying, botany, chemistry, astronomy, the arts, and so on.

The artists studying Western arts were called Yokufaga, or "Western-style painters." Their art works are "Ranga" in Japanese. Western-style painters worked in various districts of Japan, such as Nagasaki, Edo,

Akita, and Sukagawa. Western-style paintings in the Akita domain, called the Akita school, played an important pioneering role in the Tokugawa period of national isolation.

Satake Shozan (1748–1785) and Odano Naotake (1749–1780) were representative artists of the Akita school, the latter a samurai and also Shozan's retainer. At first, both studied the Kano school style of painting and later became founders of the Kita school of Western-style painting. Aiming to rebuild the local finances of the Akita domain, Satke Shozan invited Hraga Gennai to Akita to give advice on local copper production. This invitation provided Odano Naotake with a chance to study Western-style painting.

Hiraga Gennai (1728–1780) was a multitalented man whom contemporaries called a prodigy, because he produced novels and dramas of the puppet play, wrote books of natural history concerned with scientific classification of animals, plants and minerals, experimented in making asbestos cloth and thermometers, and produced oil paintings. It was reported by Shiba Kokan that Gennai made great sacrifices to collect Dutch books and bought them by selling off his own household effects and bedclothes. In fact Gennai possessed Western books of a high price: Rembertus Dodoneaus's *Kruydt Boeck*, Eberhard Rumpf's *Amboinsche Rariteikamer*, Jan Swammerdam's *Historia Insectorum Generalis*, Francis Willughby's *Historia Piscium*, Jan Jonston's *Nauekeurige Beschrijving van de Natuur*, Gererd de Lairesse's *Grot Schilderboek*, *Zee-Atlas*, *Nieuw Atlas*, and so forth.

Although Gennai's journey to Akita in 1773 did not produce good results in terms of copper production, Gennai became acquainted with the young artist, Odano Naotake. It is said that Gennai taught Naotake techniques of Western-style painting, particularly chiaroscuro and the technique of shading, explaining an expressive difference between a circle and a ball. In December of 1773, Naotake moved to Edo, and took up residence in Gennai's home. While seeing illustrated Dutch books in Edo, Naotake learned the theory of Western-style painting from Gennai, and rapidly achieved artistic success. He not only studied human proportion modeled on Lairesse's *Groot Schilderboek*, but also in 1774 was chosen to illustrate the *New Book of Anatomy* (Katai Shinsho) by Sugita Genpaku and his fellows.

The New Book of Anatomy, translated from the Dutch book, *Ontleedkundige Tafelen*, which was based on a German book, was the first Japanese translation of a Western book. The book accelerated the epoch-making progress of Dutch learning, because it raised great interest in Dutch surgical knowledge among Japanese physicians. *The New Book of Anatomy* was composed of five volumes; one volume for anatomical charts and four volumes for the text. When Naotake illustrated it, he referred to many

Dutch anatomical books: J. A. Kulmus's *Ontleedkundige Tafelen*, Steven Blankaart's *Nieuw Hervorme Anatomie*, Godefridi Bidloo's *Anatomia Humani Corporis*, and so forth.

Ondano Naotake faithfully copied anatomical charts, mainly from the *Ontleedkundige Tafelen*. But its frontispiece is quite different from that of the *Ontleedkundige Tafelen*, and refers to the *Vivae Imagines Prtium Corporis Humani*, written by Juan Valverde de Hamsco, who was the outstanding Spanish anatomist belonging to the new Versalian school of anatomy (Isozaki, 1979b). On the center of this woodblock frontispiece is written "Kaitaizu" (an anatomical chart) flanked by a naked male and female standing on both sides of the pedestal. One nude, holding up a pig, is Adam and the other Eve. Adam and Eve created by God were expressed as naked covering their private parts with their hands or with leaves. According to medieval typology Adam prefigured Christ, Eve foreshadowed Madonna, or alternatively the church itself. Neither the authorities of the Tokugawa shogunate nor the public at large would have been able to discover that figures of this frontispiece were depictions of Adam and Eve. If they had, the publication of the *New Book of Anatomy* would not have been permitted because of the series of edicts prohibiting Christianity during the period of national seclusion.

Odano Naotake illustrated the *New Book of Anatomy* in 1774 with woodcuts. While illustrating, he must have learned a theory of human proportions, including a geometrical scheme. He taught Western painting and its theory to Satake Shozan, who was a feudal lord of the Akita domain and became a founder of the Akita school of Western-style painting. Satake Shozan, produced *Gist of the Art of Painting* (Gaho Koryo), *Understanding the Art of Painting* (Gazu Rikai), and *Red and Blue, Types of Pigments* (Tanseibu) in 1778. In *Understanding the Art of Painting*, Shozan included nine diagrams illustrating Western linear perspective. He also learned how to render the shadows cast by poles at equal and regular intervals in sunlight, how to make a regular octagon, how to describe the perspective of an octagon, how to draw the perspective of a circle, how an object placed high above a horizontal line should be made so that it appears equal to an object placed a little above the horizontal line, and how to describe a pair of double stairs.

The last diagram is of double staircases, on which two persons, the one ascending the other descending do not give the impression of an imminent collision. Double stairs or spiral staircases are often found in sixteenth- and seventeenth-century treatises on perspective, such as *Le due Regole della Prospettiva Practica*, written by Giacomo Barozz da Vignola (1507–1573), *Leçons de Perspective Positive* by Jacques Androuet Du Cerceau (ca. 1520–after 1584), and *Perspective* by Jan Vredeman de Vries (1527–ca. 1604). As double staircases were not in existence in the Japan of those days, Shozan was probably interested in them as a rarity, and produced an elevation and a plan of them. Shozan divided a semicircle of the plan into twelve equal parts, and then drew perpendiculars from every one of the points in the semicircle to each respective step (see figure 1.2). This diagram described by Shozan closely resembles the "description of a pair of double stairs," in *Practical Perspective* written by Joseph Moxon. This book was useful for painters, engravers, and architects, and was published in London in 1670. About double stairs, Moxon writes: "They are also set forth by Vignola, in his *Book of Perspective*, from whence this is taken" (1670, p. 47). In brief, Moxon also borrowed the description of double stairs from *Le due Regole della Prospettiva Practica*, written by Giacommo Barozzi da Vignola. I do not know whether Shozan saw Moxon's *Practical Perspective*. Shozan probably saw a diagram closely resembling Moxon's double stairs recorded in a certain Dutch book, because it is hard to imagine Dutch traders importing English books into Japan.

Two leading members of the Akita school, Naotake and Shozan produced superb sketches, whose subjects included animals, birds, insects, flowers, and grasses. Both Western-style painters grasped that what constituted the characteristic feature of Western art was a realistic style. They learned techniques, such as perspective and chiaroscuro, to make the representation of objects fit closely to reality, rendering an illustration more realistic than a mere representation.

The Pursuit of Realism and Rationality in Western Art

Theories and techniques of Western-style painting continued to be pursued by a considerable number of successors of the Akita school artists. The Tokugawa shogunate kept the Dejima Dutch trade under its direct control. Shogunate regulations forbade the Dutch to leave Dejima and ordinary Japanese people were barred from entering Dejima. However, there were exceptions. Japanese traders were permitted to enter Dejima when laden Dutch ships came to Nagasaki harbor. The Dutch not only gave gifts to the Shogun, but also sold Western books, etchings, and curiosities to Japanese Hollandologists (Rangakusha) at a high price in order to fill their own pockets. The easier Dutch books were within the Hollandologists' reach, and the more Dutch books were imported, the greater the progress the Japanese made in their studies of Western art and science.

Shiba Kokan (1747–1818) was an artist and innovator who made remarkable achievements in Western-style painting. He was not only an artist, but one of the pioneers who intended to Westernize Japan, as opposed to the closed and conservative intentions of the Tokugawa government. In 1783, he created the first copperplate etching in Japan, based on

FIGURE 1.2

Satake Shozan. Double staircases (from his "Sketch Book"). Sumi on paper, 1778.

the techniques probably translated from a Dutch encyclopedia.

Besides Western art, Kokan was eager to investigate new fields of Western science. He actively worked to transmit Western scientific information to the general public, informing them about the world outside Japan and of heaven and earth. Referring to Dutch books and maps, he etched copperplate maps of the world; one of his representative works is *Complete Map of the World*, executed in 1793. He also directed his attention to astronomy and introduced Copernican theory to the public, adding explanatory diagrams, copperplate etchings, and text. Consulting Dutch books, he explained the revolutions of the earth and planets, and the heliocentric theory, in a Tokugawa society imbued with the contrary, Confucian order, which already provided explanation of both the metaphysical and the physical.

However, Kokan mainly pursued a painting career throughout his life. He obtained various Dutch books and etchings. Following hints from Jan Luyken's *Menselijk Bedrijf*, which was one of his favorite books, he produced many works of art: *Seaman*, a drawing in black and white on silk in 1784, *Coopers*, an oil painting on silk, around 1794, *Peat Digger* in thin coloring on paper, around 1790, and so on (Isozaki, 1979).[2]

Kokan interpreted the primary aim of Western art as to produce a true representation of reality based on a spirit of rationalism. In contrast, Japanese and Chinese paintings were always produced without turning attention to the actual appearance of objects, rather focusing on the lively mood and feeling of objects or with the impression given by the brush technique. Western artists, pursuing the spirit of reality and rationality, could correctly represent distance, space, depth, and dimension by employing perspective and shading. For example, when man carefully looked at Western botanical books, man became aware of the importance of illustrations with which it was possible to acquire an accurate understanding of the appearance of a flower. Illustrations were as important as words. Kokan judged that Western illustrations or pictures were useful ways to clearly teach people about the appearance of things.

Aodo Denzen (1748–1822) was ordered to acquire the technique of copperplate etching by his patron and his feudal lord, Matsudaira Sadanobu. Denzen became one of Kokan's pupils to learn this technique. But he was soon expelled by his master because of his slow-witted progress in the copperplate etching technique. Accordingly, he was forced to learn the technique from the Dutch-learning scholars (Rangakusha) serving Lord Sadanobu, who had already acquired a knowledge of etching through some Dutch books such as Egbert Buys's *Nieuw en Volkomen Woordenboek van Kosten en Weetenschappe* and J. A. de Chalmot's *Mastering the Technique of "Stopgroun."* He managed to perfect etching (Isozaki, 1980).[3] He put etching to practical use rather than using it for aesthetic enjoyment.

Katsushica Hokusai (1760–1849) was one of the great masters of full-color woodblock print. He was interested in Western painting in the early 1800s, and studied rational and formative elements in the Western arts. Perhaps he got a kind of Dutch schematic drawing book, which showed simplifications of various figures in an illustrated form. I cannot state definitely what this book was, but there is a possibility that it was *Het light der Teken en Schilderkonst,* written by Chrispin de Passe (see figures 1.3a–b). Hokusai did sketches of animals and humans and explained schematics of drawing, for example, of a horse or ox seen from behind, in his book, *How Quickly Man Sketches Objects.* Many Western-style painters, including Hokusai and Shozan, had learned a great deal from illustrated Dutch books, including the idea that all things in nature originally have order, which consists of geometry such as a square, rectangle, circle, triangle, cube, and so on.

These artists' attitude of pursuing rationality in art was to contribute greatly to the support of new ideas in the coming Meiji restoration. Moreover, their concept that Western art followed a rationality relying on geometry, perspective, proportion and so on, was applied to the first textbook on art, *Teaching of Western Painting* (*Seiga Shinan*), published in 1871.

The Institute for the Investigation of Western Books

While the active study of Western learning was advanced by the research of individual scholars of Dutch learning, the Tokugawa shogunate established an Institute for the Investigation of Western Books (*Bansho shirabesho*) in 1811. The institute belonged to the astronomical observatory of the Tokugawa shogunate, where the main work was to correct a time lag of the lunar calendar. It was the first formal institution for study in scientific and technical books of the West, and for teaching Western languages. Naturally, the first language of teaching and learning was Dutch, which was joined later by English, German, and French. Because the institute attached importance to military subjects, courses of study were made up of surveying, navigation, naval architecture, and metallurgy to include geography, chemistry, geometry, and physics.

Kawakami Togai (1827–1881) entered the Institute for the Investigation of Western Books around 1857, and became a lecturer in the course of the art of painting. His course on Western art and instrumental drawing was probably based on the translation of Dutch geometrical books, judging from Dutch books owned by the shogunal institute: Jacob de Gelder's *Handileiding tot het meetkunsting teekene,* J. W. Schaap's *Architectur-perspectief,* and H. Strootman's *Groden der beschrijvende meetkunst,* among others.

Takahashi Yuichi (1828–1894) studied Western art under Togai, after

FIGURE 1.3

a. Katsushika Hokusai. Birds and schema *(at left)*. Illustration from *How Quickly Man Sketches Objects*. Woodcut, 1812.

b. Chrispin de Passe. Schematic simplification *(below)*. Illustration from *Het Light der Teken en Schilderkonst*. Etching, 1643.

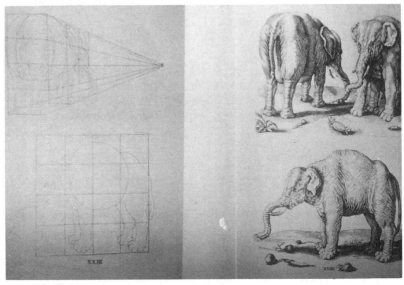

entering the institute in 1862. The institute underwent various changes of name, as times changed.[4]

The mid-nineteenth century of Japan was also a time of diplomatic and political crises; social and institutional disquiet grew more intense. It was caused by economic insecurity brought about by series of famines, and by the strong approach of Western powers such as the Americans, Russians, and British. Above all, it was the impact of the unexpected naval mission to Japan by the American Commodore M. C. Perry that ended the Tokugawa shogunate policy of national seclusion in 1853.

Restoration of the Meiji Era

The dawn of the new age came in 1868 when the Tokugawa shogunate was brought down by antishogunate forces, which declared the formal return of political power from Tokugawa shogunate to the emperor. It was the Restoration of the era named Meiji, which meant *enlightened rule*. The Meiji period was the beginning of the Japanese modern period, which saw the transformation of feudal Tokugawa-Japan into an emerging civilized, industrialized, and military nation. The leaders of the Meiji government intended to take in everything new, not from the traditional Confucianism, but from the West. While Confucian instructional models had fallen, Westernization came to the front. The Westernization of the Meiji period was prepared and realized by scholars of Dutch learning under the patronage of feudal lords. They had already tried the diffusion of Western learning, sometimes warning of possible dangers from the West, and privately criticized the Tokugawa shogunate policy.

At the beginning of the Meiji period the new government powerfully proceeded toward the achievement of unity and centralization and the establishment of a modern educational system. In 1872, universal schooling was proclaimed, and European and American curricula were introduced into Japan. In the beginning it was the translation of European and American textbooks that came to be widely used in schools. There were no restrictions on the compilation and publication of textbooks.

The First Textbook on Art

The first textbook on art, *Teaching of Western Painting*, was published in 1871. It consisted, in the first part, of two volumes, and in the latter part, of two volumes and an illustrated supplement (see figure 1.4). The first part was a translation of *The Illustrated Drawing Book*, written by an Englishman, Robert Scott Burn, and the latter a translation of various Dutch books.

毛筆或ハ灰筆ヲ以テ臨畫スル圖

FIGURE 1.4

Kawakami Togai. Illustrations from *Teaching of Western Painting* (Seiga Shinan). Woodcuts, 1871.

This textbook was produced by Kawakami Togai, lecturer on Western art at the Institute for the Investigation of Western Books. The contents of the book covered how to draw lines, curves, parallel lines, a bisector, how to make a regular triangle, a regular square, a rectangle, a circle, and an ellipse, how to draw a window, a cask, a wheel, a handcart, a box, and a book, and so forth, in the application of geometrical shapes, how to cast shadows, how to draw human figures, and how to make perspective easily.

The textbook showed that a pupil could correctly draw objects and figures as they actually appear, having worked by the rules of instrumental drawing. It is apparent that an important aim of the textbook was not to develop a child's originality and aesthetic mind, but to train the child's hands and eyes. It was finally to produce practical and useful men, who were indeed required by the Meiji government, because the new government had abolished conservative Confucian thought and values and had adopted Western ideas and values under the slogan "Civilization and Enlightenment."

The first textbook on art, *Teaching of Western Painting*, was one of the remarkable achievements produced by Western-style painters of the Tokugawa shogunate in order to aim at the idea of rationality in art. At the same time, it was also a result of educational policy determined by political and national structures of the Meiji period. However, a reaction against the uncritical adoption of Western civilization set in around 1880 and new educational ideas were developed in cooperation with the publication of new textbooks on art.

Notes

1. A live Indian rhinoceros, sketched by A. Dürer, was sent as a gift from the king of Cambodia to King Emmanuel of Portugal in 1515. After this animal had remained for six months in Lysbon, it was shipped as a present from Emmanuel to Pope Leo X. However, the ship sank with the rhinoceros on board near Genova. After it washed ashore, it was stuffed and presented to Leo X (Isozaki, 1979a, pp. 57–59).

2. Kokan also copied Dutch proverbs written on pages in "Het Menslijk Bedrijf": e.g., *Soeckt in u selfs den Schat, van't aller schoonste Vat* (Seek in yourself the treasure of the most beautiful cask) and *Het Stof, en Slyck der Aar, en is den Twist niet waard* (The dust and the mud of this world are not worthy of the dispute).

3. The Catalog of Aodo Denzen Exhibition covered all items of profitable knowledge: medical treatment, agriculture, pharmacy, geography, etc. Among those items was an article entitled "Etsen" (etching) that was valuable for Denzen and Kokan. This article made etching in Japan possible. Today there exist many editions of *Huishoudelijk Woordenboek* in Japan.

4. This institute was renamed *Yosho shirabesho* (Institute for the Investigation of Western Books), and later *Kaiseijo* (Institute for Development). The new Meiji government reopened the institute as *Daigaku Nanko* in 1868. Mitsukuri Gempo (1799–1863) was appointed an official interpreter in the Tokugawa shogunate's Office of Astronomy (*Temmonkata*) in 1839. In 1865 Gempo became an important instructor in the institute.

2

Doug Boughton

Australian Visual Arts Education

Long-Standing Tensions between Sociocultural Realities and Governmental Policy

This chapter briefly describes the cultural origins of the peoples comprising the Australian nation and the early history of ideas about art education derived from European sources and transformed in the Australian context. It would be difficult to understand the meaning and significance of visual expression in contemporary Australian life without stories of the broader cultural context. The long-established traditions of Aboriginal visual culture is one of these stories. A second story is about the British invasion of Australia in 1788, which imposed a conflicting and initially separate tradition of visual culture and the subsequent diffusion of British cultural potency by the immigration of peoples from many diverse backgrounds following World War II. The collision and subsequent intertwining of these stories provides the framework for an analysis of contemporary art education issues.

The Early Years

Viewed from a European perspective, the history of Australian art education is a very short one of just two hundred years from the first British settlement in 1788. In contrast, viewed from an Aboriginal perspective, art education might be as old as sixty thousand years (Roberts, Jones, & Smith, 1990). To properly understand the context in which both education and art education developed, a brief survey of Australian social history is important.

The Impact of Invasion on Aboriginal Peoples

Probably the most significant feature of the story of European invasion of Australia is that until 1993 white law in Australia was predicated on the doctrine of *terra nullus* in relation to Aboriginal land rights. Under Australian law, the country was uninhabited at the time of the white invasion. National legislation was passed in December 1993 to revoke *terra nullus* following an historic high court decision in the Mabo case in June 1992, which at last recognized the right of Aboriginal land ownership. This decision has been heralded, almost universally, as a turning point in the history of the nation (Wolfe, 1994; Harris, 1994), although skeptics (Poynton, 1994; Wolfe, 1994) have argued that little is likely to change as a consequence.

The theme illustrated by the Mabo decision is the long-standing pattern of colonialism entrenched in the social ethos of the nation that can be traced back to its roots. According to Wolfe (1994), there were three basic settler-colonial strategies: confrontation, incarceration, and assimilation. Confrontation immediately followed the seizure of territory and was characterized by indigenous mortality following from homicide, sexual abuse, disease, and starvation. This period was short, lasting from six months to ten years, depending on the location of new territories settled within the colony. The long-term effect of war, disease, and despair was the reduction of the initial population, estimated to be 1.5 to 2 million Aboriginals, by 90 percent in the first one hundred years (Poynton, 1994).

The second phase, incarceration, saw the indigenous survivors of the first phase gathered into fixed locations on mission stations and reservations. While the intention here was not directly homicidal, it was consistent with the theory of elimination—to free the land for pastoral settlement. Aboriginal labor was exploited in every phase of settler colonization (Curthoys, 1982).

However, despite the blatant opportunism displayed by the colonists in their use of native labor, the underlying assumption was that the race was dying out. This teleological view of evolutionary racism is reflected in these observations by the editor of Captain Cook's journal. Writing after almost one hundred years of settlement, he described Aboriginal people in this way (cited in Pearson, 1994):

> Their treachery, which is unsurpassed, is simply an outcome of their savage ideas, and in their eyes is a form of independence which resents any intrusion on their land, their wild animals, and their rights generally. In their untutored state they therefore consider that any method of getting rid of the invader is proper. Although treated by the coarser order of colonists as wild beasts to be extirpated, those who have studied them have formed favorable opinions of their intelligence. The more savage side of their disposition being, however, so very apparent, it is not astonishing, that brought into contact with white settlers, who equally consider that they have a right to settle, the Aboriginals are disappearing. (p. 2)

The third phase of settlement according to Wolfe (1994) followed the peculiar legislation of 1900 which, in the same instant, decreed colonists to be Australians, and Aboriginals to be non-Australians, by virtue of their exclusion from the provisions of the new constitution. A problematic outcome of this legislation was the (potential) expansion of the "half-caste menace," a rapidly growing group of people resulting from the sexual exploitation of Aboriginal women by white men. The offspring resulting from these encounters invariably grew up with their mothers, being identified initially as "native" rather than "settler." The official response to the "half-caste menace" was to redefine people of mixed descent as "settler," thus leading to the forced separation of them from their maternal kin on reservations and the beginning of a series of assimilist policies. Child abduction, undertaken by whites as part of a program of "improvement" became the icon of the assimilation phase. The missionary rhetoric of uplifting and civilizing was applied to the "stolen" children who were to be provided with the same privileges and opportunities as whites (Wolfe, 1994).

In the early 1900s, Aboriginality was considered an ideological issue. However, definitions of Aboriginality hinged on formulas of generational diffusion. The first generation of mixed blood was half-caste (one white and one Aboriginal parent), second generation was "quadroon" (one white and one half-caste parent) and "octoroon" was third generation (assuming one white and one quadroon parent).[1] Beyond quadroon one could be defined as white. Over time, the simple mathematical logic of these definitions, of course, became diffused by the various intermarriages and the introduction of different racial groups into the Australian cultural mix. As a result, a consequence of early assimilist policies was genetic, rather than ideological, assimilation.

In contemporary Australia, the notion of Aboriginality is a complex construct that defies genetic definitions. In the context of post-Mabo land claims, an authentic connection to the land has to be proven by the claimants, and the parameters for compensation include a "consideration for Aboriginal special attachment to the land" (Poynton, 1994). What constitutes "Aboriginality" and "special attachment to the land" remains to be determined judicially in light of pending Aboriginal land claims. The contemporary notion of Aboriginality in art and education is an even more complex issue that I will return to later.

Art Education in the Australian Colonies

The hundred years following the first settlement were not characterized by any systematic or widespread formal art education programs in schools. It was not until the 1870s and 1880s that centralized state systems of education were put in place in most Australian states. While the timing of developments was different in each state, the general pattern was similar. Prior to the late 1800s, instruction in art and design was obtained by colonists largely through self-education and opportunities provided by private teachers, and later through public elementary schools and public art galleries (Young, 1985). Art schools were established in Victoria in 1870, Hobart in 1889, and Western Australia in 1900. Each of the state schools provided drawing lessons for children, and trained artisans, teachers, and art masters (Chalmers, 1990).

It is not surprising that English colonists looked to artistic accomplishment as a way of providing evidence of cultural refinement in their harsh new surroundings, as well as a link to home (England). As the colonies developed and settled into patterns of agricultural and industrial life, interest in formalizing education to serve the commercial interests of the new economy became stronger. In an effort to establish and maintain standards of education that were not inferior to that provided in England, each of the Australian states moved toward centralized control of the schools. Curricula and examinations were imported from England.

By this time, throughout Australia the most powerful influence in art education came from South Kensington in England. South Kensington was the home of the School of Art and Science, formerly the British Department of Practical Art. The South Kensington philosophy of art education drew from German ideologies, which tended toward utilitarianism. The proponents of this approach "espoused a view of drawing as being utilitarian, ornamental and mechanical as opposed to an aesthetic atelier training in the French and Italian academic traditions" (MacDonald, 1970, p. 227). Based on geometry and technical drawing, this drawing syllabus demanded mechanistic processes of imitation. The basic intention was to discipline and train the hand and the eye. The overall program was broken into four divisions, which in turn were divided into various stages totaling twenty-three altogether. Twenty-one of those stages comprised copying exercises from the flat, the round, or from nature.

The power of South Kensington derived from the overall administrative responsibility held by the Department of Science and Art, which installed a structure of state-controlled and state-supported art schools. The driving interest of this structure was directed toward the national interests of British trade, through the education of the tastes of artisans and consumers. Not only did the Department of Science and Art supervise the teaching of art throughout the country, it also was responsible for the examination of generalist teachers of art and trained art masters (Chalmers, 1990, p. 71).

The influence of South Kensington in England, in British colonies (Canada, New Zealand, and Australia), the United States, Brazil, and other parts of the world was nothing less than formidable in the latter part of the nineteenth and early twentieth centuries. This influence is well documented (e.g., Aland, 1992; Barbosa, 1984; Chalmers, 1985a, 1985b, 1990; Hillson, 1987; MacDonald, 1970; Young, 1985). The work of Walter Smith, who became state art director of Massachusetts and director of drawing in public schools in Boston in 1871 and applied the South Kensington system to his programs, created such an impact that the programs were used in other American states and Canada (Hillson, 1987). Smith's work did much to convince Australian colonists that the South Kensington style of education was appropriate for Australia.

The significance of South Kensington and its impact in Australia and New Zealand cannot be underestimated. Teachers who were trained at South Kensington were sought by the colonists and often imported at high cost. Drawing masters moved from colony to colony. The four major art schools in New Zealand were affiliated with South Kensington in the late 1800s, and students sometimes traveled to one of the Australian colonies to take the London examinations (Chalmers, 1990).

In 1882 Harry Pelling Gill, a South Kensington graduate with qualifications in mechanical, geometric, and architectural drawing, was employed in South Australia to teach drawing and design in the context of manufacture within the South Australian School of Design. High expectations were held for his contribution, not only to the proposed drawing programs of the School of Design but to art training generally in South Australia (Aland, 1992). Gill remained in South Australia until he retired due to ill health in 1913, but his influence remained well into the 1920s. Gill assumed enormous power during his career playing a central role in the School of Design, the School of Art, the art gallery, teacher education, and the inspection of accredited teachers of art in public schools (Aland, 1992).

In 1889, Frederick Woodhouse was brought to New South Wales to become the new superintendent of drawing at a salary of five hundred pounds, fifty pounds a year more than the principal of the Training School received. A reasonable conclusion following from this indication of high status was that Woodhouse was expected to become the Walter Smith of Australia (Hillson, 1987). In Queensland, the first art master to teach at Brisbane's School of Art was Joseph Augustus Clarke, a graduate of South Kensington, who had previously taught topological drawing to the Indian army.

It is interesting to examine the reasons why the mechanistic approaches to drawing and design, typical of the South Kensington approach, held such appeal in the colonies. For example, Aland's (1992) analysis of the situation in South Australia reveals that the concern of pressure groups—such as the South Australian Institute, the Chamber of Manufactures, and the South Australian Society of Artists—was to prepare the colony to compete in industry. At this time, the growth of mining, agriculture (and related manufacturing industries), and the building industry, demanded a workforce with a background in technical education, an important element of which was technical and disciplined drawing. The drawing curriculum of schools was viewed as an essential instrument of industry to educate students appropriately for the workforce. In the 1880s, the lobby groups in South Australia influenced the Central Board of Education to introduce drawing as a compulsory subject in all public schools (Aland, 1992).

A secondary theme of art education was evident in the years immediately following settlement. This involved the study of art to refine public taste, and "to develop artistic talent in young colonists to reform and improve life in the colony" (Young, 1985). This form of art education was promoted through the art societies of the colony and was usually dependent on volunteers. The model was similar to provincial English art societies and drew, through committee memberships, on the voluntary services and support of prominent citizens. Young (1985) described the situation in South Australia:

> The belief in art as a moral, refining influence and a sign of respectability and prosperity was apparent in public discourse, and influential in art and design education in South Australia. Membership of the S.A.S.A. [South Australian Society of Arts] became a sign of respectability and may have provided some S.A.S.A. supporters with an opportunity for greater social mobility. (p. 221)

During this early period, little interest was taken in the art of Aboriginal peoples, except as a curiosity. The fierce commitment to the establishment of the colonies' economic base left no room for contemplation of the meaning or significance of Aboriginal artifacts, which were viewed as primitive.

The influence of South Kensington lasted in Australia until World War I, although its practice was complemented to some extent by the addition of manual training at the turn of the century. This included wood and paper work, and emphasized the development of manual dexterity. Needlework crafts originating from nineteenth-century Russia, Germany, and Scandinavia were also introduced at this time (Hammond, 1981). The powerful theme of education as an instrument of industrial revitalization reemerged with renewed vigor in the Australian national context in the late 1980s.

The Later Years

Art Education between the World Wars

The overall pattern of development in Australian art education after World War I was similar to that in North America and Europe, but with a significant time lag between overseas developments and observable effects in Australia. Ideas in education generally were imported from overseas and this was particularly the case in art education. The links with Britain remained solid until the end of World War II, diminishing slowly under massive immigration programs.

After World War I, art education in Australia entered a transition phase, moving away from the rigid disciplines of the "hand-eye" training doctrines of South Kensington. By the late 1930s, the word *art* was used, rather than *drawing*, to describe the subject, although interest in drawing was evident till the late 1960s (Boughton, 1987). Franz Cizek's ideas about the creative potential of young children, and the belief that the child's mind was qualitatively different from that of the adult's, spawned a methodology and approach to instruction in art that was in many ways antithetical to the South Kensington pedagogy. A Scottish-trained art educator, Mary Harris, lectured on Cizek's philosophy in 1922 and published an article in the *South Australian Educational Gazette* (Harris, 1923) that described Cizek's ideas. However, it was not until 1940 that any evidence of change could be seen, and that was manifested in Western Australian curriculum documents (Mandelson, 1985). Despite the widespread changes taking place in Britain, Europe, and America, it was not until the 1950s that evidence of acceptance of the liberal doctrines of the creative self-expression movement could be clearly seen in schools in all states (Boughton, 1987). In Britain, for example, Cizek's ideas arrived in 1921 and were firmly established by 1931.

The inertia of Australian educational bureaucracies may be understood in relation to social and political circumstances. The changes in art education that occurred, for example, in New York between the world wars were not reflected in Australia. Art education in the United States was influenced by European refugees, a nationalist movement focusing on cultural leadership, and the emergence of Abstract Expressionism as the center of the fine art community shifted from Paris to New York (Freedman, this volume). In Australia, the cultural and intellectual focus of the colony remained England. The inevitable penalty of this relationship was time delay in the transportation of ideas. Energies were devoted to industrial survival and growth and, to a large extent, the service of economic and political interests of the mother country.

During the 1940s the writings of Read and Lowenfeld laid the groundwork for the changes that were to come later. The final turning point was a UNESCO seminar—*The Role of the Visual Arts in Education*—held in Victoria in 1954. The seminar was attended by artists, teachers, inspectors, and administrators who met to formulate policies for the future of art education, reflecting a commitment to the development of creativity in the students of Australian schools.

Aboriginal Art

Returning to the theme of Aboriginal culture, I must first make a comment about the term *art* used in connection with Aboriginal culture. Some scholars question the appropriateness of the term *art* as applied to Aboriginal artifacts. Rogers's (1994) research with the Adnyamathanha people in the Flinders Ranges in South Australia indicates that artifacts, which may be viewed by Europeans as art, simply resemble objects commonly recognized by that description in European culture. Adnyamathanha people do not separate art from culture, nor do they have a tradition of description or specialized language to deal with independent notions of "art" or "creativity."

Little attention was paid to Aboriginal art or artifacts in the school curriculum until the 1980s. By the beginning of the twentieth century the impact of the white invasion had altered the nature of the "art" objects made by Aboriginal peoples. Early settlers looked upon artifacts as something to acquire, which led to Aboriginal people increasing and adapting their production to suit the purposes of trade, rather than to serve traditional cultural purposes. While this influence was noticed immediately following the first settlement, the economic impact of this trade did not become significant until the 1920s (Rogers, 1994).

This phenomenon is a well-documented scenario for first nations peoples who have experienced European invasion in other parts of the world. The impact for Aboriginal peoples was culturally significant, the full effect of which is difficult to determine. Rogers's (1994) oral history research in South Australia has revealed some examples of the adaptations made in response to the tourist trade in the 1920s.

> Researchers in this project have only just begun to look at the Adnya-mathanha people and the 'tourist trade', but respondents have already pointed to a variety of influences. A number of Adnyamathanha people carve emu eggs. The techniques used were not possible before Europeans brought metal tools. Boomerangs were decorated with a wider range of designs and were made in different sizes in order to meet the demand of the market for a decorative rather than a practical tool. . . . Many were made during the nineteen-thirties. Times were bad and it was possible to trade artifacts with the station owners for extra rations. The missionar-ies too acted as "middlemen" providing a link with any tourists. How important an influence this was on the Adnyamathanha still needs to be determined. (p. 19)

The Adnyamathanha group is only one of many Aboriginal groups in Australia, and considerable regional differences of experience exist. How-ever a confronting cultural issue for Aboriginal peoples is highlighted by the trade of artifacts. Rogers (1994) points out in his research that Western cultures assume that the artist is the intellectual owner of his or her work and that the work has financial, intellectual, and/or aesthetic value because of its uniqueness. Traditional Aboriginal peoples did not hold this assumption. Individuals were not necessarily the creators of ideas. Instead, Aboriginal societies viewed individuals as being the temporary "custodi-ans" of ideas, which were passed on to others within a society characterized by oral traditions. Ownership of intellectual property in this sense is col-lective and ageless.

Of great significance for Aboriginal people was the rise to attention of Albert Namatjira, the first nationally prominent Aboriginal artist. Namatjira learned to paint with watercolors in a European style. He was taught by artist Rex Batterbee in 1936 and painted his own country in the interior of Australia. His work did much to elevate the status of Aboriginal people and to demonstrate artistic capacity in terms that the Eurocentric population could understand. While his work at first impression appeared to be entirely derivative of European traditions, closer examination reveals similarity with early Western desert "dot" painters (Neale, 1993). Because Namatjira's work resembled European art, his paintings were included as content for study in school programs in the 1950s.

World War II to the 1980s

Following World War II, Australia began a virtual cultural revolution, brought about by a massive immigration drive. In July 1945, Arthur Caldwell, the first Minister for Immigration, announced the broad objective for Australia of a population of twenty million, to be achieved through immigration. This sparked a drive for non-British as well as British immigrants in all states.

Following the lifting of the "white Australia" policy in the mid-seventies, immigration from Asia increased significantly. Between 1971 and 1986 Australia gained a total of 1,108,164 people from immigration comprising 36 percent from Asia, 27.3 percent from the United Kingdom, 13.8 percent from New Zealand, 6.2 percent from Eastern Europe, 4.6 percent from Africa, and 4 percent from Pacific Island countries.[2]

Since the end of World War II, Australia has accepted more immigrants per capita than any country, other than Israel. Forty percent of all Australians are the product of postwar immigration (Grassby, 1978). Figures from the 1981 census show 12 percent of school-age children were born overseas and another 12 percent are the children of parents who were both born overseas. Overall, the Australian population is composed of over 140 cultural groups, 90 languages (not counting an estimated 200 Aboriginal languages), and 80 different religions.

The rapid cultural transformation brought about by immigration placed enormous pressure on bureaucratic educational structures that were developed to deal with an essentially monocultural population. By the 1970s, pressure had been brought to bear on the government to shake off its colonial perspectives and to recognize the multicultural mix that now constituted its population. In 1973, the government committed itself to a policy of multiculturalism. This policy has been exercised within the arts and education in various ways through funding agencies.

Despite the commitment of these funds, a review submitted to the Commonwealth Schools Commission in 1984 reported that of the 2,871 funded multicultural projects in 14 percent of Australian schools, almost one quarter were judged to have been unsuccessful. The report commented on the sheer difficulty of the task of implementing a philosophy of multiculturalism in Australian schools (Executive summary, 1984). Ethnic subgroups within society survive only because they are composed of individuals with strong emotional ties to such groups. Promotion of multiculturalism may be regarded by these individuals as a threat to their own survival, and instead of improving understanding and tolerance, may stimulate ethnic dissent and division. The simplistic approach of the Australian Government—development of a policy and allocation of funds to implement it—was simply inadequate and did not recognize the complexities inherent in cultural issues.

From the mid-sixties to the eighties, practical art teaching in secondary schools underwent a transition from a focus on process to a studio product orientation. This required a disciplined study through studio practice of traditional fine art and craft disciplines including drawing, painting, printmaking, sculpture, ceramics, fiber crafts, film, and metal crafts. The approach was skill based, and the conceptual content of most state curricula was derived from modernist concepts of Abstract Expressionism, primarily the elements and principles of design (Boughton, 1987).

Art appreciation and art history have been consistent themes in Australian education since settlement and by the seventies were firmly embedded in the senior school curricula of all states. By the late 1980s, art became accepted as one of the subjects students could use for university entrance examination, with art theory or art history being a substantial required component (up to one half of the syllabus content). Assessment of senior school final examinations is public and centrally administered by state departments or boards of education. The early belief in art knowledge as a sign of moral virtue and cultural refinement transmogrified during the eighties into a belief that knowledge of art in social contexts promotes cultural understanding.

The 1980s and National Curriculum Reforms

From the mid-eighties many of the previously discussed elements of Australia's cultural history combined with newer economic/industrial and political forces in the context of government-initiated curriculum reforms. The increases in immigration from Asia following revision of "white Australia" policy reflected a heightened consciousness of the proximity and power (particularly economic) of Australia's closest Asian neighbors. Ethnic tensions within urban communities threatened national unity, leading to nationalist rhetoric and government-initiated debates about republican status. Poor economic performance of Australian products on overseas markets led to sweeping microeconomic reforms in industry and the development of competency frameworks for the assessment of immigrant (and domestic) workers' skills. Education was swept up in these government reforms in order to bring schools in line with the requirements of the workforce. The principles of student performance expressed as standardized competency frameworks (profiles), against which teachers' report outcomes formed the centerpiece of the national curriculum reform movement. The visual arts were forced to fit these government-inspired patterns of curriculum structure, forcing a crisis of identity for the discipline (Boughton, 1992).

The Australian national curriculum movement had its origins in a concern that the country could not effectively compete in an international market without massive restructuring in industry and concomitant educational reforms to provide appropriately skilled labor. The logic expressed by government officials is characterized in this statement by the Federal Minister for Education in 1988:

> The schools play a critical and central role in the nature of our society and economy. They provide the environment through which the children of Australia pass as they move on to technical and further education, higher education and employment. There is little to be gained from adjustment to the structure of our nation and the way we live and work if the central position of the schools is ignored. (Dawkins, 1988, p. 1)

The National Industry Education Forum reiterated this view in 1991:

> If we truly believe that Australia's future depends on becoming competitive then one of the first things which must surely be set right is the education system. (Loton, 1991, p. 1)

The Minister's recommendation for national curriculum reform was taken up by the Australian Education Council (AEC), an intergovernmental committee of federal and state education ministers. In 1989, this group published *Common and Agreed National Goals for Australian Schooling*, a statement identifying eight key learning areas, one of which was the arts. The AEC also established the Australian Curriculum Corporation to facilitate and promulgate the resulting national curriculum statements and profiles, and recommended a national approach to teacher education and accreditation. The AEC also established CURASS (a curriculum and assessment committee) to negotiate collaboration between the states for the purpose of developing national approaches to curriculum and assessment.

Each of the states and territories participated in the development of national curriculum statements and profiles for all subjects. The brief for the arts curriculum was completed in June 1992 (Emery and Hammond, 1992), and the statements and profiles were completed in 1993. The centerpiece of the curriculum document was the "profiles," a framework describing the expected trajectory of the "typical" student through eight levels of schooling from entry at about age six to exit at Year 12. The levels of expected performance were expressed as outcome statements. Each of the arts shared three common components (domains): (a) making/creating/presenting; (b) past and present contexts; and (c) criticism and aesthetics. The purpose of the profiles was to provide an agreed-on national framework for teacher reporting of student progress.

Strong pressure was applied from industry to exercise control, not only upon curriculum standards but on accountability measures for teacher quality. The national Industry Education Forum in 1992 expressed this goal illustrating the pressure on education to apply a similar competency-based approach to education that was employed for industry:

> By 1995, school systems throughout Australia are to have in place a comprehensive system of performance and accountability measures which will allow for valid and reliable assessments of *student and teacher* performance as a basis for national and international comparisons. [emphasis added] (NIEF, 1992, p. 4)

In July 1993, the national curriculum reform movement lost some of its impetus at a meeting of the Australian Education Council called inter alia to accept and adopt the completed national curriculum documents. Instead the curriculum documents were referred back to the states for individual interpretation, and the federal government lost control of the national agenda to some extent.

The theme evident in the national curriculum reforms is a familiar one. In the late 1800s, drawing was seen by the administrators of the colony as important to industry and was incorporated into the curriculum to serve this purpose. In the late 1900s, the agenda of government is derived from neocorporatist principles, the state acting in the national interest drawing together representative groups and establishing a working relationship among them (Grundy, 1994).

In the 1880s, the needs of industry resulted in the inclusion of art (drawing) in the school curricula of the colony. In the 1990s, the needs of industry have forced the arts to be described within a curriculum framework more suited to other disciplines and at a level of specificity unsuited to the nature of the field. It is unfortunate that at this moment in Australian history the move toward centralized control of education, characterized by application of uniform standards and an interest in developing performance-based descriptors of competence should occur within an intellectual climate sustained by postmodern discourse.[3]

One of the key elements of postmodernism is the notion that ideas from different cultures can be accommodated together in the context of pluralistic societies. Old distinctions within and between cultures are breaking down. In Australian society the struggle of diverse ethnic subgroups to retain their core values, supported by a government policy of "dynamic but lasting multiculturalism" (Boughton, 1986, p. 95), is thrown into sharp contrast against the search for a distinctive Australian national identity.

Contemporary Issues for Aboriginal Art Education

Following the 1992 Mabo High Court land rights decision, Aboriginal groups assumed a political profile and influence disproportionate to their population base (about 1 percent of the total population). Education in Australia is grappling with social justice, multiculturalism, and nationalist issues—for which the Aboriginal debate has assumed lighthouse status on all fronts. Work by Aboriginal artists has moved out of museums of natural history where it was once displayed as a curiosity into high-status national galleries.[4] Daniel Thomas (1988) observed that

> Australian Aboriginal art, admired by the European art world as art throughout most of the twentieth century, is in the 1980s a very conspicuous reason for the white community's new respect for Aboriginal culture generally. The Aboriginal people are re-conquering the minds of their invaders, as the Greeks re-conquered the ancient Romans. (p. 12)

Aboriginality as a concept in art is becoming blurred as Aboriginal transitional artists take up European materials and forms of representation, demand ownership and financial reward for their intellectual property, accept recognition as creative individuals, and exhibit in galleries in the European tradition, isolated from their cultural roots. The contemporary definition of Aboriginality is a complex, ideological issue, making the study of traditional forms relatively simple in comparison to contemporary works of urban Aboriginals.

Conclusion

The complexities of curriculum development are intimidating for teachers faced with teaching Aboriginal groups not only about traditional Aboriginal art and culture but transitional art, as well as European, Asian, and other world cultures. Added to this problem is the fact that Aboriginal students fall into three distinct groupings: (a) those living in traditional areas of Australia, such as the Pitjantjatjara Lands and Yalata, where Aboriginal culture and values are still observed; (b) Aboriginal communities where traditional ways are not observed; and (c) minority groups of Aboriginals living in urban situations (South Australian Aboriginal Education Consultative Committee, 1983).

Government-inspired national curriculum reforms have done nothing to address the complexities of these cultural issues. Contemporary curriculum profiles in the arts reflect modernist Eurocentric definitions of artistic practice and analysis, and, while paying lip service, do not accommodate issues of Aboriginality, or non-European artistic traditions, such as the growing Asian and Muslim populations in Australia. (Vestiges of paternalistic colonial ideologies persist in government, it appears.) In effect, contemporary industry has driven government demands for a curriculum to define predictable and regulated pathways in the arts and set up a conflict of sociocultural, ideological, and political forces that remains to be resolved.

Notes

1. See Wolfe's (1994, p. 113–16) extended discussion of this issue.

2. The source of all statistics is Crowell International (1990), *The Concise Encyclopaedia of Australia & New Zealand.* Sydney: Horwitz Graham Pty.

3. See Efland, Freedman, & Stuhr (1996) for a comprehensive analysis of the impact of postmodernism in art education.

4. A prime example of the high regard held for both traditional and contemporary Aboriginal art work is the Aboriginal and Torres Strait Islander Collection held at the Art Gallery of New South Wales. See Margo Neale's *Yiribana* (1993).

3

F. Graeme Chalmers

Teaching Drawing in Nineteenth-Century Canada—Why?

C anada is a great band of land across the top of North America. Of its indigenous, French, and British origins, it was the British influence that was to most affect the teaching of drawing in nineteenth-century Canadian schools. The recent Quebec referendum shows how fragile the Canadian confederation is, and how dominated and conquered many French-speaking Québecois still feel. The British colonies of Canada East (Quebec), Canada West (Ontario), New Brunswick, and Nova Scotia became Canada in 1867. Prince Edward Island waited until 1873. The western provinces and territories were next to join the confederation, although with the exception of Nunavit in the far north, many First Nations and Inuit land claims have yet to be settled. Newfoundland, with its parallel systems of denominational schooling, joined the Canadian confederation in 1949.

The indigenous populations of what we now call Canada had many

47

needs for art in their lives and had well-developed apprenticeship systems of art education for both girls and boys long before contact with European colonizers from the two so-called founding nations. The nineteenth-century industrial drawing curricula taught by missionaries and others in Indian residential schools certainly did not acknowledge either the art or the instructional systems that were already in place.

This chapter examines some ideological influences on the teaching of drawing in preconfederation and postconfederation Canadian schools. Nineteenth-century Canadian schools embraced ideas transported from Britain and France, but it was a selective and conservative embrace. When we consider Victorian art education, in Canada and other European colonies and dominions, we find a plethora of dull and arid drawing and copy books containing "little more than banal and repetitious geometric exercises, [with little] that could be related to modern notions of art education, self expression and child art" (Ashwin, 1981, p. 3). Such was certainly the case in Canada, and in this chapter, I investigate *why*.

Drawing as a Means of Social Control

Whereas nature and "art" were suspect, copy-book "drawing" was seen as particularly useful by nineteenth-century Canadian public school promoters, many of whom, as practical Methodists or dour Presbyterians in English-speaking Canada, had little time for the "fine" arts. In conquered French-speaking and Catholic Quebec both the hierarchy and the provincial government—which some would argue was one in the same—also supported this view; although some boys destined for a career in the church, law, or politics received a classical education, and girls of the upper classes attended elite urban convents where a different view of art and art education prevailed. In such institutions girls were taught polite accomplishments, and boys were introduced to the cultural heritage of western Europe. In contrast, children (both boys and girls) in *public* and *parochial* schools needed to conform and be obedient; to be seen, but not heard. Powerful elites saw the boys who attended public and parochial, rather than private, schools as future artisans predestined and confined to their agrarian, working-class, or lower middle-class roles and stations. In England, Earl Granville (*Art Journal*, 1857) even suggested that girls destined for domestic service should study drawing because of "the precision and neatness it leads to" and "that to lay a knife and fork perfectly parallel to one another required the sort of eye which was perfected by a drawing lesson or two" (p. 353). Drawing was training. It involved discipline, particularly self-discipline. Most nineteenth-century drawing manuals, in Canada as elsewhere, deliberately begin with drawing *straight* lines.

In the eyes of growing commercial and industrial elites, drawing in nineteenth-century Canadian schools helped to produce efficient, well-trained, peaceful, neat, well-behaved, compliant workers and, consequently, along with other aspects of the curriculum, served as a powerful means of social control. According to Efland (1983) in the United States, and Soucy (1986) in Canada, the nineteenth-century entrepreneurial classes supported an industrially based system of drawing instruction in schools because it, in turn, supported their own economic interests. These entrepreneurs, who were exclusively men in Ontario and to a certain extent Quebec, instituted a system of certificates and publicly and privately funded prizes that especially recognized diligence and perseverance, rather than creativity or knowledge about high art. As with the British South Kensington system, these government certificates supposedly offered access to jobs.

In Canada, drawing was first taught in the mechanics' institutes established from the 1830s through the 1880s. In contrast, "art" for "gentle" cultural refinement, was taught only in elite boys' schools and in "ladies" colleges and urban convents. With the exception of a few schools for girls, these elite institutions were not greatly supported by the growing Methodist and Presbyterian middle-class majority.

By the time that a British Royal Commission on elementary education reported in 1887, drawing was compulsory in the publicly supported schools of the provinces of New Brunswick, Nova Scotia, Ontario, Prince Edward Island, and Quebec. It had been introduced and was growing, although was not mandatory in Manitoba and British Columbia (Royal Commission, 1888).

Drawing was introduced into Canadian public schools using rationales that linked it with penmanship, utility, and mechanical and industrial progress. There were no exorbitant claims; nothing about creativity. Drawing was not to be a great civilizing or humanizing force. In 1851, the same year as the Great Exhibition in London, the first superintendent of education in Nova Scotia stated: "Drawing is worthy of introduction into every school, as a means of training the eye, the hand, and the observing faculties, independent of its use in many mechanical pursuits" (Dawson, 1851, pp. 56–57). But, despite this rhetoric, it was *industrial* drawing that school systems eventually embraced.

Embedded in what became an increasingly narrow and utilitarian view, drawing was a means of social control and cultural hegemony. Not only would evening drawing classes in mechanics institutes supposedly keep male artisans away from street corners and even more pernicious surroundings (Smith, 1883a), the teaching of drawing in public and parochial schools would be good for the working classes "whose children constitute so large a majority in our schools" because, according to one Nova Scotian writer, it would appease their ambition and make them contented peaceful workers. In 1879, Emil Vossnack, a civil engineer, included the following in his letter to the Nova Scotia Council of Public Instruction and the City of Halifax School Commissioners:

> Our schools have furnished the heads tolerably, but have left the hands comparatively powerless and hence have steadily sent into the active world multitudes who were sufficiently educated to be dissatisfied with their social stations, but who have had no capability of using their knowledge in improved forms of labor, *which should at once appease their reasonable ambition, and make them contented to be honest work-people.* (p. 2, my emphasis)

Competing "fine arts" ideologies related to both aesthetic education and notions of refining the masses, along with "moral elevation" that eventually led to the turn-of-the-century picture study movement, also existed. However, practical industrial aspects of drawing were most emphasized in Canadian schools. For example Vossnack's letter continued:

> The moral elevation which results from familiarity with beauty and grace in nature and art is also a considerable element in [drawing] instruction, not to be under-valued, *but the most hopeful immediate consequences are to be looked for in the improved efficiency of Canadian artisans*—a life question for them—whose field of opportunity will be enlarged in proportion as their fingers are trained to deftly execute the commands of an observing eye; eye and hand being especially educated in drawing. (Vossnack, 1879, p. 3, my emphasis)

Where "beauty" and "grace" were included in drawing curricula, these concepts followed learning to draw straight lines, curved lines, and vases with "subtlety of proportion." But, it was *rules*, such as the "rule of thirds" that were taught. In nineteenth-century public schools beauty was not in the eye of the beholder, it was defined by the drawing masters, who were the servants of the captains of industry.

Teachers were trained to perpetuate the system. Typical Canadian teachers' examinations from the 1880s required teachers to be able to explain, by reference to the all-important approved drawing manual, the best mode of teaching reduction and enlargement and to be able to state when the blackboard should be used in teaching drawing. Conformity was much more important than individuality. Teachers were to state the advantages of class, rather than individual instruction in drawing by dictation exercises and memory exercises. They were to give methods for drawing straight lines, curved lines, and trial lines. They were to give an example of a drawing lesson suitable for the blackboard, and finally, so that they could also teach the working classes "good taste," as defined by their betters, each was to draw a vase "exhibiting subtlety of proportion and curve" (Public Schools Report, 1889, pp. 97–98).

In 1875 John Jessop, the superintendent of public instruction in British Columbia, a Methodist and ex-student of Egerton Ryerson in Ontario, turned to an "eminent authority" and brought the following to the attention of the British Columbia Legislature and public school promoters:

> Almost everything that is well made now is made from a drawing. In the construction of buildings, ships, machinery, bridges, fortifications, nothing is done without drawings. It is not enough that there be draughtsmen to make the drawings: the workmen who are to construct the objects required should be able, without help, to interpret the drawings given for their guidance. This they cannot do without instruction that acquaints them with the principles on which the drawings are made and so trains the imagination as to enable it to form from the given lines a vivid mental picture of the object required. The workman who lacks this knowledge and this ability, as it is probable that nineteen twentieths of . . . artisans now do must work under the constant supervision of another, doing less and inferior work and receiving inferior wages. But it is also essential that the workman himself be able to make at least a rude working drawing whenever, as frequently happens, an emergency requires it. (Public Schools Report, 1875, p. 15)

Efland (1985) and other historians of art education have argued that "statements referring to education that is useful or practical often had the ulterior purpose of shaping the education of the pupils around those duties and responsibilities assigned to their present class" (p. 136). Such was the case in Canada.

Methodism and the South Kensington System in Canada

One of the first Canadian public school educators to think about drawing in this way was the Reverend Egerton Ryerson. Ryerson was the leading intellectual figure in Wesleyan Methodism in British North America between 1825 and 1860. He was, successively, a circuit rider, founder and editor of the *Christian Guardian*, pastor of Newgate Church in Toronto, principal of Victoria College (now part of the University of Toronto), and provincial superintendent of education. His association with Britain's Department of Practical Art (the beginning of the South Kensington System) and subsequent influence on art education in Ontario deserves attention and can be profitably examined in the light of his Methodism.

Methodism, even in Wesley's lifetime, showed signs of becoming predominantly middle class. Wesley wrote "Methodists in every place grow diligent and frugal . . . consequently they increase in goods" (Southey, 1930, p. 175). Inglis (1963) and other historians of church and class conclude that "in the early nineteenth-century the [Methodist] movement drew its largest number of adherents from the middle classes who had made and been made by the industrial revolution" (p. 9). By 1830, the Methodist Church was the largest of the Protestant churches in Central Canada. It was this class whose sons and daughters became public school teachers in English-speaking Canada and whose Protestant values allowed *drawing*, but not *art*, to be taught in public schools.

Methodists, like many other nineteenth-century Christians, generally believed that capitalism and social justice were wholly compatible. As chief superintendent of education for Upper Canada, Ryerson had traveled in the United Kingdom and Europe and was familiar with developments in art education, particularly drawing, at South Kensington in Britain following the Great Exhibition. He established an educational museum in Toronto "founded after the example of what is being done by the Imperial Government as part of the system of popular education . . . training the minds and forming the taste and character of the people" (Chief Superintendent of Education, 1860, p. 14).

Rather than the morally uplifting "pictures for the poor" endorsed by some British clergy, Ryerson praised drawing in his 1859 report as "exerting a very salutary influence." He specifically mentioned the South Kensington system as imparting instruction in drawing to the British working classes. It was Ryerson who, in 1857, fourteen years before Walter Smith arrived in Boston, arranged for John Bentley, a graduate of the Macclesfield School of Art in England, to be paid his South Kensington Certificate allowance to teach at the Government Model School in Toronto. Ryerson made sure that his art master was a practical man from the industrial and nonconformist (Methodist) heartland of England. The Reverend Dr. Ryerson was true to his Methodist roots. Bentley was to teach industrial drawing, not art; "art" was a "worldly amusement."

The rigid system of drawing instruction and examinations promoted by the British Department of Science and Art at South Kensington has been explained by a number of writers (e.g. MacDonald, 1970; Thistlewood, 1986). Minihan (1977) has bluntly stated that

No beguiling dreams of high art distracted [the South Kensington Art Masters] from their daily tasks. They were practical men working to include art in the national elementary school curriculum and to educate the tastes of artisans and consumers alike in the interests of British industry and trade. (p. 96)

South Kensington's system was characterized by the South Kensington-trained Massachusetts state supervisor of drawing, Walter Smith (1883a), on one of his visits to Canada in the following way:

> Led by that great man, Prince Albert the Good, the consort of our beloved Queen, the nation went to work to remedy past deficiencies, to provide for a national system of education in elementary art and science, and to sustain the civilization of the country at its weakest point. Every child was to be taught how to draw; every boy or girl was to have a chance; every stray genius was to be carefully husbanded; every mechanic was to be given the choice or whether he would spend his evenings profitably in a school of art or science, or waste it at street corners or in even more pernicious surroundings. (pp. 16–17)

Learning to Draw and the Protestant Work Ethic

For Methodists, idle hands were the devil's playground. In his *Handbook of Practical Art*, British clergyman R. St. John Tyrwhitt (1868) claimed that

> All success must be won by hard and systematic exertion, which will save him from lower desires. . . . Nobody expects the whole of the working classes will at once take to drawing and entirely renounce strong liquor—but many may be secured from temptation to excess. . . . Teaching children good drawing is practically teaching them to be good children. (MacDonald, 1970, p. 151)

Ryerson and other public school promoters in Canada probably shared this view. To them, beauty equaled holiness and moral righteousness rather than art and they wanted order and a lack of chaos. They would have agreed with Scottish-born Thomas Braidwood who, when he opened his own School of Design for Artisans in Philadelphia, distributed a brochure stating: "Schools of Design improve the moral condition, by training the mind to things of beauty and order, rendering sin, in all its chaotic hideousness, more and more repulsive" (Braidwood 1853).

Temperance and evening classes in drawing were often linked in the nineteenth century. John G. Grace (1870) told a meeting of British "art workmen" that, by spending their evenings in drawing classes rather than bars, they could save, travel, and see major art works in Europe. "For many a man, by abstaining from drink and by careful economy, may save up thirty pounds, and every man can learn to draw" (p. 21). Such was Ryerson's view.

Before leaving England for North America, Walter Smith likened evening drawing classes to Bible classes, temperance rallies, and other alternatives to music halls, pubs, and dance halls. His published lecture on *The Importance of a Knowledge of Drawing to Working Men. A Lecture Delivered in the Mechanics' Institution, Keighley, November 24, 1859* (Smith, 1860) was dedicated

> to the members of the Drawing Class in the Keighley Mechanics' Institution, that little band of workers who endeavor by self-denial and self-improvement to increase their own value as citizens and their own happiness as men, who, I hope and believe, are setting an example of temperance, perseverance, and work, both to their families and their fellows. (p. 2)

In Ontario particularly, as in Britain, an elaborate system of education department drawing examinations was developed (see Chalmers, 1993). Administered by Ryerson's lieutenant, Dr. Samuel Passmore May, the system included certificates in primary, advanced, and mechanical drawing as well as industrial art. The examinations could be entered by students in public and private secondary schools as well as in the mechanics' institutes, teacher-training sites such as model and normal schools, and schools of art. By 1890, drawing was taught in Ontario in all of the publicly supported elementary schools, art schools in six towns, twenty-one mechanics' institutes, twenty-five high schools, and seven private girls' schools.

It is significant that in an 1890 directory for Toronto, when the religion of a public school principal is stated, which along with his politics was almost without exception, it was invariably either Methodist or Presbyterian. Inglis (1963) and others have shown that the issue of "worldly amusements" became a common theme in nineteenth-century nonconformist discussion. For many nonconformists, museums and art galleries, especially if open on Sunday, constituted a particular threat to salvation. However, classes in drawing were a different matter and the South Kensington system was far from a worldly amusement.

Walter Smith in Canada

Evangelists of the South Kensington system other than Walter Smith came to North America, including Canada West's Bentley in 1857, Forshaw Day to Halifax and then Kingston in 1862, David Blair to British Columbia, and, in 1873, a South Kensington trained art mistress, Elizabeth Croasdale, became principal of Philadelphia's School of Design for Women. However, as supervisor of drawing in Boston schools and state director of art education in Massachusetts, Smith was most responsible for bringing

South Kensington's rigid system of industrial art education across the Atlantic through his many publications and demanding lecture circuit. Although he never lived in Canada, he did visit, and much of his work was republished in Canada. Walter Smith's curriculum materials were reprinted in Montreal, St. John, Toronto, Truro, and Winnipeg (Conseil des Arts et Manufactures, 1878; Normal School of Nova Scotia, n.d.; Smith 1878, 1883b, and 1884). His influence was considerable.

In Quebec especially, his drawing manuals were viewed as catechisms. At the same time that Smith's manuals were being rejected by urban Massachusetts Unitarians they were being translated into French for use in rural Quebec. Roman Catholic, French-speaking teachers may have found teaching from the conveniently packaged French edition of Smith's drawing book (Conseil des Arts et Manufactures, 1878) rather familiar, and not unlike teaching catechism. For example, Sister St-Théotiste (1878), a member of the Congrégation de Notre-Dame in Montreal, prepared a complementary booklet about linear and geometrical drawing "after the method of Walter Smith" that was organized in exactly the same way as a catechism; it contained 112 questions and answers.

Smith himself viewed teaching as a religious vocation. He was raised in one of the first rural "Catholic" parishes within the Anglican Church. Influenced by the Oxford Movement, he believed in salvation through "good works," not by faith alone or predestination. In northern English towns, he had worked with many Methodists and other nonconformists, but he also understood Catholics. In slow and deliberate English he told students at l'École Normale Laval in Quebec City that in teaching drawing they should be "true and faithful to the great ideal which has been set before [them] by the Great Teacher, the Son of God," and that consequently they may "be poor, laborious, obscure; be the plaything of politicians . . . ; be misunderstood and be misrepresented, and die and be buried in the silence and darkness" (St-Théotiste, 1878, p. 27). Smith's lectures in Quebec were arranged by S. C. Stevenson, a Presbyterian printer who became a Montreal City Councilor, president of the Mechanics' Institute, and president of the Quebec Council of Arts and Manufactures.

Nationalizing South Kensington
Made-in-Canada Drawing Books

Late nineteenth-century art education in much of Canada implied a system of social control based on the South Kensington system, which was centralized in each province's education bureaucracy. It was also controlled by men of the governing classes, who, as members of boards of trade and education, and individual manufacturers, awarded prizes for conventional industrially related art work. As a result, in both English and French, Walter Smith's drawing manuals were influential in Canada until the middle of the 1880s. However, as they became more difficult to obtain, they were replaced by "made in Canada" expressions of the South Kensington ideology.

In the Canadian textbooks, the distinction between drawing and art was maintained. The term *art* referred to something completely different when applied to the artisan than when it was applied to the upper and educated classes. For the rich, it meant the fine arts of painting and sculpture, for the poor, it meant the crafts and industrial drawing. This difference was never stated, because being understood and accepted—at least by the upper classes who did the defining—as O'Brien, McFaul, & Revell, (1885) made clear in their series *The Canadian Drawing Course* (p. 9), it never had to be.

O'Brien, McFaul, and Revell's (1885) series was followed by McFaul's (1892) *The Public School Drawing Course*, authorized by the Ontario minister of education in 1892 and also used in British Columbia and Nova Scotia. A related secondary school series *The High School Drawing Course* (Casselman, 1894) was used in the same provinces. These series, as well as the less successful *Progressive Drawing Course* (Selby and Company, 1895) were modeled on Smith's work. Although Casselman opposed "copying from the flat" and included patterns for building the requisite cylinders, prisms, cubes, cones, and pyramids, it was still a familiar version of "South Kensington in Canada."

One of the first home-grown drawing manuals in French-speaking Canada, a four-stage "National Method of Drawing" was designed, significantly, by a teacher of drawing in a *commercial* school (l'Académie Catholique Commerciale de Montréal), and appeared in 1886 (Templé, 1886). Within a few years, Templé's work was approved by the Council of Arts and Manufactures and the Council of Public Instruction in Quebec and in 1892, S. C. Stevenson, who had earlier brought Walter Smith to Quebec, translated the teacher's manual into English (Templé, 1891). By this time, Templé was also professor of drawing at the Jacques Cartier Normal School in Montreal. Possibly criticizing Smith's work, and in the manner of the "drawing book wars" in the United States, he wrote:

> Our Canadian youth is generally endowed with superior natural talent; advantage should be taken of cultivating this aptitude in order that the greatest possible success may be attained. . . .
>
> Some methods are too long and contain too many useless preliminary exercises, which are detrimental to progress. There are other systems, which can be taught only by the authors; a generally satisfactory result from these is almost an impossibility. (Templé, 1891, p. 3)

Although still providing "suitable progressive instruction and information for every branch of trade" (p. 3), Templé reflected growing nationalism and used drawing to impart a knowledge of history and cultural pride, as well as to teach object lessons. For example:

> We have . . . taken all the subjects and scenes in this beautiful Canada of ours. They consist of houses in which distinguished sons of the soil were born, and ruins of certain habitations around which twine some facts of history. Instead of European foliage, often unknown here, we have substituted our own Canadian leaves, our wood-lands, our enchanting villages; while the shores of the St. Lawrence and Ottawa supply their contingent of charming subjects. (p. 4)

The Ontario drawing manuals of this period also introduced familiar "Canadian" objects. Marie Currie (1990) has effectively compared pages from *The Canadian Drawing Course* (O'Brien, McFaul, & Revell, 1885) and *The Public School Drawing Course* (McFaul, 1892) with illustrations of sideboards, shoes, and pocket knives in the T. Eaton Company catalogues of the same period. Eaton's was, and is, one of Canada's major department stores.

The idea that drawing was mostly for boys attending other than academic classical colleges was overtly acknowledged. Brother Felix, superior-general of the Brothers of Mary, an order that taught such nonacademic youth, wrote that he found the *Méthode national de dessin* "well adapted to diffuse a knowledge . . . so beneficial to the industries of the province of Quebec. It is to be hoped that every teacher may avail himself of a copy of this work, and that it may be used in all our schools" (in Templé, 1891, p. 54). Some evidence exists that the brothers may have used the Canadian material in their industrial boys schools in Chicago. Templé also suggested the following: "Certain parts of the ornamental course may be used as models in embroidery, for young ladies attending convents and schools" (p. 5).

Although art was also taught as a refined accomplishment, especially to "ladies," even in a few Methodist and Presbyterian colleges, it was rarely taught as a liberating force in the world. When it was taught as a liberating force, it was always a cause for conflict between those proposing it and the "System." Institutional discipline and the perpetuation and legitimization of social differences among classes, through particular types of schooling, can certainly be found in approaches taken to art education in nineteenth-century Canada.

Some nineteenth-century drawing manuals were still used until the 1920s. In British Columbia, David Blair's *Canadian Drawing Series* (1903) continued to rely on the South Kensington approach and was similar to any series published in Canada twenty years earlier. Graded drawing books continued to be produced until the 1930s. In some provinces, such as British Columbia, *drawing* did not become *art* education until the 1930s. Charles H. Scott (1922), who was supervisor of drawing in the Vancouver City Schools, stated, "Drawing can be taught because Drawing is a Science. Art cannot be taught because it is an expression of the spirit or soul" (p. 14). In the nineteenth century, Canadian children were expected to exhibit only rule-governed obedience and conformity. They were not to express "spirit."

Conclusion
Changing Conceptions of Childhood

Although some nineteenth-century ideas, such as Pestalozzi's views of the value of drawing in general education, appeared to challenge the status quo, they were not widely embraced in Canada until the beginning of the twentieth century. By 1900, the ideologies surrounding drawing in Canadian schools were changing. Although in his *Hints on Drawing*, S. J. Latta (1900), the principal of the Colborne Street Public School in London, Ontario, still divided his manual into four parts (freehand and practical design, mechanical drawing and illustration, object drawing, and applied perspective, grouping, shade, and shadow), for the first time in Canada the illustrations had a much more childlike feel about them. There is direct reference to "the image in the mind" and to the applicability of the psychological work of William James. Latta (1900) wrote:

> We deplore the too prevalent neglect of proper method in the teaching of this fascinating and important subject. We believe that the particular side of the child's nature it should seek to develop is, in many respects, by the means commonly employed, retarded rather than fostered. (p. 11)

4

Fernando Hernández

Framing the Empty Space

Two Examples of the History of Art Education in the Spanish Political Context

I have often tried to organize the main approaches to art education in Spain from a historical point of view (Hernández 1994a, 1994b, 1994c, 1995). From these attempts, two dominant forms of synthesis have emerged. One illustrates a description of facts and events from the dominant trends throughout historical periods. The other pays attention to specific examples, such as case studies, where the interrelationship among educational, artistic, political, and ideological conditions can be examined. Art education phenomena are connected with other social, political, artistic, and educational events that create bodies of knowledge and a structural network which provides a level of understanding influences beyond the content of the field (Freedman, 1987).

It is from this second approach that we can discuss a critical historical approach to a curriculum subject such as art. From such an approach, the study of school subjects is discursive and practical forms of power can be used to build teachers' and students' consciousness.

In this chapter, I will construct the historical discourse from the second approach, illustrating it with examples of the first two periods or divisions we use to organize this fragmentary picture, which is Spanish art education. These periods are organized around the "names" adopted for the subject during each historical period:

1. Drawing (since the end of the nineteenth century)
2. Handicraft and Geometric Drawing (since 1940)
3. Plastic Education (since 1970)
4. Visual and Plastic Education (since 1990)

The research presented in this chapter is an attempt to build a puzzle made of different fragments that the reader can use to construct new relationships or complete with more references and different interpretations. This is a risky strategy because the history presented herein is incomplete. Some other pictures have not been included, such as teachers education and examples of art education practices conducted in schools of different ideologies. However, the purpose of this chapter is not completely finished. This is not due to the fact that the pieces included are not enough, but because other strategies to interpret these fragments may be developed in other ways. In this sense, I am offering the present text as an open discourse to be completed both by the reader and by forthcoming historical research.

A Frame for a Big Picture

Writing history of art education is not only a professional decision but, in cases such as the Spanish one, it is a pioneer adventure, due to the circumstances surrounding the history. Broadly speaking, Spain lacks historical research on the curriculum subjects, and in the case of art education this is due to the attitude of Spanish society toward arts learning. The idea that art skills are the result of a natural gift and the tradition of considering the artist as a genius has influenced this lack of interest toward art education in the Spanish society (Arañó, 1992).

However, and as a consequence of the interest shown by art history scholars toward the figure of the artist and the recent tradition (since 1976) of doctoral studies in the Spanish fine arts faculties, we can find some interesting examples under the descriptive and long period approach to research in the last fifteen years, especially on the history of the artists' education. Calvo Serraller (1982) on the Spanish academy, Cabezas (1984) on Spanish treatises about perspective (1526–1803), Pérez Sánchez (1986) on drawing history in Spain, Arañó (1986) on fine arts teaching in Spain, and Repliger (1989) on artistic thought in the romantic magazines (1835–1855) can be considered examples of research where art education historians have found many useful sources and references to explain the changes in the ideology of the subject. Other studies have been related more specifically to historical periods, geographical locations, or art institutions. These include work by Ruíz Ortega (1986) on the Design School of Barcelona (1775–1808), Porral (1991) on art institutional teaching in Galicia (1886–1986), Domínguez Perela (1990) on aesthetic behaviors, and Llorente (1995) on art ideologies of Franco's regime (1939–1960).

Some of these works dealt with only one figure whose influence established a particular tendency in arts teaching, such as the case of the study of the painter Francesc Galí by Masip (1995). In this study, we find that at the beginning of the present century, relationships were established between the ideals of a part of the Catalonian bourgeoisie and the way young workers were trained in art education skills.

The studies we may find on the specific sphere of art education related to compulsory education are rather limited. The work done by Cuenca (n.d.) on drawing teaching in colleges of education between 1839–1986, and some papers by Arañó (1989), constitute some of the very few examples in this area.

Interest in this field has recently been expanded with two symposia on the history of art education, held in Barcelona in 1994 and 1996 (Hernández & Trafí, 1994; Hernández & Planella, 1996). During the first of these events, I (Hernández, 1994a) presented a paper that described an organizational frame of four main periods so as to show the relationship between social and political events, educational development, and the content of the subject. Special attention was paid to the relationship between the names that art education has been given in school curriculum.

In order to situate the context of the research developed in the present chapter, the following paragraphs present a historical frame by organizing the general picture of art education in Spain according to two main cultural references:

1. Art education as a strategy to create a working-class culture of reproduction near the turn of the twentieth century.
2. Handicraft as a school subject and the creation of a kitsch and national taste under the influence of the conservative ideology of Franco's regime throughout the 1940s and 1950s.

This division has been made by following not only the chronological criteria but also connecting the dominant trends in art education ideology and practices with the significant political, educational, artistic, and social events that influenced them. Figure 4.1 shows a frame of some of the relationships during the first period of cultural history of Spanish art education.

FIGURE 4.1

Social and Cultural Influences on Spanish Art Education from the
Mid-Nineteenth Century until the Spanish Civil War (1936–1939)

Period	Art Education Content	Values	Socioeconomic Relations	Debates	Influences	Names and Books
From mid-nineteenth century until Spanish Civil War	Drawing	Discipline values and reproductive skills	Workers should be qualified enough	Drawing from nature or copying from models and illustrations	The rise of industries (related to Industrial Revolution) vs. taking nature itself as source of inspiration	Drawing manuals: Adsuar (1899), Masriera (1917), Blanco (1919)
	Expressionism	People's internal world becomes their source of inspiration so as to reflect a vision of reality	Human beings are good in nature and can be educated	Aesthetic education versus artistic education	Developmental psychology	New School movement: Rousseau, Pestalozzi, Froebel, Montessori, Dewey, etc. Institution for Free Teaching (Madrid), Mancomunitat's and Racionalist schools (Catalonia)

Art Education and the Culture of
Reproduction in the Nineteenth Century

Throughout the nineteenth century, members of different groups with a liberal ideology, as well as some philanthropists, had a common aim. They believed that it was the state's duty to extend schooling to all citizens. The ideological and political confrontation between these groups and the conservative forces (always with the strong support of the Catholic Church) was a constant condition in the modern history of Spain. Members of these two political groups were alternatively in power and, on many occasions, their ideological differences were different in the arena of schooling reform.

During the nineteenth century, some members of the liberal groups tried to adapt schools to social changes going on at the time. These changes were affected by the process of urbanization and industrialization and the emergence of new ideas regarding the society and culture from some other European countries. These ideas and experiences affected the taste and the aesthetic values of some minor groups, especially in such areas as Catalonia, where this initial industrial development took place. These groups were different from those belonging to the ruling social classes up to that period, the nobility and the Catholic Church.

Martínez Cuadrado (1974) pointed out that this change made the confrontation of two forms of understanding and interpreting reality possible:

> The Catholic and populist traditional culture had ruled over the world image, spare time and the myths of the majority of Spanish social classes until the first half of the nineteenth century. Since the political revolutions of 1854, 1868 and the social revolution of 1873, popular groups from working and rural social classes . . . were replaced by the traditional culture with other cultural conceptions, materialist or idealist. The penetration of federalist, anarchist, libertarian-communist and socialist ideas substituted slowly but with an inexorable process the traditional mentality of large popular groups. (pp. 533–34)

The bourgeoisie was divided into four main tendencies, which enriched the Spanish cultural spectrum versus the traditional unitary pattern. First, the elitist and rationalist group, included, for example, the founders of the Free Teaching Institution (the role of this institution shall be commented on later). Another group comprised elitist nationalism and nonliberal trends. Other sectors were grouped under a populist ideology, and the last group represented what Martínez Cuadrado called "crypt-anarchism." Each of these groups tried to impose their ideas and beliefs on education, and, tangentially on art education.

However, it is possible to find a common twofold purpose. On the one hand, art was to develop drawing skills with the aim of qualifying workers for industrial needs. On the other hand, art has always played an important role as part of the ideology intending to produce a new human being close to the ideas of the philosophers and social reformers from the Age of Enlightenment. These were the main streams in art education in the industrial countries; but at the end of the century, although Spain had good intentions, few liberal, educational reforms were promoted by industrial groups.

Some examples of these reforms are Moyano's Law for the Reform of both School and Teacher Education, approved in 1857; the Law for Freedom of Teaching, passed in 1868; Pedagogical National Museum, created in 1882; and the first Conference on Pedagogy, held in Madrid that same year. All the normal schools were economically sponsored by the state in 1886; the reform of secondary education took place in 1895; and the Ministry of Public Instruction and Fine Arts was created in 1900.

However, most of these initiatives did not fully succeed, due to the lack of funds. On top of this circumstance, and in the particular case of art education, school practices and teacher education were affected by the deadness of the members from the arts schools, always reluctant to any kind of reforms, and their traditional ways of representing artistic objects.

The influence of the French absolutist idea of the state under the monarch rules was specially felt in Spain due to two main reasons: the Spanish kings had belonged to the Bourbon French dynasty since 1700, and the great fear the nobility and the members from the church showed toward any influences coming from the liberalism of the French Revolution. It is important to remember that it took almost a century to put an end to the privileges and the rules of the academy: from 1755, when the Law of the Academy of Madrid was passed, to the Royal Decree of 1844 which put an end to the official taste and manners of the academy.

The Industrial Revolution in Catalonia and the Relevance of Art Education

In addition to these two causes of the situation of art education at that time, it is necessary to pay attention to the way the industrial revolution took place in Spain. About the second half of the nineteenth century both the industrial changes and their social consequences were visible, especially in the area of Barcelona, where 40 percent of the industrial capital of Spain was invested in the textile sector (Artola, 1976, p. 115), as well as in some parts of Catalonia and the Basque Country, where steel began to be produced. Due to these circumstances, arts schools linked to industry had only minor relevance in some parts of Spain. In Catalonia, however, the teaching of drawing, together with the development of the manufacturing textile industry and the training of artisans and artists, had acquired relevant importance since the eighteenth century.

In 1847, the Industrial School was founded in Barcelona with the aim of qualifying workers to become craft specialists. In 1874, some artistic and professional schools were established in Catalonian towns, such as Barcelona, Sabadell, Terrasa, Mataró, and Manresa. The School of Noble Arts of Barcelona was founded in 1775, and it was not until 1877 that its studies became officially recognized. All these initiatives were strongly criticized by the defenders of liberal arts, who were contrary to applied arts.

Two Reform Movements
The New School and the Free Teaching Institution

Monés (1994) stated that there are no references about the role played by art education during primary and secondary school years before the Liberal Triennium (1837–1840). He also proposed a hypothesis about the inclusion of aesthetic education as part of "adornment subjects" and that the teaching of drawing should be done by copying pictures. He provided the example of the Valldemia school, founded in 1855 in Mataró (during the Progressive Biennium 1854–1857). At this school, drawing was a subject close to physical education.

However, this situation partially changed in the second half of the century and with the commitment of a moral transformation within the Spanish society. A group of liberal and democratic intellectuals founded La Institución Libre de Enseñanza (the Free Teaching Institution) on 29 October 1876, under the management of Francisco Giner de los Ríos. The aims of this institution were initially close to the Free University of Brussels, where "new" human beings could be educated with no ideological constraints from the state or the Catholic Church. Ethic rigor and individual austerity were the main characteristics of this regenerative movement, aimed at the promotion of personal moral criteria versus dogmatic values. The influence of the German idealist philosophers (Fitche, Schelling, and Hegel) was adapted for the Krausist movement (Krause, 1883) by the philosopher Sanz del Río and by Giner, director of La Institución Libre de Enseñanza. However, this independent enterprise did not succeed from the economic point of view and its mentors decided to devote their energies and time to educate primary and secondary students regardless of religious ideas, philosophical, and political pressures.

Manuel Bartolomé Cossio was one of the main figures of the institution and responsible for the educational program where the references of the role of drawing were explicit. Under the inspiration of Froebel's ideas, drawing activities were related to the teaching of geometry and the representation of everyday objects and forms, in order to educate all the senses, especially vision and touch.

The Free Teaching Institution educators were all in favor of the importance of natural drawing as opposed to the dominant tendency of copying:

> Against the frequent opinion that pupils must copy from pictures, leaving natural drawing to superior grades, the Institution follows the criteria that children could draw what they are interested in, according to their tastes and inclinations. (Jimenez, 1987, p. 308)

Cossio was against the copying of pictures as well as the use of text books. He had the opinion that drawing teachers should be skilled enough to develop children's capacity of vision as well as that of copying from nature and everyday objects. Cossio's ideas of art education were close to Krause's aesthetic approach, the characteristics of which were the development of good taste, beauty feelings, and the enthusiasm to produce it.

For a better understanding of the context of these initiatives, Jordi Monés (1994) remarked on the importance of the Universal Exhibition held in Barcelona in 1888 as well as the influence of foreign ideas on education. These ideas came mainly from Rousseau, Pestalozzi, Froebel, and Tolstoi (the latter the less evident). Later, Dewey and Montessori became the most relevant names of this movement. Their influence enlightened some of the debates and new initiatives in art education. I shall briefly discuss some of these new insights, particularly in teachers education and school practices regarding drawing and handicraft skills.

The way the ideas of some of these educators were adapted to the Catalonian situation was studied by Monés (1994). The naturalist conception of Rousseau questioned the practice of copying, and paid more attention to the drawing of objects, people, and animals, namely, natural drawing, and the importance given to the education of the senses reinforced the importance of drawing in order to develop vision and touch.

Pestalozzi's ideas on art education were tied in his approach to moral and religious education in which notions of universality, simplicity, harmony, and the education of these senses were essential. Drawing, as a part of the educational process, was relevant in Pestalozzi's approach to education in different ways: as a helpful tool for any teaching method; as a base for reading and writing, especially due to the importance of the role that illustrations from books played in this process; as a medium to facilitate children's contemplation of the world around them and to develop their motor skills; and as a tool in the measuring process.

Froebel considered art as an internal attitude and part of the interior life. Drawing, forms, color, painting, and expression were close to his ideas of human development and to their being cultivated during the school years. Tolstoi was in favor of the importance of drawing in the educational process, stressing the discipline given to children rather than its artistic values.

These authors, together with their ideas and examples, were important in some of the reform initiatives that took place in Catalonia in the second half of the nineteenth century and up to 1939. The ideas of the New School movement (*Escuela Nueva*) that emerged in Europe at the end of the nineteenth century, exerted an important influence, particularly in Catalonia, where the process of industrialization and its social, political, and economic consequences were reflected in the ideas of educators such as Ferrer i Guardia (founder and director of the rationalist Modern School, 1901–1906) and Pau Vila (founder and principal of the Horaciam School, 1905–1912).

The initiatives taken by the Town Hall of Barcelona, the Mancomunitat and the autonomous Government of the Generalitat between 1900–1939 to reform teacher education and the pedagogic quality of public schools were inspired by the authors mentioned above. The Spanish Civil War (1936–1939), whose origin was a military rebellion against the constitutional government, put an end to all these reforms. Once the civil war was over, a new historical period of social and cultural repression under Franco's dictatorship started.

An Art Education Debate
Spontaneous versus Reproductive Drawing

The year 1898 has a symbolic relevance in Spanish History, since it set the end of the Spanish colonial empire (after Cuba's war), and many intellectuals and popular groups started to search for the regeneration of their own society. According to the studies by historians of education (Gay, Pascual, & Quillet, 1973; Solà, 1976; Monés, 1994) there was a popular movement in Catalonia related to the promotion of culture and education during the last fifteen years of the nineteenth century.

This movement favored the creation of a large number of schools linked to groups, political parties, or associations, with cultural, educational, and social purposes. These schools, which were not controlled by the state, did not follow any particular method and teachers were not required any qualifications.

The so-called Modern Schools were probably the most popular in these movements. These schools were created and adminstered by the Anticlerical Confederation of the Free Thinkers League. Into this stream, Ferrer i Guardia opened the first Modern School on 8 September 1901 (Ferrer, 1912, 1913). This school movement was an expression of the Anarchist ideal of the world conversion through education (Gay et al., 1973).

This interest also affected art education. As Alexander Galí (1982) stated in his book on art institutions and cultural movements in Catalonia: "We have the suspicion that at the beginning of the century there was a spontaneous movement, so personal, in Art pedagogy, and parallel to that of Primary Education" (p. 12). This interest in art education received, as was mentioned earlier, some theoretical reinforcement from the ideas of Rousseau, Pestalozzi, and Froebel. However, the main notion related to the importance of freedom and spontaneity for the education of young children was often questioned in practical experience, especially in the field of art education. In some ways, this movement could be interpreted as a response to industrialization in Spain, as happened in other countries.

Art education was considered an educational rather than instructional subject, which provided subjects such as maths or grammar (the traditionally so-called thinking subjects) with an equilibrium. Oliver (1923) clearly expressed such concern:

> It is necessary to find an equilibrium, a balance between Art and Aesthetic Education on the one hand and Grammar, Calculus, Orthography . . . on the other. It is important to emphasize the danger of converting Art into a teaching subject. It will be contrary to a truly aesthetic concept, the dissection of Art into rules and notions that will convert it into one more of the school's tortures. . . . If in some place a child's individuality and sentiments have to be respected it is particularly in Aesthetic Education. (p. 62)

In 1931, Cassià Costal, in his report on the situation of the Catalonian schools, also described a critical picture of art education:

> There is no painting, there is no modeling, there is no drawing according to a child's living interests. There is no good teaching of singing and music (with some exceptions), there is no feeling and understanding of beauty. There is no showing to children the natural beauties, countryside, the sea, the rising sun, the starry nights. (Cassià Costal, 1931, Pedagogy Seminar Report, quoted by Monés, 1994, p. 28)

According to Vall Alberti (1933), the methodology used to develop aesthetic feelings in children and adolescents should follow five steps: (a) to arise aesthetic feelings; (b) to give form to figurative dimensions; (c) to stimulate the creative capacity; (d) to open a critical spirit, and (e) to go beyond preexisting artistic forms. The main stream of this proposal is based on the notion of generating a new human being through education.

The core of the discussion during these years was set around the relevance and the limits of free expression in children's education. In the case of art education, this debate was fixed on the dilemma between spontaneous or directed imitation. Traditional education assumed that children have an experiential background but do not know how to express it, because they do not have the skills to represent the forms of reality. Such will be the main aim of family and school education. The debate beyond this traditional position was centered on showing that form and content were not independent, and that teaching the skills before the conceptual development had no empirical and research evidence to support it. Drawing was considered to be a positive strategy in order to develop observational skills, although the educators belonging to the Modern School movement were against teaching drawing skills per se without an educational framework. To solve this dilemma, educators such as Cousinet (1912) defended the importance of free drawing in the education process: "School loses its artificial character and is transformed into an extension and explanation of life. . . . The teaching of drawing has a place in this implication" (p. 312).

Even though some voices defended the importance of total freedom in children's education, some innovative educators expressed concerns regarding the use of drawing for this purpose. In the beginning, the idea of free drawing as a form of free child development was accepted as a dogma, partially due to the new democratic ideas on education, and partially to the importance of art and the artist's role as cultural medium of a new free society. This new approach to teaching was accepted by progressive educators almost without discussion.

However, the extreme positions tried to find an equilibrium since there had been some excesses or because some educators identified these ideas with those of the Modern School movement, which were almost anarchist. There emerged a strong reaction against free education and the use of drawing and arts as a means to promote it.

The "equilibrium position" sustained the belief that there was not a contradiction or opposition between free drawing without a pattern and drawing from a model. The explanation of this synthesis came from the psychological notion of internalization: a child could not express him/herself without a preexisting internal image. Expression was only free if this image spontaneously provoked a reaction.

Galí (1982) quoted in his study the words of Francesc Labarta from a children's exhibition of natural drawings in 1914:

> We will continue believing that teaching will be faulty, if drawing comes directly from objects—as it is wanted now—and not taken from natural forms as it has always been done, and the interest of teaching is not focusing on the interpretations of forms made by each pupil. (p. 60)

Francesc Labarta, who founded the Superior School of Fine Professions in 1914 with the sponsorship of the Diputació of Barcelona, was far more explicit, stating in 1916: "It does not matter if the pattern is a picture, a sock, an alive being, or a dead object: an apple painted by Cézanne is more alive than an instant photograph of a Marathon runner" (p. 58).

Freedom and spontaneity were also two main ideas renewing the education that affected the teaching of technical drawing. Carles Pi i Suñyer (1923), one of the most well-known personalities in the training and vocation-educational movement, expressed this concern:

> It is necessary to provide workers with the weapon of drawing . . . as a natural capacity and not as an artificial skill. In opposition to old academicism . . . it is necessary to infiltrate into disciples' souls a new sense, to make the view of space more intuitive. . . . Once graphic intuition is acquired, it shall never be lost and it makes possible that representation springs up as a spontaneous act. (p. 25)

Under the Dictatorship
The Creation of a Conservative Taste

After the civil war, the new political regime gave the control of the school system to the Catholic Church and the arts to the female section of the Falange, one of the groups that supported Franco's rebellion, which supported ideas quite close to the Italian fascist movement led by Mussolini. By the passing of the Law of 17 July 1945, primary education was regulated with the explicit recognition of the Catholic Church's control of the educational system. No specific qualifications were required to become a teacher, only a certificate accredited by a Catholic Church authority. Progressive teachers belonging to the New School movement were killed or purged because of their ideas.

As Rodríguez Perela (1990) pointed out in his study on the aesthetic and taste values during Franco's regime, the components of this trilogy were the essence of the philosophy of the new art education: "One of the signals of this period is the inseparable union of the Catholic Church, the State and Education, where Truth, Goodness and Beauty are the recurrent trilogy" (pp. 51–52).

Domínguez Perela also illustrated this influence with the anachronistic debate about the legality of abstraction. Spanish educational and cultural authorities reinforced art educational practices of mimesis and academic and figurative forms in painting. According to this point of view, the main aims of the art subject in primary school was to train pupils in the mimetic copy of illustrations and standardized patterns.

The importance of geometric drawing was not only due to its utilitarian use, but, as Sánchez Mazas wrote in 1942, due to its being a vehicle used to reinforce the aesthetic and moral ideas of the new regime: "More than for its content, rhythm, tune and style, the spirit of harmony and geometry of this type of drawing shows the values of the New Spain" (quoted by Domínguez Perela, 1990, p. 29).

However, the most significant signal of the influence of dictatorship art educational values was represented by handicraft education, particularly through the promotion of a new division of sexual roles. Figure 4.2 illustrates some of the cultural and historical connections to art education during this period.

The Relevance of Handicraft Education

During the Spanish Civil War, one of the first laws (4 September 1936) approved by the rebels to the Republic was to abolish coeducation. With a similar aim, another law was imposed in Madrid (1 May 1939), stating that the abolition of the pedagogic system of coeducation was because it is antipedagogic and antieducational for boys and girls. Education must reflect the principles of a healthy moral and agree with the postulates of our glorious tradition.

Members of the Female Section of the fascist Falange and the religious schools were in charge of girls' and women's education. Since its beginning on 28 December 1939, home teaching was a compulsatory subject for girls. Nice handicrafts, as a vehicle of the new universe of representation, particularly for women, were the dominant practice in Spanish schools during this period. The interest in producing these kind of objects came from the time previous to the civil war, when under a progressive conception, this activity was linked with the importance given to hand development and, of course, girls' education.

We can find an example of such an attitude in the program of the 1914 Summer School of La Diputació (a provincial administrative institution) of Barcelona:

> The object . . . will not continue with the same old concept of handicraft as school subject, but to reinforce its educational value. . . . Educational handicraft is, at the same time, an auxiliary procedure for schooling methodology . . . it is also a synthesis of the education of the hands and the senses; it gives taste, the routine and the love for work; helping to develop the individual genius. It is a continuous exercise of persistence, meaning that they should be educational by their realization more than utilitarian by their finality. (Diputació de Barcelona, 1914, p. 5)

FIGURE 4.2

Social and Cultural Influences on Spanish Art Education from the
Spanish End of the Civil War (1939) until the Passing of the General Education Law (1970)

Period	Art Education Content	Values	Socioeconomic Relations	Debates	Influences	Names and Books
From the end of the Spanish Civil War (1939) until the passing of the General Education Law (1970)	Handicraft; copy of illustrations; geometric drawing	Art and culture were used as the channels through which the values of Franco's dictatorship could be spread (e.g., women—as the "weak sex"— were only educated to become perfect wives, housewives, and mothers from an early age)	Strict separation of roles/sexes at schools; new social and cultural order appropriate to the régime's view of life, society, etc.	Academicism vs. abstraction	Art as a media of propaganda; fascist aesthetics	Drawing and handicraft manuals

Handicraft was used in the case of boys to develop their skills for a professional job. In the case of girls, the production of nice objects was close to a female home education, with a little touch of technical science. In the program of handicraft and home teaching, published by the School Patronage of Barcelona's Town Hall in 1931, it is possible to find good examples of this idea.

> The work of female schools must follow a spatial orientation adapted to women's lives and missions. A Girl's handicraft shall be considered a way of expression necessary for the rest of the school subjects as well as home teaching. (p. 105)

The attitude of the new dictatorial regime regarding women was clear from its beginnings.

After the copying of pictures, geometric drawing, and handicraft as dominant art education practices, we reach the positive economic situation and social changes of the sixties. The relationship of this culture and social values affected the Spanish society, which continued to fight for democracy. A new technocratic approach to economy and education was the answer of the régime to the new domestic and international situation. This movement affected art education, and by the 1970 curriculum reform, the aims and contents of this subject in primary education were close to expressionism and the development of creativity. Facts, reactions, and consequences of this new trend should be explained some other time in another history.

II

Cultural Ideals

The Effects of Visions and Values

Cultural values influence art education from many directions, particularly through the channels of dominant conceptions of art and education. The field is constructed not only through what is said about children, but what is valued as art and selected for inclusion in curriculum in a particular country. As progressive artistic and educational communities have attempted to reform themselves as part of efforts to improve social life, the influence of cultural ideals has been reflected by both discourse about the field and its visual character. The chapters in this section reveal that art education in the past has reflected people's hopes and dreams for the future.

Connections between art, education, and cultural values, such as the conception of individualism prevalent in early twentieth-century United States, are discussed in the chapter by Kerry Freedman. The growth of the fine art community in New York City, the emergence of progressive education, increasing altruism, the introduction of psychotherapy through Freud's work shortly before World War I, and cultural responses to that war, all influenced the transformation of art education. As ideas about art became internalized and naturalized to the extent that children, once thought incapable of making art, became representatives of artistic expression, art and art education in New York became representations for a culture of individualism in the United States.

As Steffan Lovgren and Sten-Gosta Karlsson explain, art education in Sweden also shifted historically as a result of cultural values. Before World War II, the purposes of art instruction were based on aesthetic influences from central Europe, as well as strong feelings of nationalism. After the war, a belief in the strengthening of democracy through education and freedom in expression became prominent. Then, in the 1960s, an awakened interest in children and youth culture, and concerns about the influence of mass media, moved art education toward a focus on visual communication.

The chapter by Lucimar Frange focuses on the deep cultural relationship between art and art teaching in Brazil. The author discusses a rich art-and-craft tradition, but argues that a lack of cultural institutions in the country inhibits the growth of art education. As a result, the visual arts remain neglected by both the culture industries and education, which she argues weakens feelings of citizenship and social cohesion. The author hopes that art education can be used to improve social conditions by enabling intimate contact between individuals and cultural groups.

The chapter by Jordi Pintó and Khalid El Bekay discuss influences of cultural politics and Islamic tradition on art education. The authors establish a connection between economic improvements in Morocco and the increase of art lessons taught in schools. The transition took place between 1961, when formal art education was available to only 2 percent of the total population, and 1988, when the percentage dramatically increased. They describe similarities and differences that currently exist between the art education in public and private schools, linking them to economics and the worldwide trend of educating people for a global market.

5

Kerry Freedman

The Importance of Modern Art and Art Education in the Creation of a National Culture

New York Roots

I n the United States, World War I marked the beginning of collaborative efforts by several groups to define American art and culture. No place in the country was this more apparent than in New York City and no place was more influential on art education in the United Stated during the first half of the twentieth century. Ideas about the importance and definition of modern art and education met in New York in a progressive milieu. These ideas grew up together in the city, only to reach maturity decades later as they were enacted in classrooms across the country.

Early in the twentieth century, artists and intellectuals gathered in Manhattan's Greenwich Village to discuss the possibilities of cultural change through the expressive potential of the arts. The discourse about fine art, particularly modern, abstract art, became connected to diverse social and political issues, such as socialism, women's rights, free love, the elimination of racism, and labor unionism. Radical intellectuals used art to challenge Victorian limitations on acceptable behavior and borrowed from Freud to explain the purpose of breaking through boundaries of sensuality.

Several art exhibitions in the 1910s and 1920s helped to promote debate about modern art in the city. Exhibitions, such as the Armory Show of 1913 and the Metropolitan Museum's Modern Art Exhibition of 1921 were supported by New York collectors of modern art, but offended almost everyone else. A negative attitude toward modern, particularly European, art was encouraged by the New York popular press. Newspaper accounts of these shows were the public's informants. The articles were filled with horrified commentary on degradation in modern art and its negative influence on American political and economic optimism (Thistlewood, 1990).

An important aspect of these early debates in New York was whether children should be exposed to modern art and the sociopolitical ideas surrounding it. However, as American discussions of art began to move toward a focus on formal and psychological explanations of expression, modern art became increasingly depoliticized. The depoliticization resulted in art being surrounded by a new political discourse of independence, which intensified through World War II, as a realization of American democratic culture. As art was seen more and more as the creation of free-thinking individuals, artistic self-expression became increasingly acceptable, even necessary, for children in the United States.

Common Interests
Education and the Fine Art Community

As these discussions about the relationship between art, politics, and culture were taking place among artists and intellectuals, art education in New York drew closer to the fine art community. James Parton Haney (1914–1915), director of art in the New York City high schools, promoted interactions between the schools, artists, and museums. Student work was shown in a gallery used by the city art associations, and the New York Metropolitan Museum of Art loaned collections for exhibition at a local high school. Haney viewed these types of collaboration as opportunities to improve the cultural development of students.

Progressivism, Private Schools, and
Individual Expression

World War I has been called a turning point for progressive education
(Cremin, 1961). Before the war, progressive educators in New York had
begun a battle with local public school officials, influenced by the business
agenda of the federal administration, who sought to improve school efficiency through the use of business and industry management strategies.
During the war, however, progressive educators worked to shift thinking
about the purpose of education from merely a vocational training ground to
a way of humanistically shaping children's minds.

By the 1920s, several progressive, private schools were established in
New York in response to the "unnatural" education found in the public
schools. One of the foundations of progressive education was the new idea
that artistic expression was natural to children. From this perspective,
children could achieve psychological health through the process of making
art. The progressive schools sought to aid children in adapting to a disor-
derly social world by providing them with a therapeutic art education.

Walden School (originally the Children's School) was a progressive
school founded by Margaret Naumburg, who with the help of her sister,
Florence Cane, developed a progressive art education program. Naumburg
was a student of John Dewey; however, unlike Dewey, Naumburg was
greatly influenced by clinical psychology. Whereas Dewey focused on the
emergence of an individual through a social group, Naumburg was concerned with the independent development of an individual for integration
into a group, which could then be reformed by the individual (e.g., Beck,
1959; Wygant, 1988). She rejected the idea that social problems could be
solved by work with social groups. The impossibility of success of this
approach, she argued, was demonstrated by the war. She stated:

> I've lived to see that whether people fought to save democracy or imperi-
> alism does not make the profound difference I had once hoped. I've wak-
> ened to the complete realization that all social and economic groups have
> identical methods of acting and reasoning, according to whether they are
> in or out of power. (Naumburg, 1928, p. 14)

Instead, Naumburg looked to Freudian psychoanalysis for answers and
began her school based on principles developed through her own psychoanalysis (Naumburg, 1928). Naumburg's sister became the art teacher at
Walden School and together they formulated an art education based on a
Freudian expulsion of what they considered unnatural social impositions
and a mystical unity based on Jung's conceptions of cosmology (Karier, 1986).

The focus of education at Walden School, and the other progressive schools, was closely aligned to currents in the New York fine art community. This was the case, in part, because many of the teachers in these schools were practicing artists or moved in circles of the art community. Over the years, several artists and intellectuals taught at Walden (Cane, 1926; Walden School pamphlet, n.d.), as well as other such schools. For example, Lewis Hine, who later became known for his social-work photography, taught nature at the Ethical Culture School.

However, the close alignment between the progressive, private schools and the fine art community was also a result of the social milieu. For example, progressive education became mixed in New York with other methods of instruction, such as those of Viennese art educator Franz Cizek, whose students' work was shown in a well-attended and often cited (as in Rugg & Schumaker, 1928) exhibition at the Metropolitan Museum of Art in 1924. In an effort to allow students to draw on their own experience and promote free expression in his classroom, Cizek supported an education in which minimal teaching occurred and children were not shown adult works of art to copy. The subject matter of the students' work had some relationship to their lives and the method of instruction was not intended to reflect adult influence. However, Cizek's students' art resembled adult Viennese popular culture of the time because the children drew from images they remembered (Duncum, 1982; MacDonald, 1970). The case in New York was similar. Although educators such as Cane (1926) and Naumburg (1928) believed that child art should not be influenced by adults, the children's work in these schools often looked like the representational Expressionism and Art Deco popular at the time (see, for example, Rugg & Schumaker, 1928).

Social reconstructionism, the radically progressive perspective that education was a way to change social, political, and economic conditions (Cremin, 1961; Kleibard, 1987), emerged in part as a result of these discussions of the relationship of individual children to society. American social reconstructionist educators were from the beginning closely tied to the art community. For example, one of the originators of educational social reconstructionism, Harold Rugg, who was on the education faculty at Teachers College, Columbia University was part of the circle that surrounded photographer and impresario Alfred Stieglitz and painter Georgia O'Keeffe.

The Stieglitz-O'Keeffe circle included artists such as John Marin, Arthur Dove, and Ansel Adams, and critics such as Waldo Frank (who became Margaret Naumburg's husband) and Lewis Mumford. In the late 1910s and 1920s, this circle worked to bring about a new understanding of modern art and American culture, which was highly individualistic and experimental. In their struggle against conservative politics and the increasing control of business and industry in social life, these artists and intellectuals took refuge in a myth of artistic creation as individualism and innate genius. Wealthy New Yorkers joined with these members of the art community in their support of modern art and collected the greatest concentration of early modernist drawings and painting outside of Paris (Sarinen, 1958). In his gallery, Stieglitz showed the collected work as predecessors of modern American art. As was the case with previous American collectors (Freedman, 1989a), these collectors sought to educate people to appreciate the objects in which they had invested.

The collections and Stieglitz's exhibitions included black African and other so-called primitive art. The interest in collecting primitive art depended on a romantic belief that it reflected a natural freedom and independence uninfluenced by cultural socialization. This art influenced New York artists of the period, including artists who took part in the growth of African American arts known as the Harlem Renaissance. For example, painter Aaron Douglas, perhaps the most widely known of the Harlem visual artists, became acquainted with African (and some European modern art) through the collection of Philadelphia philanthropist Albert Barnes. Although such adult art was created in the context of complex social systems, associations were made between it and the art of children because both were believed to be naturally expressive.

The political economy in the United States, combined with a growing national optimism, was reflected in progressive education through the elevation of "the child" as a naturally free and independent thinker. This mythical conception of childhood became increasingly attractive in progressive educational circles in New York, but contrasted with other perspectives of children, influenced by, for example, the realities of urban economics. What was considered hidden and deep within children by progressive educators was a reflection of adult culture and social circumstance. For example, a particular class concept of self-importance was not the social reality for all people. The parents of the children taught by Naumburg and Cane valued art as cultural capital. However, for children in the public schools, less a connection with avant garde art and more a concern on the part of the teachers about vocational skills and a lack of good taste in students prevailed (Graham, 1935).

Conservatism, the Public Schools, and Socioeconomic Realities

The realities of the public school system in New York City illustrate the sociopolitical position against which the progressivism in art education movement stood. In the early decades of the century, New York public school teachers of all subjects became enmeshed in the battle between local politicians seeking efficiency in education and the proponents of progressive education

(Ravitch, 1988). As the battle progressed, strict discipline became the focus of commentary by some educational reformers, while others advocated a more liberal, child-centered approach. Teachers were faced with poverty, violence, and shameful working conditions.

> City children brought their street behaviors, beliefs, and resistances to school with them, and New York schools [in the 1910s and 1920s] were rocked by incidences of student riots, robberies, and murders. In the spring of 1922, students in Brooklyn schools made glass bombs out of wartime military equipment and exploded them in their classrooms. Teachers also met young students in both elementary and secondary school that were sexually promiscuous, chronic liars, and troublemakers, as well as children . . . exhausted from lives of poverty. (Rousmaniere, 1994, p. 59)

In contrast to the focus on expressionism in the private schools, public school art education typically focused on skill training. For example, students in high schools did posters and advertisements based on Arthur Wesley Dow's book on composition, which had editions from 1899 until 1940. The illustrations in his book supported an art education that focused on compositional design and had elements of Art Nouveau and Art Deco. Dow, who became the director of fine arts at Teachers College in 1904, developed his influential program around Japanese pictorial arrangement. His concept of art education was also based on a scientific reduction of elements of design, such as line, notan (light and dark), and color in order to produce pleasing form. While these elements were not new, Dow presented them in a formalist instructional system that was new to New York (Sargent, 1921) and met the demand for a commercial design curriculum.

The negative public response to modern art made it clear that art education would be required to help people understand its importance in the creation of a new American culture. The Museum of Modern Art (MoMA), which was founded in 1929 to publicly display the growing accumulation of modern works of art in New York and make the city the world's center of modern art, soon became a teaching institution (Thistlewood, 1990). Art experts, such as historian and the first director of MoMA, Alfred Barr, and patron and theorist Albert Barnes (1925, 1928), pointed to connections between modern art and accepted European artistic traditions in writings and lectures in an attempt to make modern art acceptable.

While relating modern art to European tradition aided in educating the general public toward understanding and acceptance, some New Yorkers, such as artist and art educator Ralph Pearson (1925), stated concerns about a lack of the production and appreciation of a particularly American culture:

The principle at stake centers in this. Has a nation an ethical right to associate *only*, or principally, with the art of other ages and civilizations—in other words, to borrow instead of create its culture? Borrowing evidences lack of internal resources, if not of poverty, and borrowing peoples become negligible in history. Borrowing is the vogue at present because it is a means to display of (sic) wealth, because it is an easy way of escaping individual judgment and the attendant chance of making mistakes, because vicarious respectability attaches to it, and because former art is, in many cases, greater than our own of to-day. Shall the children be taught to borrow their art, or to share in its creation, or both? (pp. 202–3)

The public discourse that emerged from these fine art community influences helped to shape art teachers' understanding of modern art in New York. Although private school art educators began to use modern art concepts and techniques, opposition against the use of modern art existed in the conservative public schools. To some educators, modern art and the art and intellectual community signified the influx of European ideas, such as socialism, and they worried about the influence of these ideas on students. In the public schools, art education was still to provide (capitalist) vocational skills and good taste based on a Victorian aesthetic. Also, the radical politics and bohemian lifestyle of modern artists was of concern to many of the city's teachers.

At one level, the notion of the importance of artistic expression in children may have seemed merely an attempt to enable individuals to escape psychologically oppressive social boundaries reproduced in the public schools. However, at another level, it was a sociopolitical stance that made sense in the context of attempts to redefine American democratic culture based on creative self-expression as a representation of individual freedom. In the following section, these emerging conceptions of art and education are discussed in the context of the social, political, and economic environment of the 1930s.

Artists, Intellectuals, and Education during the Depression

During the Depression, the language of progressive education in New York shifted from the extreme individualism of Freudian psychology and the bohemian art community, toward a social consciousness reflected in social reconstructionism and John Dewey's work (Cremin, 1961). The connections between education and the fine art community also changed as attention to the political economy increased in both professional groups. This resulted in a resurgence of radicalism and an emphasis on individual responsibility, as well as individual expression.

For John Dewey (1931), the union of fine art and social life was vital. He rejected the traditional notion that aesthetic experience was something set apart from daily life and experience. Dewey viewed art as the expression of the relationship between material, process, and ideal. As such, art was created from human desire and embodied the realization of the interaction between people and their environment. His focus was on the interaction of process and product and the social aspects of artistic experience, not just free self-expression or individual artist intent. However, Dewey had a particular conception of the social aspects of art that did not necessarily include social commentary. He asserted "art should be accessible to all is a demand by the side of which the personal political intent of the artist is insignificant" (p. 344).

Dewey's ideas about the social qualities of art learning and art knowledge were interpreted in highly individualistic ways. This interpretation was consistent with the extreme individualism that enabled an emphasis on individual responsibility for social and economic conditions to became part of national, political discourse. This focus involved a neglect of the important social aspects of art that Dewey considered a vital part of artistic and aesthetic experience. It also involved conflicts of conscience as educators became enmeshed in the problems of the relationship between child and adult art, evaluation of children's artistic expression, an increasing national interest in personality and talent assessment, and standards of judgment and taste.

In the 1930s, the scientific management, therapeutic, and social reconstructionist themes of education that emerged in the 1910s and 1920s continued. Interest in scientific, educational testing grew, psychoanalytic progressivism remained in educational discourse, and an educational social consciousness had been raised. These three streams of thought were reflected in art education (Efland, 1990). However, the boundaries between these perspectives increasingly blurred in the United States as the battle between social influence and individualism shaped curriculum.

Modern Taste as American Culture

In the United States, children's artistic expression was generally discussed in progressive literature of the 1930s as if unrelated to adult standards of judgment, which were plainly stated as paramount in earlier art education discourse. However, the development of "good taste" in children maintained importance during the Depression in the guise of consumer education. Art education was used to train people to buy tasteful commodities at economical prices (Freedman, 1989a). Art experts represented art appreciation as helping people to focus on "high" values and "lofty" goals, such as purity, competitive excellence, and nationalism, so that they would not be drawn to revolutionary (socialist) activities during the economic crisis. The interpretation of these social goals as individual responsibilities in public school art discourse supported the development of a peculiarly American culture that associated independent thinking with democracy in the United States.

The desire for promoting a national culture through art grew even stronger among artists and intellectuals during and after the Depression. Art educators like Ralph Pearson (1941) criticized teachers who allowed work in their classes that resembled commercial art or adult realism because he denied that realistic art was expressive. Pearson viewed teachers who promoted realism as maintaining an old (European) tradition, rather than helping to create a progressive, cultural style.

The promotion of modern art as good taste necessitated a universalized art education for the general population. The New York City museums continued to take responsibility for part of this education. In exhibitions at MoMA held in the 1930s, Alfred Barr juxtaposed modern art and non-Western (such as Meso-American and African) art to illustrate "universal" art concepts. This strategy met with some success, in part, because a growing social movement had emerged that promoted attention to the similarities between people in response to the pre-Depression focus on socioeconomic differences. Rejection of industrial urbanization, attention to the "primitive" unconscious, and the federal government's focus on nationalism and the cultural values reflected in the New Deal, resulted in an increasing interest in the visual culture of native peoples, especially Native Americans (Rushing, 1995).

"Realism" as Political Art

As economic and political problems increased at home and abroad in the 1930s, nationalism focused on cultural leadership to promote faith in United States enterprise. At the same time, a new generation of radical intellectuals, those born in New York ghettos to Eastern European and Russian immigrants, looked to Marxism as a European solution to problems of American capitalism (Diggins, 1992). This group largely accepted Soviet communism before the invasion of Poland and viewed it as a positive alternative to the fascism that threatened Europe. Through local periodicals, these intellectuals developed American perspectives of Marxist theory. In doing so, they rejected as bourgeois older American leftist perspectives, such as bohemianism, and the support of artistic free self-expression. By the 1930s, Soviet communist art was strictly controlled to promote Social Realism, and in New York, those who supported free self-expression through abstraction battled the political "realism" of the Regionalists. The

Depression was the greatest period of socially conscious art in the United States (Von Blum, 1982).

These radical, intellectual perspectives provided a source of debate and inspiration in the New York fine art community, generated in part by the Federal Art Project. The project gave artists an opportunity to work; but social and cultural agendas were at work as well. The artists in the project began working in the representational forms, muted tones, and rural subject matter of Social Realism and Regionalism as the new representations of national culture. Many of these artists, such as Jackson Pollack, who had studied under William Bentley, were sympathetic to Marxist ideas and organizations during the Depression. Social Realism and Regionalism were thought particularly appropriate by New York artists and intellectuals, because they signified a rejection of elitism in favor of art for the masses. These styles of art were supposed to be easily understood and appreciated by the public. However, the rural communalism of Regionalism was inconsistent with the urban consciousness of most New Yorkers, and some New York artists, such as Lewis Hine, Edward Hopper, and the Ashcan group, including Reginald Marsh, focused on urban life in their work. These artists represented a humanistic perspective of the complexities of urban industrialism, from the crushing crowds to loneliness and alienation, which clarified the contradictions of American individualism.

One reason for the eventual shift in focus to abstraction in the New York fine art community was the influx of European artist refugees, several of whom had been experimenting with abstract art before arriving in the United States. For example, some of the Federal Art Project artists attended Hans Hofmann's Eighth Street school where Hofmann, a German refugee, presented a vital urban alternative to rural Social Realism. Hofmann explored abstract forms, vibrant colors, and the idea that art could emerge completely from within an artist. Some of these artists, such as Pollack, Lee Krasner, and Willam de Kooning, became part of the first generation of Abstract Expressionists.

The influx of refugees combined with other events to continue to fuel interest in a national culture. The growth of an influential art community in New York was enhanced by its physical distance from World War II. While Paris was the unrivaled center of the Western fine art community during the 1920s and 1930s (and drew several influential U.S. expatriates), the destruction of Europe during World War II made the continuation of a European artistic center impossible. New York cultural activity and study were sustained, in part, by the work of refugees and first- and second-generation immigrants who sought assimilation and social mobility through educational, artistic, and scholarly work. At the same time, concern about the influence of increased immigration emerged among groups of U.S. citizens, strengthening their nationalism.

In part, as a result of the conflict between European politics and United States democratic ideals, the psychological conception of the free and democratic individual grew stronger in the fine art community and art education. This psychological concept contained what appeared to be objective, scientifically determined definitions of health and appropriate behavior, in contrast to the arbitrary determinations of socioeconomic class and political ideology. Art education reflected the belief, inherent to American progressivism, that a science of the human mind could solve social problems, including the sense of alienation of human beings in general and artists in particular. Social scientists, artists, and educators viewed this sense of alienation as imposed upon children as well.

The Triumph of "Free" Self-Expression

In 1941, Raymond Faulkner, who had become head of the Department of Fine and Industrial Arts at Teachers College, and Edwin Ziegfeld, then assistant professor of fine arts at that institution, having recently left the University of Minnesota, published *Art Today* (with Gerald Hill). Their book was based on work done as part of a project in Owatonna, Minnesota, during the 1930s. The Owatonna Project focused on art in daily life and was supported by Carnegie Foundation funding from New York. The book made a case for including appreciation of "functional" arts, such as in architecture, furniture, and photography, in curriculum.

The continued support of functionality in art education from, for example, poster design early in the century to art in daily life, became extremely important as New York City school art became a tool for producing cultural unity. As the time approached for the United States to enter World War II, members of the arts community implored teachers to enlist in a cultural war against European fascist attempts to repress artistic experimentation and progressive thought.

Victor D'Amico (1942), who promoted teaching children through the studio production activities of fine artists, was a prominent New York art educator at the time. He had headed the Fine Arts Department of one of the progressive, private schools and then became director of the Department of Education and Peoples Art Center of MoMA in 1937 (Lynes, 1973). While on the faculty of Teachers College, he edited the 1942 Teachers College staff and student annual journal, *Art Education Today*, in which the lead article, "Art Education, Democracy and the War," explained that the purpose of school art was to promote national strength:

> The attack upon us is cultural as well as military . . . fascism finds it
> necessary to "silence" the creative artist whenever it comes to power. It

recognizes the spirit of freedom which art not only implies, but which it generates. We have heard fascism's echo in our country, in campaigns against free education, against popular culture, against the experimental and progressive in both art and education. . . . Let us be certain about this, that in war and peace, art belongs to the people. It is theirs to use as a weapon in their struggle for freedom. (p. 2)

In 1943, D'Amico headed a Committee on Art in American Education and Society, which was formed to centralize the national focus of school art and provide expert advice in defining an appropriate wartime art education (Staff and Students of the Department of Fine and Applied Arts, Teachers College, 1943). The committee supported the view that, during wartime, art education should become propagandistic and promote the liberal Western traditions, loyal citizenship, and national security that were threatened by the Axis powers. Coercive imagery in art education, which had been instrumental in the rise of Nazi politics in Europe, was represented by the committee as "one of our most powerful weapons" (Staff and Students of the Department of Fine and Applied Arts, Teachers College, 1942, p. 3). The propaganda of art education in the United States, however, "in its honesty of purpose and message" was believed to have "nothing in common with that of the fascist nations" (p. 3).

The overt support of nationalistic interests in school art influenced the aesthetic focus of curriculum. Prescribed political formulas and mottoes were not those of the fine art community, but the style of Madison Avenue commercial art, particularly posters. The advertising style was used in school to teach students how to develop convincing nationalistic messages.

Abstract Expressionism
The New York School

By the middle of the 1940s, artists, intellectuals, and educators formed a new coalition in New York. Lectures and discussions were held concerning political and philosophical issues involving painters, writers, composers, and people associated with literary magazines, museums, and universities. These interactions enabled New York painters to become increasingly acquainted with clinical psychology and Surrealism, based on the revelation of the unconscious. Familiarity with the childlike symbolism of European artists such as Klee, Miro, and particularly Kandinsky, grew through reproductions and exhibitions of their work. New York artists adopted the Surrealist practice of automatism, or automatic writing, as a release of the unconscious, and went beyond these methods to include chance and unconscious gesture to explore new possibilities for abstract imagery.

The renewed attention to formalism and expressionism was not merely the result of change within the fine art community. It was an extension and result of the ideological milieu (Guilbaut, 1983). From these social relations and artistic experimentation emerged the ideas and images that developed into Abstract Expressionism, which is generally considered the first American avant garde art movement. Unlike the group around Alfred Stieglitz, who would not have considered attempting to shift the center of the fine art community from Paris, this later New York circle intended to do just that (Trachtenberg, 1989).

The work of art critics Clement Greenberg and Harold Rosenberg illustrate debates concerning the influence of social science and social politics on the fine art community. Both critics supported the New York School and viewed it as a representation of national culture. Greenberg's formalist support for Abstract Expressionism was based on an evolutionary, "objective," scientific reductionism in which the social context of a work of art was considered unimportant. Greenberg's focus on objective standards of formalism was to free art from the influence of mass culture banality (Greenberg, 1940), which were particularly illustrated at the time by Nazi and fascist regimes. Rosenberg took a different, but also apparently asocial approach. He focused on existential self-realization and the production process. For Rosenberg, Abstract Expressionism provided an opportunity for purification through human expression in an alienating world. It was hardly a coincidence that feelings of alienation pervaded Western culture during economic depression and war.

Paradoxes in Greenberg's and Rosenberg's work reflected conflicts in the New York art community. Although the critics denied ideological qualities in Abstract Expressionism, the artistic style was a response to sociopolitical conditions. As was the case with other modern art, it was to be a weapon against authoritarianism. The emergence of Abstract Expressionism became possible in and was part of a milieu that focused on formalistic analysis, as well as personal self-expression, and upon democratic freedom, as well as individual isolation; an idiosyncratic production process was valued as well as a common materialism. In the artists' and critics' attempts to depoliticize their work by focusing on formalism and individual expression was a political statement that emerged in the context of fear. That political statement was no less a part of the creation of national culture than the overt efforts of the New York intelligentsia earlier in the century or the hunt for communist sympathizers among artists and academics that was to follow.

In art education, however, the vital sociopolitical roots of the New York intellectual and fine art community were left behind as the language of self-expression was embraced in classrooms across the country. In schools, the focus on formalism was reflected in an emphasis on design, based on commercial art, at the same time as expressionism was maintained and strengthened to facilitate the development of a democratic personality in children (Freedman, 1987, 1989b). Through the well-intentioned efforts of art educators like Viktor Lowenfeld (1947), who, himself, had narrowly escaped from Austria as the war began, political tendencies were represented as psychological conditions and personality traits because fear existed that fascism resulted from an authoritarian personality developed as a result of certain schooling techniques. Educators sought to remedy the situation by allocating time during the week for "freeing" experiences in art. An art education promoting extreme individualism emerged by the 1960s that was to maintain children's "natural" democratic personality in a world thought to decisively impose unhealthy, undemocratic principles on weak individuals. Art education was to prepare children for social life and, at the same time, protect them from it.

Conclusion

The intention of creating a modern, mainstream culture of the United States, based in part on an ideology of individualism, was reflected in the dialogue between educators, intellectuals, and the members of the fine art community in New York during the first half of the twentieth century. The apparent contradictions of the culture, such as a focus on individual psychology to solve social problems, scientific group analysis to determine individual characteristics, an elite socioeconomic group defining a culture for all, and a national culture based on individualism, seemed of little consequence.

However, it was these contradictions, or more appropriately, these dualities, that enabled the social and historical conjunctions to occur that set art education in the United States on its present course. This is illustrated by the fact that the same individualism that once was intended for white males has been appropriated by women and men of color. As a result, art education in the United States now focuses on debates in which a faint ring of the discussions held in New York in the early 1900s still can be heard. Now, art communities, issues of diversity, and the economic and technological results of industrial capitalism have been given new attention.

Art educators in the United States have seriously struggled with the implications of modern art and culture for children, a struggle that has seemed to become less important in a postmodern society of outcome-based assessment, access to global technologies, and a loss of innocence. The field moves toward a convergence of production with appreciation, concepts with skills, and technique with meaning. Today, as in the past, art education in the United States changes in relation to its contexts and enriches them in the process.

6

Staffan Lovgren
Sten-Gosta Karlsson

From Art Making to Visual Communication

Swedish Art Education in the Twentieth Century

A rt education was gradually introduced into the Swedish school system during the late nineteenth century as a practical subject. During this period, a radical change took place in Sweden. Industrial production had rapidly expanded and the process of manufacturing demanded new skills. The production of handicraft and other trades followed new principles as well. School authorities, technical colleges and industrial leaders agreed that education in drawing was an important qualification for labor in crafts and industry. Thus art education was accordingly designed to fit production in these areas.

At the same time, however, a reappraisal of fundamental existential principles took place all across Europe. The expanding labor movement shook social, economic, and judicial foundations across nations (Seyler, 1983). Influential groups at all levels of society called for law and order and a strengthening of nationalistic feelings. As a result of these changes, the Swedish flag received its modern design and became a unifying symbol for the people of the nation, poor as well as rich. Exhibitions of handicrafts, like the flag, seemed to rise above social conflict and were accessible to the general public.

Art as a practical subject in school was challenged by the movement for "education through art." As early as 1882, Conny Burman argued for art education for the sake of good taste, beauty, and aesthetic appreciation. In 1897 Thorsten and Carl G. Laurin founded "the Association for Embellishing the Schools with Works of Arts" (Pettersson & Åsén, 1989, p. 81). The interest in aesthetic education had its origin in central Europe and was manifested at the big world exhibitions at the turn of the century. These conditions had a great bearing on the National Curriculum of 1905. It stated for the first time that one of the goals for teaching art in schools was the development of good taste and a sense of beauty (Key, 1899).

Visual Descriptive Drawing on the Black Board

At the end of World War I, new winds of democracy swept through the nation with the introduction of universal suffrage, a dawning secularization, and an increasingly strong Social Democratic Party. Sweden was changing from a country of producers to one of consumers. Domestic production of arts and crafts gave way to industrial goods, urbanization, and all the problems of socialization, that developed during this expansion (Pettersson & Åsén, 1989). New educational methods were gradually incorporated in a growing feeling of national heritage that guided art education toward becoming integrated with local geography, history, and folklore. In classrooms, the repetitive practices of drawing lines and points that had prevailed since the turn of the century, were gradually replaced by studies of the home environment and depictions of real objects (Isling,1988).

Hugo Segerborg, director of the department of the College of Art Teacher Training in Stockholm for twenty-six years, became one of the most influential scholars in introducing these new methods to Swedish art education. Segerbord was influenced by ideas from England, Germany, and the American progressive movement (John Dewey's and Liberty Tadd's books had been translated into Swedish at the beginning of the century). He stated:

> Around us, in the cities and in the country, at home, in the workshops, in the stores etc., there are a number of objects, which could be particularly suitable for usage in the art room. Among those things the choice should be the best ones. As a rule the choice will not be difficult, as our time endeavors to produce beautiful and functional forms even in the most

everyday ordinary object. A cover of a book, a tool, a can, a globe, a pitcher etc., they could all, provided they are correctly chosen, fulfill propounded requirements. (Segerborg, 1916, p. 5)

Segerborg endorsed the instructional method of the teacher drawing free-hand on the blackboard in front of the students who were expected to copy the drawings. The drawings were intended to visualize thoughts and ideas that the teacher wanted to convey to the students. The main purpose of this method was to teach students to observe and visually describe things, depict correctly, and learn aesthetics.

> The students . . . would like to be able to see how the pictures along with the oral explanations gradually grows on the black board. It will draw their attention to the delivery and increase their interest. Here, if ever, the well known phrase, that the competence of a teacher can be measured by the quantity of chalk he will consume in his act of teaching. (Segerborg, 1916, p. 18)

The Teacher Had to Know How to Draw

At the end of World War I, Sweden was still an agrarian society, but it was also involved in a fast transition toward mechanization and industrialization, a growing population, a strong movement from an agricultural to an urban society, the organization of the great national popular movement and the decreasing power of the church (Richardsson, 1990). A national-romanticism movement grew out of the expanding interest in the beauty of the native country. This interest was nurtured by a group of artists and writers led by Zorn Heidenstam and Carl Larsson, who focused on cultural heritage, folk art, peasant culture, and the dramatic beauty of the Swedish countryside. Open-air museums were inaugurated at a number of sites throughout the country and professional and amateur research in local study was carried out (Sjöholm, 1961).

In this context, the National Curriculum of 1919 introduced a new form of art education to the Swedish elementary schools called *local study* (*hembygdskunskap*). Local study involved research into the local neighborhood and reading, writing, and speaking combined with an extensive amount of art and image making in class. Thematical studies in such areas as food, the clock, summertime, and communications lead the students to studies of nature and the nation. Themes like these, where representational drawing and illustration played an important part, were to awaken students' interest in and love for their country. Flags and other national symbols as models for drawing became fundamental educational tools for a patriotic education. Simultaneously, local studies became an important part of the modern society's struggle to teach its younger generation the virtues of diligence, thrift, tidiness, and decency.

Behind the development of this new subject were two teachers at the Elementary Teacher Training College in Gothenburg: L. Gottfrid Sjöholm and A. Goes. As early as 1914, Sjöholm had studied new directions in education in Europe and come across the concept of work schools. He was influenced by Seinig's discussion of artistic production as part of the overall knowledge-seeking process. (Sjöholm, 1961).

However, the most influential person among the pedagogues of the work schools during this time in Germany was Kerchensteiner. Teachers and other educators, among them members of the Swedish Elementary Committee, the founders of the 1919 National Curriculum, journeyed to Germany for his seminars. The most revolutionary idea of these pioneers was the emphasis on individual studies through manual work, which penetrated all school subjects.

Sjöholm and Goes (1916) designed a number of assignments that aimed at sharpening the perception and observations of the individual child. Sjöholm and Goes's "silent exercises" were to draw on the interests and experiences of the child and were aimed at teaching the children how to make fast drawings to depict the essential form of the subject with a simplicity of design (see Figure 6.1). This method required the teachers to know how to draw on the blackboard. It also included instructional handbooks on local study and a collection of reproductions used between 1920 to 1950. With these teaching aids, the school presented art by the most influential artists of the country that depicted cultural and aesthetic values that suited the aims of school authorities for a nationalistic educational program.

By the early 1930s the shift in art education from technical-practical training to aesthetical education was completed. This coincided with the fast growth of unemployment and economical unrest that spread across the country. As a result of these changes, more time on the schedule was given to aesthetic training and education in arts and crafts (Pettersson & Åsén, 1989).

Toward "Free Expression"

The notion of "child art," which emerged shortly before the turn of the century, did not reach the educational world in Sweden until the middle of the 1920s. The first to present these ideas to the Swedish educators was the Austrian art educator, Professor Richard Rothe, in his book *Kindertümliches Zeichnen*. Rothe's method was based on the achievements of developmental psychology and focused on different levels of growth of the child. Rothe believed that the most important task of the teacher was to adjust

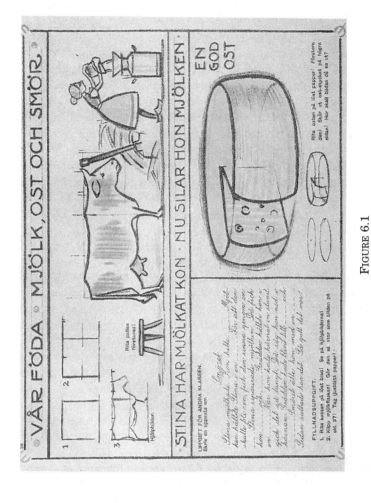

Figure 6.1

A page with the title "The Farm" from one of the workbooks in local study by Sjöholm and Goes.

pace and degree of difficulty to the developmental level of the child. The role of the teacher became supervisory so as to not interfere with the creative process and "the organic growth of the child." The free expressive drawing of the child soon was enclosed by a system of rules, similar to a "safety net" in order to save the childishness of the picture.

> All drawing must be clear and distinct, every line has to belong to a solid encircled shape, flying marks, which do not enclose a shape, should not be allowed. This and other figures are indoctrinated and unwanted images that children mainly imitate from commercialized reproductions, without understanding them, possibly in order to reach a closer likeness to the achievements of adults in society. (Rothe, 1937, p. 76)

After the devastating experience of World War II one of the most crucial issues in the countries of Europe was the restoration and fortification of democracy. This issue was important on all levels in Swedish society as well, and the coalition government made up by the Social Democrats and the Farmer Union initiated political reforms that sought to ensure this development. Social changes included an expanding mobility from agriculture to industry, from country to city life, from nationalism to internationalism.

In this context, art education became immersed in the notion of free expression. New winds of democracy and freedom swept over the country and influences from United States and England were felt in every part of society. Fine arts and the art community increased in importance in art education, particularly at the secondary level. Abstract Expressionism made its debut and many art teachers worked simultaneously as artists and teachers.

The reconstruction of democratic ideas in the postwar era merged closely with Lowenfeld's and Read's philosophies regarding the political and educational importance of stimulating individual expression in art. The greatest impact on art education at this point was the writing of Herbert Read and his book *Education through Art*, which was translated into the Swedish language. Read, who wrote his book during the most fearful times of World War II, advocated democratic education as the most important way to fight an authoritarian school system and totalitarian society.

During the 1950s, the methods of the free-expression movement were developed by many teachers in Sweden, particularly by Nils Breitzholtz, who as a director of the art education department at the College of Arts and Crafts in Stockholm, perceived teaching art as a way to extend art appreciation to young students. Based on his supervision of an art school for children, he published a book on free-expression methods for elementary classroom teachers (Breitzholtz, 1962). However, another art teacher, Jan

Thomaeus (1980), opposed the notion of institutionalizing the method of free expression. He also disliked the idea of high art as part of education and argued instead that students should spend their time studying expressions of free activity and experiment with different materials.

The National Curriculum of 1955 established the method of free expression in the nation's art programs. It emphasized the image as an expression of students' own experiences, emotions, and imagination, along with a development of appreciation of beauty and fine arts. Emphasis on depiction and realism, drawings of objects, and geometric drawings gradually diminished due to the new goals that stressed education through art and art appreciation. Simultaneously, the teachers were given new directives, where their own attitudes and personalities were decisive factors regarding the students level of activity and their enjoyment in their own work.

The National Curriculum of 1962 stated that the method of free expression should become the supreme goal for art education, and the teachers received well-defined directions on how this would be accomplished:

> The teacher has his most valuable aid in his own oral performance, the ability to paint with words, with a few but essential strokes. Stimulating activities should, particularly when they involve materials from other subjects, aim at activating the imagination of the students and not project images from their remembrance of the pages of the textbook. Illustrations, pictures and wall charts should not be shown as models for depiction. . . . Copying from drawings on the blackboard should not be existing in connection with free expression. (LGR, 1962, p. 310)

From Drawing to Art as Communication

In the early 1960s, a lot of young art student teachers felt that the ideas and methods of free expression were becoming obsolete. They were part of a society that was rapidly changing and images were becoming more and more important in the process of communication. Through movies, television, and newspapers, the whole city environment was getting crowded with commercial images and propaganda. The art teachers realized they did not have the knowledge to meet this new situation and felt that art education must change direction (Nordström, 1967). Discussions took place in the professional journals of the teacher association called *Drawing* (*Teckning*) and by the most committed art teachers.

The 1960s were a time of political and educational revolts in Sweden as well as other places in the world. The students at the universities expressed their protests against unwanted changes in higher education through demonstrations and "occupations" of university buildings. This reaction was provoked by a governmental commission that sought to professonalize college education. The change was intended to enable a centralized bureaucracy to take charge of college education, which would result in restricted admission to higher education and adaptation to short-term demands of the labor market. The students felt that behind these demands they could detect the Social Democrat government and the interests of capitalism. The Minister of Education at the time, Olof Palme, was forced to defend these changes in the educational system. The opposition was represented by sympathizers from both left and right. During this time the leftist movements had grown particularly strong in the country and they were attacking the society that Olof Palme and his party represented.

In this political and educational turmoil, the art teachers focused their struggle against the committee of the teacher education (LUK). The fight against LUK lasted for more than four years and took place in the streets, the schools, and the mass media. Many teachers and students took part in the events. One of the leading personalities in this struggle was Gert Z. Nordström, a teacher at the College of Arts and Crafts in Stockholm, later the first art person to be appointed professor of art education in Sweden.

During this time, the Vietnam War rallied students all over the world as well as in Sweden. Olof Palme again found himself in the middle of the attention, however this time on the same side as the young protesters. He took part in demonstrations and officially criticized the United States. His radical position in this controversial issue caused a lot of protests, both at home and abroad. However, such action from an official person influenced young people to take positions in complicated issues and stand up for their opinions in their encounters with the establishment.

Politics and Art Education

The world and its problems were felt to be close as a result of the mass media and for the students in art education, it became clear that the content of art education was too limited. The student teachers wanted the presence of everyday life to be included in the artworks of the children. A statement of this position was published, to the dismay of the older teacher education faculty, in a 1967 issue of *Drawing*. In a proposal for lessons in visual arts communication for the secondary level, the teachers were encouraged to use current newspaper clippings describing the bombings of Vietnam as a commencement for making art (Karlsson, Nordström, & Wikell, 1967).

During 1960s, new media and its content began to influence Swedish art education. Film making grew in popularity. The national movie industry during this period expanded its market. A group of Swedish film directors, headed by Ingmar Bergman, had gained international reputations through their experimental and creative productions. The Swedish Film Institute, a governmentally funded cultural organization, became actively involved in introducing film into the schools. In the classrooms, students began making art with movie cameras and camcorders. In the beginning, it was a slow process, not because of lack of interest or determination, but rather due to a shortage of resources. However, in order to hasten the development of film-making programs, instructions involving integration across the curriculum were published and distributed.

Changes to the National Curriculum

The National Curriculum of 1962 had to be revised, and the new proposal of 1969 became a battleground for new and old ideas. The challenge was to devise art education programs for the 1970s and establish new goals for future work in the school subject. The result became a powerful change of direction in the teaching of art, which continues to have an impact on art education in the country.

In the curriculum of 1962, instructions for all levels in art education began with an item called "activities in free expression." In the curriculum of 1969 this formulation was omitted. For the first time, the goal statements required that interpretation and picture study should involve other images than works of fine art. Some of the titles of the art courses now were "Images as Communication" and "Environmental Studies." These titles were soon to dominate the discussions of the practice of art education and, as it later turned out, "Environmental Studies" became the most practical of all art education to be handled by classroom teachers.

Environmental Studies in Art Education

At the beginning of the 1970s the Swedish trade market declined in a remarkable way. Employment was affected and the amount of foreign trade decreased for the first time since World War II. The government, led by the Social Democrats, began to increase governmental funding of housing and road projects and the great change of the urban environment was allowed to continue unrestrained. Blocks of old houses were torn down, streets were widened and new housing projects commenced. *Buy, wear, and throw away* became the most popular motto of this time (Larsson, 1970).

Protests were loud, both in the media and out in the streets. Critical voices advocated a more flexible style of living. One of the leaders of this movement, Lena Larsson, a teacher at the College of Arts and Crafts in Stockholm, quickly implemented educational strategies to promote critical thinking about the environment in the training of art teachers and the national curriculum. "Environmental Studies" created meaningful and solid assignments that could be included in local art programs throughout the nation's schools (Wikell, 1967; Jarenskog & Svanvik, 1968).

Art as Communication

In the late 1960s images for communicational purposes developed rapidly in the Western world. Television, advertisement, film, newspapers, and comics were all part of popular culture and were new channels of communication in an expanding multimedial society. Particularly important for this increased utilization of pictures in the communication system was the expansion of television and techniques in printing and copying.

The National Board of Education established a commission to produce materials that focused on art as communication for teachers' in-service training. The model of communication that was the basis for this material depended on a system of classification of images according the intentions of the sender. In this system the teachers obtained an objective tool of classification, which enabled them to survey pictures. Distinctions between types of images made classroom planning easy. The classes of images governed teaching aids produced during the 1970s and constituted the foundation of the national curriculum of 1980. The categories included images in which the intention of the sender is to convey knowledge, report, entertain, propagandize, advertise, give an aesthetic experience, provide information, or warn. The model for analyzing these categories has its origin in theories and models of communication (Bengtson, Karlsson, & Eklund, 1970).

In 1970, a new book was published that had great impact on art education, not only in Sweden but also in the other Scandinavian countries. In *Images, School and Society (Bilden, skolan och samhället)* Nordström and Romilsson (1970) argued that the use of pictures in society was related to the political situation at large and art education in general. This was a convincing argument for a new direction in art education. In their book, Nordström and Romilsson (1970) presented a new instructional method focusing on the student as a *conscious* critical individual. The method was called *The Polarizing Methodology* and its basic idea was that the student, through extensive work in interpretation of images and producing art, should examine a concept from as many different perspectives as possible. Nordström and Romilsson argued that the best way to reach an understanding of the world would be to study the intrinsic contrasts in all things and phenomena (see Figure 6.2). Their pedagogical model was a form of problem-oriented studies that rested on the foundation of analytical studies and research in Marxist methods. The model emphasized the communicative qualities of the image over the aesthetic or artistic aspects.

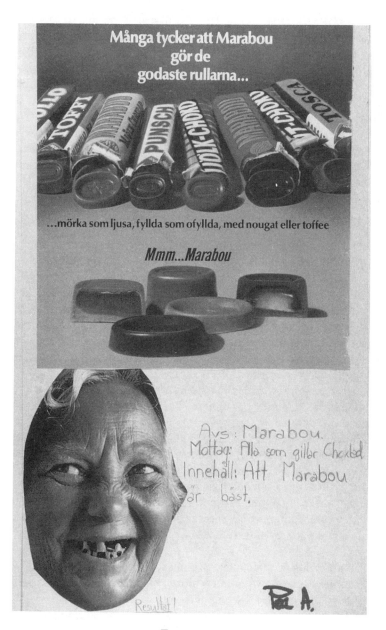

FIGURE 6.2

Collage using the Polarized Method. Made by boy twelve years of age. The boy had chosen a commercial ad to analyze. Next he identified the sender and the message. He then created a work of art that included a "counter" message.

Since 1970, a continuing critical discussion of the image as a linguistic system has emerged. Viewing art as language meant an acceptance of a collective system with rules and regulations, independent of individual desires, which were possible to test and include in the teaching process. When the art teachers in the early 1970s were laying the foundation for a new way of teaching art, theories of semiotics drew most of their attention. The first time art education was presented inside the borders of semiology was in the book *Bild och form (Art and form)* (Hansson, Karlsson, & Nordström, 1974). The new development that now took place was the application of linguistic theory to images, which placed the communicative qualities of imagery on a level equal to that of verbal language.

The Child and Youth Culture

The political discussions and the protests against society and its establishment during the 1960s and early 1970s engendered a "ideological-critical" point of view in national art education. This view was mainly directed toward the way the cultural sphere of children and youngsters were presented in the media. School authorities and the establishment had traditionally used culture, in the form of high art, as an important part of the education of the child. By this time, they felt they were up against an overpowering antagonist in the shape of commercialized products, often internationally manufactured, which had flooded the market and were aimed directly at children without the consent of adults.

In Sweden, a number of commissions and investigations developed to suggest actions to take in the area of child culture. Child culture was on the governmental agenda and the peak of the engagement came in "the year of the children," proclaimed by the United Nations in 1979. The image of the environmental situation for the urban child as it was expressed in the public discussions was dramatic. The social and cultural environment of the child was drained and the vacuum was filled with a loud and threatening media culture. A number of proposed solutions to the problem were summarized in a strategy of three levels:

1. Protect children from a deteriorating cultural consumption.
2. Emphasize alternative forms of culture, which show solidarity to children.
3. Increase the possibilities for children to work creatively.

(Hansson, Karlsson, & Nordström, 1992)

These discussions were similar to those of the 1940s. However, many issues separate the cultural debate of the 1940s from the one in the 1970s. For example, the latter was considerably more politicized, while both focused on the concept of *culture created by adults for children*. Not until the late 1970s was the concept officially enhanced to include a culture that was their own, *culture made by children* (see Figure 6.3).

In the 1980s the choice of cultural products by the youngsters became equal to the concept of youth culture (Statens ungdomsråd, 1981). This extension of the concept of youth culture made adults realize that children were caught between the interests of the commercialized industry and the ambition of the general public to educate them. For educators, the problem was to be on the side of the children. The aesthetic values of adults, which had been practiced on child art for generations, was now questioned.

Art teachers reacted to the fact that it was only the experience of the teacher and the traditions of the school that determined the content of education. The culture that came from the children themselves was characterized by the application of a collective pattern, therefore the school should acknowledge and conform to it. They argued that children do not separate different forms of language, but draw, sing, talk, and dramatize indiscriminately and simultaneously, without looking at any separate parts. This was the model schools should follow, they argued. Between 1977 and 1980 a research project led by Hasse Hansson at the Uppsala University established the following principles for education:

1. The development of the child's linguistic production has to originate from the child's reality, culture, and language.
2. The development of the child's linguistic production is improved through the integration of different expressions of words, images, sounds, and movements.
3. The development of the child's linguistic production is encouraged by collective activities.

(Hansson & Qvarsell, 1983, p. 17)

Changes in Art Education in the Preschools

The Museum of Modern Art in Stockholm had an exhibition in 1981 that introduced Loris Malaguzzi's approach to preschool education in Reggio Emilia, Italy. This pedagogy became an alternative educational system aimed at stimulating all of the senses of the child through methods that included investigation and research (Arvas, 1986). Between 1963 and 1985 Malaguzzi was the head of the municipal child-care program in the city of Reggio Emilia. During World War II, the city had been the center for the antifascist movement and it was in this atmosphere of democracy that the first preprimary schools emerged. With a little financial support from the Italian Communist Party, these early preschools were run by a voluntary

FIGURE 6.3

Youth culture has its own form and content, which is not always appreciated by adults. Quite often, it is their choice of images and the way they dress that is criticized by the older generations. In Uppsala, a school for graffiti artists was started in the early 1990s called the Aerosol School. The city authorities wanted to take control of the movement and have them perform "legal" work instead. The students received an education and were allowed to decorate various places in the city.

female staff until they gradually became part of the municipal childhood system.

Mallaguzzi's philosophy of quality and creativity in child care, as well as his charismatic leadership, played a decisive part in the successful development of the communal preschools of Reggio Emilia. The preschools were intended to play an important part of society and not become isolated from it. Malaguzzi advocated thematic studies of the city, its structure, and its tradition of cooperation and collaboration to ensure the young citizens' education in democracy and equality.

In Sweden, the pedagogical model of Reggio Emilia primarily drew interest through the formidable production of child art and stimulation of creativity. The concept of cognition and its expression through the art of children inspired teachers and started them on long journeys to the red plains of northern Italy.

In Sweden, the Social Democratic Party had fought for the rights of women to work outside the home since the early 1960s. In order to obtain this struggle for equal rights between men and women and make it possible, the Social Democratic Party had acted for common child care for all children. The only way to accomplish this was the building of municipal preschools across the country.

Since art education in the Swedish nursery schools traditionally was built on the pedagogy of Fröbel and the free-expression movement, this pedagogical model meant great changes in the planning of the activities. The shift from tradition to social consciousness, from spontaneity to research, were the characteristics of the work at the preschools inspired by Reggio Emilia. Knowledge, advocates argued, is created between people and therefore the adult educator is considered a challenger and a "fellow researcher." Children want to grow and understand and take responsibility for their own quest for knowledge. Thus, they argued against the notion of the child as nature and its division into different developmental stages according to the law of nature (Wallin, 1993, p. 105).

One of the great myths in art education, according to Elliot Eisner (1973–1974), is the notion that a child is able to see things more clearly than adults. Consistent with the Reggio Emilia perspective of art education, Eisner advocates that perception must be constantly exercised in order to be able to distinguish and create all the hues in our surroundings. The pedagogy of Reggio Emilia helped to establish the idea that education today must be directed toward the complexity of modern society. Modern society demands the development of social and communicative competence in children and youth to respond to societal changes from production toward information and knowledge (Dahlberg & Åsén, 1993).

Conclusions

Art education in Sweden has reflected the political and social changes in the country during the twentieth century. The purpose of teaching the subject in the schools has changed, not only because of certain ideas and ambitions but also as a result of political parties and social events. During the first part of the century, nationalism and the love of country dominated the intentions and purposes of art education. These ideas were challenged by strong winds of democracy after the World War II, which paved the way for the foundations of a free society and free expression in the arts. The ideology of free expression was questioned primarily by the art students, who took part in the political events that challenged all political institutions during the 1960s. Finally, the postmodern movements that grew both inside and outside the art community had a decisive effect on the new direction of teaching art.

From a national standpoint antireactionary forces, the disintegration of moral codes, emphasis on rational consideration of the curriculum, and introduction of developmental and psychological theories have, during the past twenty years, created a more child-oriented educational system (Pettersson & Åsén, 1989). The fast development of the mass-media industry with music videos and popular culture has demanded a growing need for democracy in teaching. In art, this will mean the development of knowledge about newer media, such as video, computer graphics, and graffiti (Lovgren, 1992).

7

Lucimar Bello Pereira Frange

Brazilian Connections between Fine Art and Art Teaching Since the 1920s

t is necessary to refer briefly to the Brazilian "project" of art in education, and to note at the outset that the epistemology of art, art criticism, and even debate, are practically absent from our schools. This condition results in the neglect of a potent educational force, for knowing art—making art, thinking about art, criticizing art—is founded on a dynamic, sceptical self-questioning, which is described by Paulo Freire in *Por Uma Pedagogia da Pergunta* (Towards a Questioning Pedagogy) (Freire, 1985). Art consolidates and manifests itself paradigmatically: ethically—aesthetically—politically, where to be ethical is to dwell in the here and now, to be aesthetic is to invent and reinvent the world as a work of art based on philosophical concepts, and to be political is to deploy imagination as an instrument of war against malignant forces (see Guatarri, 1990).

We are immersed in such forces, which have been imposed on us, and we must transcend them. For such institutionalized elements generate further institutionalizing elements and, in order to resist them, an individual and collective transcultural anthropophagy (cannibalizing) is needed.

Thus, Brazil's anthropophagous movement was created by Oswald de Andrade. Its meaning is: "one who eats," who does not ignore the influences exerted on him/herself but deliberately eats them as though they are food, digests them, and produces new knowledge, new actions, and new questioning (Baddeley & Fraser, 1954, p. 20). This movement is *instituting* rather than instituted or institutionalizing: to be an instituting element is to be anthropophagous. Space and time and color and structure are in this sense instituting elements. The artist works in the instituting field. And the so-called art education? It is more appropriate in relation to the Brazilian experience to speak of art and art teaching. Art is art. Education is education. Creation is transdisciplinary.

The whole of Latin America, with its diversities—geographical, ethnic, cultural, political, economic and social—is surreal, that is, beyond an established reality, imaginative and instituting. The search for cultural identities, roots, and authenticity often connects avant-garde art and popular art, and interrelates disparate experiences. The images of our everyday life must permeate our curricula and our school.

But what relations may we establish between art, knowledge, intuition, and imagination in our programs? Because the artist transcends conventions in order to continuously create, his/her intentionality, desire, realization, and reflection include intuition, thoughts, memories, emotions, perceptions, and feelings—in other words exactly the kind of holistic existence that should be the very basis of education.

Herbert Read, who has been exceptionally influential in Brazil, said that the artist is endowed with extreme sensibility, intuition, and restlessness. He/she is an individual constantly alive to the new, perfecting his/her techniques precisely for this purpose. The work of art is an intuitive image—imagined, invented, and consolidated—which acts as a bridge between actual experiences and intellectual thought, both of them connected with education (Arnheim, 1989, pp. 10–16). Intuition, intellect, and thought are the basics of the cognitive process, spanning between the most elementary records of feeling and those more sophisticated records of human experience. They cannot exist apart. Their existence is a continuum, from simple perceptions to the most complex theories (Arnheim, 1989, pp. 13–20).

To construct works of art is to construct images and forms with a Borgeslike taste, where (in his Chinese encyclopedia) an imaginary division of animals provides a bizarre new encounter with the unusual: spaces become ruins, enumerations are quotations of innumerable and impossible things (see Foucault, 1986). Works of art are spaces turned into ruins. Human life is intrinsically insecure because it consists of instituting moments. The crisis of the twentieth century is thus a crisis of the everyday, broken down into three parts: (a) crisis of identity, (b) crisis of familiarity, and (c) crisis of security. The everyday is the space of immediate circumstances, in which we familiarize ourselves with the world, and what is extraneous becomes intraneous.

While insecurity characterizes human life everywhere and at all times (Kujawski, 1988, 54–59), the vision we all have of our lives is one of uniqueness, nontransferability, and preciousness. Finding ourselves is knowing who we are, that we are unique. The uniqueness of being turns into questioning and becomes an enquiring conscience (Paz, 1961, p. 1). This questioning, in general, is the very basis of art in education. The artist is aware of enquiring into realities, and blends the extraneous and the intraneous as he/she affirms, doubts, denies.

Regina Machado (1991), responding to *Labirinto da Solidão* by Octavio Paz, puts forth the following question:

> What prospect does our educational system offer to adolescents towards providing them with an enquiring conscience? The adolescent has to be able to get hold of his/her uniqueness, aptitude, dreams, anguish and quests. I think that he/she can—provided he/she can express, or construct in a significant manner, his/her reflection on his/her "marveling at being." (p. 28)

The artist is deliberately marveling at the infinite prospects of being unique in a complete, creative, and fruitful process. Contemporary artists transcend equivalencies, affirmations, representations. Images antagonize texts; texts antagonize images. Examples can be seen in the works of Magritte, Duchamp, Oiticica, Botero, where similarities multiply in uncertain, undefined, confused, and daring relationships. These are not contradictions; they are the affirmation of other ways and other places, of the nonpresent in the present.

The work of art is the infinite within the finite, according to Ferreira Gullar. Its entirety results from its completion and must therefore be considered not as an enclosure of an immobile and static reality, but rather as the opening of an infinite that is added to the form (Gullar, 1978, p. 60). Art is the uniqueness of imaginably being and of people being themselves in a collective dimension. Art is to make and to maintain the doubt of what has been made, as Miró and Picasso did when they compulsively questioned their agreements and disagreements. As Foucault says:

> To paint is not to affirm.
> To create is not to affirm.
> To create is to accept doubt!

Today we value both the event and the rupture. The period known as postmodernity draws up the past, reinscribing it and questioning it in accordance with present traditions. The possibility of a major investment in critical perspective and cultural significances exists, as the "contemporary aesthetic experience is mainly remitted to the imaginary, considering the evanescence of the symbolic inscription" (Favaretto, 1993, p. 49). Contemporariness is here understood as fields of performance open to uniqueness and as interpretation of modern residuals.

Knowledge is not and cannot be discursive. It is also communicative, expressive, cultural, symbolic, imaginary, nonverbal. Suzanne Langer, for example, defends a presentational knowledge, which corresponds to this entirety. Art and art teaching in our present time—if we are to accept postmodern theory—are beyond words, as there is an incorporation of actions, intuitions, interlineations, and deep and time-consuming quests: "Teaching derived from art is reached through ascesis, initiation, through a lengthened look, an attentive listening" (Coli, 1984, p. 58). Art education, according to Ana Mae Barbosa, is epistemology of art, and therefore, it is the investigation of the manners whereby learning and art learning are achieved in basic and medium-level schools, in colleges and in the intimacy of ateliers (Barbosa & Salles, 1991).

Historical Considerations

In order to find the origins of what I have called the "Brazilian project for art in education," it is necessary to address the beginning of modernism in this country. This is usually considered to have been marked by the so-called Week of Modern Art in 1922. However, I maintain that three key events preceded this—an exhibition of Lasar Segall's modernist paintings; an exhibition of Anita Malfatti's expressionist and cubist images; and the revelation of a new artist, Victor Brecheret, as one of our nation's major sculptors. I believe these events were of a positively Brazilian nature, whereas in the Week of Modern Art, the participants denounced such characteristics, maintaining as a commonsense that Brazilian art's purpose was to be imitative. Manoel Bonfim attributed this attitude to a lack of power of observation, but Silvio Romero supported it in his literary studies, creating an impression that Brazil was to be an *entrepot* of social, political, and cultural products from other countries.

In the 1930s—during one Brazilian crisis, the change from an oligarchy to a democracy—a reformation of the educational system implanted the idea of free expression in the public schools. "The leaders of The New School Movement—John Dewey, Claparède and Decroly—affirmed the importance of art in education for the development of imagination, intuition and intelligence" (Barbosa & Salles, 1991, p. 14). The New School movement placed a great emphasis, in regard to the teaching of art, upon perception, expression, psychological conditions of individuals, and their experiences, as well as upon the disclosure of emotions, insights, desires, and inner motivations experienced by individuals (Fusari & Ferraz, 1991, p. 28). The first specialized schools of art were established as an extracurricular activity for children and adolescents. It was in this decade that the University of São Paulo (USP) was created as the main institution responsible for expediting the discussions and the theoretical fundamentals for art and art teaching, on both a national and international level.

These changes were, of course, consistent with contemporary political changes. Government sought to consolidate social development, bringing forth the need for a new interpretation of Brazil. The 1930s were thus decisive for a reorientation of the Brazilian historiography (Ortiz, 1985, p. 40).

In 1948, the Escolinha de Arte do Brazil (an art school for children) was created in Rio de Janeiro by Augusto Rodrigues, where children were permitted to create freely in the expressionist climate prevailing in the postwar period. Around 1958, twenty such schools existed in Brazil, coordinated by teachers who had received guidance from Augusto Rodrigues and Moemia Varella among others. Until 1973, these schools were places of apprenticeship and reflection for children, adults, and teachers from all over the country (Barbosa & Salles, 1991).

The São Paulo Biennial of 1951 extended the horizons of Brazilian art. Established after the fashion of the Venice Biennial, it promoted an international gathering. We benefited from the presence of work by Picasso, Mondrian, Klee, Munch, Ensor, Laurens, Moore, Marini, Calder, along with Cubism, Futurism, Neoplasticism. The subsequent biennials brought works by Léger, Morandi, Chagall and Pollock. In the 1960s, the Museum of Modern Art of Rio de Janeiro administered courses to children and adults and prompted *Domingos de Criação* (Creativity Sundays).

A New Cultural Cycle

The 1960s, beginning with Pop Art, marked a new cultural cycle. In the antiart trend, called the postmodern, Brazil became a forerunner, not a follower. The young Brazilian Neoconcrete artists took up their movement prior to Pop or Op movements. In the plastic arts, the *Neoconcrete Manifesto* incorporates new propositions, which become visible in such works of art as "Domingos de Criação," by Frederico Morais, and "Parangolés," by Hélio Oiticica. In these works of art, values properly plastic were absorbed by perceptive and situational structures. Expressiveness in itself was not of interest, nor was the hermetic individual aspect of Pop Art, so much as the objectivity-in-itself of Pop and Op. Hélio Oiticica was the youngest among the Neoconcrete artists. Mario Schemberg said that Oiticica was the anthropophagus of his own and that he, Oiticica, was the most Brazilian of all artists.

Of fundamental importance in the sixties was the action of the Centro Popular de Cultura, which was closely related to the National Students Association of Rio de Janeiro. Two points are worth mentioning: (1) political effervescence lead to a revolutionary reformation movement in art and culture; and (2) nationalist ideology pervaded Brazilian society as a whole and solidified different social classes and groups (Ortiz, 1985, pp. 47–48).

In the early 1970s, upon approval of Law 5692: *Diretrizes e Bases da Educação* (Directives and Bases for Education), the teaching of art was proposed on a multivalent basis, which created serious misunderstandings and was a real disaster. Training courses were created with a duration of two years, after completion of which teachers would be entitled to teach plastic arts, music, dance, and drama. Numerous were the meetings, at national and regional levels, and many were the representations to the Ministry of Education, for the purpose of denouncing how such short periods and low-cost courses would merely benefit their administrators and be highly prejudicial to, and very expensive for, both students and teachers— all poorly informed and lacking competence as to the process of creating art and reflecting on it. Echoes from the past can still be heard today—but denunciation of this state of affairs persists, and proposals are put forward every now and then for art and art teaching courses to be administered by professionals who have experienced college level courses in art in a specific language and with a minimum duration of four years.

> Redeeming specific languages is contrary to multivalence. The problems of multivalence have brought consequences both to the formation of teachers and to the pedagogical exercise, contributing to depleting the so-called Artistic Education proposed by Law 5692/71. We advocate art in basic education because we believe that it is, par excellence, the school space for an effective action towards enlarging the student's cultural and artistic universe. Art is the space for the establishment of a project of democratization of, and access to, art and culture. (Penna, 1995, pp. 21–22)

In the 1970s, a program of art education was established at the Museum of Contemporary Art of USP. At this time only a few states provided training assistance to art teachers, in which the following institutions had a major role: the Secretariat of State for Education and Culture, the School of Visual Arts, and the Educational Centre, in Rio de Janeiro; the Art Centre of the City of Belo Horizonte, sponsored by that city's Municipal Administration; and the Escola Guignard, in Minas Gerais. One of the most serious subsequent problems faced by art teachers has been that of fragmentation, the cause of hierarchy and exclusion of quality education projects from public education. This education impoverishment process sprung from a philosophical and ideological deferral to the expansion of Brazilian industry and reflected the ideal of development (Azevedo, 1989, p. 31). This and other reasons of a political and social nature illustrate the extent and difficulty of our struggle and how extremely important it is for us to keep on, even when the progress we attain is little, in order to reverse the situation.

Beginning in the 1980s the School of Communication and Arts of USP, through national and international meetings and the implementation of postgraduate courses in art and art teaching, consolidated the political consciousness of art teachers toward pedagogies and criticism related to art. A series of important events occurred, including:

1. In 1980, the Week of Art and Art Teaching, with the participation of 2,700 art teachers from all over Brazil, during which political aspects were emphasized through debates on the mobilization and isolation of art teaching, educational policy, the cultural role of art teachers in the Brazilian reality, and the upgrading of art teachers (Barbosa & Salles, 1991, p. 13).
2. In 1984, the First International Symposium on History of Art Education, intended to permit the improvement of consciousness and identity by interconnecting historical, political-social, and cultural moments. An example of this was the symposium discussion relating to the Arts Institute of the University of Brasilia, which highlighted the history, theoretical assumptions, and operation of the old institute.
3. Also in 1984, the World Congress of the International Society for Education through Art, held in Rio de Janeiro, with a significant national participation of art teachers discussing their experiences and carefully examining the main questions and concepts on the teaching of art.
4. In 1987, the Federation of Art Educators in Brazil (FAEB), congregated the national associations at both federal and state levels (numbering fourteen at the time). Two issues were important—one (political), involved a struggle for the strengthening and upgrading of art teaching within an educational process closely connected to Brazilian identities and cultures; and two, (conceptual), involved a philosophical and epistemological approach as regards art teaching.
5. In 1989, the Third International Symposium on Art Teaching and its History, with the participation of two thousand teachers and forty-nine foreign specialists, for the main purpose of illustrating art contents through concrete experiences.[1]
6. In 1992, at the time of the Fifth FAEB Congress, in Belém, State of Pará, the First National Forum on Curricula in Art Education Courses

was held as a result of a series of discussions throughout the country relating to the number of art teachers being graduated at basic, intermediate, and college levels. Two points were raised for special debate: one, the art teacher as artist; and two, the desirability of a licentiate degree not connected with the prevailing bachelor's degree.

7. In 1994 and 1995, the first five National Forums on Appraisal and Reformulation of Arts and Design Higher Education were held, where a Document of Appraisal of Art Courses was drawn up. This document involved nationwide representation, showing courses by specialization, and was pilot tested in a number of universities. Curricular discussions were proposed to continue in 1996, constituting a great challenge owing to the ethnic and cultural diversity of the country.

Recent Methodologies

Among the methodologies developed during the eighties and nineties, it is necessary to mention the Triangular Proposal, which is an adaptation of discipline-based art education, developed by Dr. Ana Mae Tavares Bastos Barbosa of the School of Communication and Arts at USP. This is a pedagogy including the history of art (contextualizing the work studied), reading of the work of art (aesthetical and critical analysis of the artistic production), and the making of art (based on technical and aesthetic knowledge as well as on historical knowledge). Related to this is the Art in School Project, developed by Fundação Iochpe in Rio Grande du Sul in 1988, which was extended to many Brazilian states.

Another methodology, critical studies, of British origin, has been influential on various Brazilian projects. Critical studies involves enquiring into and questioning the relations and interrelations between art, school, and community. Critical studies emphasizes contemporary studies, art from the past, relationships between art and sociology, philosophy, psychology, and other areas of knowledge (Barbosa & Salles, 1991, p. 40). This suits the nature of art in our present time, located somewhere between construction and deconstruction, and featuring the permanent questioning of realities. In 1981, Rod Taylor (1987) established the Critical Studies in Art Education (CSAE) project at the Drumcroon Art Education Centre, Wigan, U.K. The project originated in a few key conditions:

1. A prevailing emphasis on the practice of art solely as activities or exercises
2. A minimization of verbal communications
3. A disregard of values on the part of students
4. A disdain for individual creativity and criticism
5. A disdain for the aspects of art, design history, and artistic skill on the part of educators in general

However, the interconnected traditions, histories, autobiographical objects, feelings, perceptions, and questions about the world's images are of fundamental importance. These connections also extend to the environment, social relations, subjectivity, and objectivity. Tradition provides us with values (Benjamin, 1991, p. 18); science widens our knowledge; technology gives us conditions for a dynamic relationship with space and time; social relations give us human dimensions; subjectivity and objectivity are connections between personalities, different realities, and magical visions. At the end of the twentieth century, we need to surpass tradition, go beyond the reception and production of information; beyond technology, beyond environmental criticism and social relations, beyond subjectivity and objectivity. We must acquaint ourselves with these areas so as to acknowledge them, incorporate them, and submit them to our anthropophagy. We must be active components of the work of art, wherein we are the producers and not mere observers.

To inhale and exhale art in a continuous spiral is a concept metaphorically similar to that proposed for critical studies. CSAE's goals are: (a) to see and perceive art as an integral part of life, and (b) to deconstruct by subjecting images and forms to a permanent process of discussion, establishing links between artists, artisans, designers galleries, museums, and other cultural and educational spaces, making it possible for original works of art to be known, and originating an adequate vocabulary for reflection, discussion, and questioning.

These objectives are similar to Elliot Eisner's demand for structure: "No doors will open if there is no structure or magic in a curriculum. If we lack structure in our curricula, we will have no automacity. Without automacity, we have no internalization. Without internalization we have no magic" (Eisner, 1988, pp. 14–25). Similar too is Robert Saunders's multipurpose approach (also highly influential in Brazil), which embodies aesthetic education, visual and verbal perception, historical changes, and self-identification. To understand a work of art we need to have a series of encounters that enable us to observe different points of view, a perceptive maturity initiated by contact with reproduction and, subsequently, the original. The original alone permits authentic aesthetic experience; a reproduction is a simulacrum of the work of art.

Art is, at all times, an expression of the particular (Pedrosa, 1979, p. 132). Art is also multicultural—of particular significance in Brazil, where ethnic differences, other cultural heritages, cultural pluralism, social diversity, and a questioning of the dominance of a privileged canon of art are all matters of prime significance (Stuhr, 1991, p. 14).

Following the efforts of educators involved with the arts in schools to absorb and practice the above principles, the Brazilian Constitution was amended in 1988 in order to establish that "teaching shall be exercised under the following principles . . . freedom to learn, teach, research and disseminate thoughts, art and knowledge." This was a victory by the teachers of art who had pressed and lobbied the parliamentarians who voted on the Constitution. However, since this time we have constantly been under threat of having the discipline of art eliminated from the curriculum of the basic and medium-level schools, a threat deriving from Lei de Diretrizes e Bases da Educação, which alleges to the effect that art does not have content.

Considerations on the Content of Art

With this in mind, I should like to highlight the following for reflection. Augusto Rodrigues, plastic artist and one of the greatest Brazilian educators in the twentieth century, in an interview with Rosza Vel Zoladz (1990) on the meaning of art, stated that:

> One of the most important aspects in the art making process is that of a confusing abundance, a pleasurable form to the senses—images that fill the eyes, music that floods the ears—and that is achieved with tools of the craft: the brush over the canvas or the pencil over the paper. . . . I have as the subject in one of my paintings the top of a large tree sheltering a violet and depriving it of the sun's rays. The little flower is eager for that light so vital for it to keep alive. However, it draws back and, in doing so, it shoots forth, grows up and, in the shade, it blooms. Its nourishment the little plant extracts from the environment situation it is in. The reason for this illustration is to convey the fact that art also attains such vitality. Man's frailty gives room to a creative power inherent to art. What I mean is that Art, as a contest of human experience, shows life's uncertainties as to the extension of that which man creates, develops and invents. It is impossible to think that art manifests itself outside our perplexity, before life's intricacy. Creative power arises out of this paradox silently experienced in its human aims. (pp. 90–93)

Barbosa & Salles (1990) state that: "Art has a domain, a language and history of its own; it consists of fields of specific studies, it does not consist of mere activities" (p. 7). In their introduction to *A Imagem no Ensino da Arte* (The Image in the Teaching of Art), they state that "art is, in postmodernity, connected to cognition; the concept of making art is connected to construction of thought arising out of images."

Language enables man to organize what is real, to establish the categories and classes of events, naming them and classifying them in a significant structure. Language makes it possible for acts and objects to be abstracted in their essential characteristics and to be represented by means of symbols. However, the real nature of feeling is something that language, as a discursive symbol, cannot express.

Art is work; it is invention turned real. It "presupposes basically the action of imagination—the realm of man's creating power" (Duarte, 1981, p. 107). Jorge Coli (1984), in *O Que é Arte* (What art is), writes:

> The "in itself" of a work is an immanence, a projection. It is us who express the "in itself" of art, that which in the objects is, to us, art. Andre Malraux, the contemporary French novelist and politician, conceived an "imaginary museum" to be provided with works of non-historical affinities—a museum of analogical subjectivity. Subjectivity has the power to disclose the artistic force which lives in the objects. (pp. 64–65)

Art and Art Teaching
Discovering Possibilities

The 1960s in Brazil was a period of cultural, political, economical, and social effervescence, mainly in the arts and literature. Conceptual artists during this period were Mario Pedrosa, Mario Schemberg, Frederico Morais, Ferreira Gullar, comprising the popular culture as a regaining of consciousness of the Brazilian reality (Ortiz, 1985, pp. 71–72). Others requiring mention are the Neoconcretists Hélio Oiticica and Lygia Clark. In fact, the Movimento Neoconcreto Brasileiro (Brazilian Neoconcrete Movement) has great possibilities for understanding and implementing Brazil's art and art teaching projects. Especially useful is the concept of antimethodology, which signifies methodologies under permanent construction, not really prepared at any one time and, therefore, never canonized. These antimethodologies are, to use the words and ideas of Haroldo de Campos about the work of Hélio Oiticica, "hang-gliders to ecstasy" (Campos, 1992).

Oiticica (1986), discussing Parangolés, states that they explain his own theoretical development of an aesthetic experience subdivided in color, structure and time. They are part of an environmental art. The spectator has total participation in their environmental totalities. The Parangolé is, in a certain way, opposed to Cubism, as it does not take the object in its entirety and in all its complexity for study, but rather accords special attention to the object's foundation. In the Parangolés, the action is sheer expressive manifestation of the work itself.

This, in a nutshell, is the Brazilian conception of art that we wish to form the basis of education. It springs from the inner rhythm of the collective. The experience of dance and of samba provided Oiticica with the exact idea of creation through the bodily act, the perennial transformation.

The Neoconcretist Manifesto offers such daring interpretations, bringing forth other movements like Neoplasticism and Constructivism. The work of Mondrian, for example, as an *oeuvre* with Neoconcretist antecedents, is antagonistic. As both painting and theory it fully integrates art and life. The theory is self-contradictory as Mondrian, demolisher of the surface, the plan, the line, constructs other space, an other surface. Mondrian deconstructs in order to construct *himself* besides his works. The work of art is conceived as a *corpus*— neither machine nor object, but a continuum whose reality is not exhausted in the external relationship of its elements, because it devotes itself fully to a direct and phenomenological approach. Time and space and structure and color are integrated as part of an indivisible *totality*. In Neoconcretist poetry, space does not flow; it *lasts* (Castro, 1985, p. 13). Neoconcretism returns to humanism in order to oppose the concreteness of scientism (Brito, 1985, p. 49).

Hélio Oiticica is one of the greatest contemporary Brazilian inventors. As an open compendium of innovating propositions and concepts, his work is a paradigm for education. He questions and reflects on international art and concepts and practices of the twentieth-century avant garde: ready-made, box form, merzbau, object, happening, antiart, events, installations, environments, and questions raised by Constructive art, Dada, Pop, Body Art. According to Frederico Morais, Oiticica's work exemplifies the theory of marginality—a radical marginality—which leads him to consider art a rebellion against all forms of oppression: intellectual, aesthetic, metaphysical, social (Oiticica, 1986).

Felix Guatarri in *As Três Ecologias* (The Three Ecologies) proposes an articulation between three ecological areas: social relations, environment, and human subjectivity. He has created an ethical, political articulation that he calls "ecosophy." Ecosophy is the reinvention of relationships between individuals, their bodies, their ghosts, of the space and time where the mysteries of life and death are experienced. Guatarri considers that there is no praxis without ruptures. Both Oiticica and Guatarri affirm the need of the human being for accepting himself/herself as he/she really is, accepting the environment, the social relations, the human subjectivity and objectivity, accepting the ruptures. Guatarri has, so far as the foundations of his theories are concerned, aspects in common with Oiticica. Oiticica, in Guatarrian terms, is ecosophical.[2]

Guy Brett (1992) says that in Oiticica invention and thought flow continuously; that he is a solitary researcher. In his New York writings there is a fusion between thought and life processes. Oiticica's order system is proposed as intimately interconnecting order and disorder, objects and bodies, and environment and architecture, incorporating that which is given and what is to be constituted, nature/human being/culture (Oiticica, 1992, p. 207). Today's artists show clearly the interconnection between art, life, science, philosophical and aesthetic concerns, that is, their concern to perform, think, question and experience art in a manner that is unique.

It is impossible to produce art without interconnections between functions, forms, images, concepts. Images, in postmodernity, are beyond functions, beyond forms, beyond concepts. In order to establish relationships, one needs to desire not that which is a representative process, but rather a "presentation" process to be constructed within arts curricula. Art, philosophy, and science must be interconnected and they must relate to the cultural manifestations of memories and traditions, metanarratives and questionings, which become the exercise of an imaginative and philosophical daily routine. We live with high technological advances on the one hand and with the production of artists and craftsman on the other hand, a production deriving from the most diverse materials and cultures. The multimedia can offer a wide range of referents, which at first glance appear to be impossible. It can also facilitate the carrying out of inquiries, mainly of the latest publications, through data banks and updated images.

The different forms of the skilled crafts—frequently innovating in spite of being regarded as popular art in Latin America—have since the beginning of this century been the subject of debates and discussions. This art is not only a social production but also economic, ethnic, and cultural, related as it is to religions and social transformation movements. The avant garde keeps turning to it on account of its rigorous force and diversity of forms and cultural identities. And such manifestations must find their way into our schools. Art and life are closely connected to the experience that springs from reality; art cannot be dissociated from the reality of environment, history.

In the work of Oiticica, landscape, samba, people, everything, have Brazilian/universal roots—multicultural, visible with their expressive and mystical forces, daring and questioning. An environmental imaginariness is being perpetually instigated, which is neither instituted nor sanctioned. Neoconcretism points to other relationships between art, school, and community. Art in the formal or informal spaces of education is knowledge in research-action and in constant questioning of multiculturalities. Art and art teaching are onthological (What I am), epistemological (What I know), and gnoseological (What I am, believe, and know socially and culturally). These investigations pervade basic and medium-level teaching, the universities, the ateliers and the community experiences, as they are the rights of citizenship and everyone's entitlement.

8

Jordi Pintó
Khalid El Bekay

Art Education and Social, Political, and Economic Changes in Morocco

I n this chapter, we link the economic improvements in Morocco with the increase of art education lessons taught at schools. We discuss the connection between Morocco in 1961, a time when art education was within the reach of only 2 percent of the total population, and 1988, when the percentage dramatically increased to 50 percent of the school population. This chapter deals with the similarities and differences between art education of children aged six to eleven in public and private schools in relation to the general worldwide trend of raising children to be suitable for a global market.

Social and Political Changes in Morocco

The process of Morocco's economic and political evolution should be taken into consideration when attempting to understand the different stages of its education system, and particularly, art education. Strange and difficult as it may seem, in 1990, thirty-four years after Morocco became an independent country and thirty years after King Hassan II had come to the throne, the essence of all the problems and the debate held between the ruling classes and the opposition were still very similar to those at the early stages of the country's independence.

Currently, the utmost, although sometimes tacit, aim of the political parties remains the promulgation of the democratic constitution and the establishment of a fully participatory political system. During the first fifteen years of the country's independence, the parties brought the controversies out into the streets, sometimes in a violent way. Now, little controversy exists and the opposition merely reminds the people of their points of view during their national meetings or on the occasion of a general election.

Two coup d'états have been attempted, which were efforts to change the political system in the country, but they resulted in the execution of the leaders. These attempts have not seemed to be extremely important in the Moroccan debate, since some politicians assert that they were merely attempts to replace the monarchy with another political system. However, the democratic constitution and its parliamentary monarchy are still supported by the nationalists in a subtle but persistent way, which has been the real source of discontent and instability during Hassan II's reign.

The struggle for a democratic constitution started in Morocco at the very beginning of its independence from the French in 1956. The influence of this struggle is still apparent on the education system in central and southern Morocco, especially in Casablanca, the city on which our research was focused.

The debate was postponed during Mohamed V's lifetime thanks to a sort of vote of confidence given by the nationalists. But at his death, on 26 February 1961, the struggle worsened. Hassan II's clever foreign policy, which adopted the nationalistic attitude, isolated ntionalists internationally and calmed them down at the domestic level. The political scenery was outlined at the early stages of Hassan II's reign, and such a scenery has prevailed up to the present. Nevertheless, the frequent periods of exception have made it difficult to get to the core of the matter.

Art Education and the Political Context

But let us concentrate on the subject of our research, namely art education in Morocco. Since 1957, after the colonization (i.e., between 1961 and 1975), young people's art education was exclusively based on geometric technical drawing and manual crafts. Political and religious reasons were behind all these limitations on art education. The most important political reason was the complete absence of freedom of speech, as well as the little importance given to plastic arts by society. At that time, only 2 percent of the total population received some type of art education, and it was always in a private schooling context for the children of wealthy parents. Poor children attending public schools had no art education.

Economic factors played an important role in the absence of art education. Most people were poor and materials were expensive and difficult to obtain, especially paper. On top of that, the country lacked the proper insfrastructure to make art education available to everybody. There were no art museums and no activities were organized to promote art.

The only artistic activities for children were manual crafts, being their only aim to imitate the country's craftmanship. Such cheap and easy-to-obtain materials as wood or mud were used in these manual crafts. These lessons were taught by the Arabic or French language teachers at school, who were not usually qualified to teach the subject. Moreover, the art lessons took place in the same classroom as the other subjects, since they lacked rooms fitted for it.

Religious reasons for the lack of art education included the old prohibition regarding the natural model, which constitutes the origin of the lack of tradition in drawing. The Koran overtly prohibited the natural model, since it stated that people from ancient times would do drawings and make sculptures seeing the images they had created as Gods, and since Islam should be their only and truest religion, people should not create fake images of God. That is the reason images were banned, and hence Islamic artists started creating geometric ornamentation, free of any figural forms.

Notwithstanding all of the above factors, Morocco as such had and does still have an enormous influence on people's art education. Light, color, and shape are all common elements in their everyday life. The rich scene around people provides them with a special sentitivity to shapes and colors, even though there may not be qualified art teachers.

Social Changes and Popular Reactions

From 1975 to 1985, some school and family improvements developed, though they were not dramatic enough. Our research clearly supports the idea that art education in Morocco is closely linked to the economic situation at that time, together with a new opening policy the government started, by providing more freedom to the people and making some general changes in order to mitigate people's general discontent. The fact that in 1985 art education gained more importance as a school subject was a direct consequence of these changes, as we will see later.

In 1979, the country's economy was already in a crisis. In its annual

June report, the Bank of Morocco admitted that growth had been inferior to 1977. There had also been a decrease in investments together with an increase in foreign debt. The report suggested that the reasons for such a crisis could have been the increase in their oil expense, the constant decrease in the prices of phosphate, the salary increases on 30 April that same year, and the great economic effort made to improve the defence budget.

According to the Moroccan Communist paper, the relationship between the lowest salaries, 300 dirhams (approximately US$43) per month, and the monthly income of the wealthiest classes was 1–332. Al Bayan stated that salaries had to be tripled so that the employee's purchasing power were the same as in 1960. Twenty percent of a total of 450,290 farming families had no land of their own and lived on an average salary of 800 dirhams per year (approximately US$115), while about 2,350 families owned 745,000 hectares (approximately 1,840,895 acres) and their annual income amounted up to 12,000 dirhams (approximately US$1,715). Nubir el Anuai, general secretary of the Socialist Trade Union (CDT), called for a 70 percent increase in the salaries of all the civil servants and employees, as well as a minimum salary for industry of 1,000 dirhams a month (approximately US$143), since prices had increased by 77 percent between 1973 and 1978, according to official statistics.

The 1981 riots had their origin in the sudden and sharp increase in the price of essential products, such as fruit, vegetables, rent, water, gas, and electricity, shortly after the government had announced the increase. Not only did the Workers' Democratic League criticize and disapprove of the government's decision, but they also claimed a general strike. The trade-union opposition thought it was the right time to face the ruling classes again. Some Moroccan Socialists thought François Miterrand's victory in the French elections would make the Government behave in a more care-ful manner. However, according to some indexes, an average eight-person working-class family in Morocco, whose average salary was around 50 dirhams per month was unable to afford any consumer goods. For example, it would take two thousand months for any Moroccan worker to save the total amount needed to buy a bike.

Only 6 percent of the rural population had electricity and only 5 per-cent had running water. Despite the fact that Morocco is one of the very few third-world countries that devotes a high percentage of its GNP (7 percent in 1976) to education, the effects are obviously scarce. In 1980, average life expectancy was about fifty-five years. Children's death rate was 130/1,000 in the cities and 170/1,000 in the countryside. Seventy-two percent of the population were illiterate. There was one hospital per each million inhabi-tants and one doctor per 12,000 people. General Secretary Anuai stated that all the increases in prices made by the government had been illegal and asked all the CDT members and the working classes to use all legal means available, including strike, to protest. It was a strike that caused the riots in Casablanca in 1981.

In December 1982, Morocco was unable to face its foreign debt. The number of people killed during the riots increased more and more, but the media ignored it since it is their policy not to mention anything until the king has done so.

In December 1983, a rumor began to spread saying that the price of some essential products would rise again. People's discontent began to be felt again, leading to the so-called bread riots in January 1984. The Moroccan people were greatly disappointed with Hassan II's policy. The situation between the government and the people was almost unbearable and something had to be done quickly in order to calm people down.

Hence, 1985 brought a series of economic and social changes to Morocco, which led indirectly to an improvement in the country's art education. Due to the continuous riots, Hassan II and his government decided to compromise so as to soften the situation. A greater freedom of trade was established, more TV stations and cinemas were created, art activities increased considerably, and the art market was restored. But we should also take into consideration that the international situation at that moment, especially the détente between the Soviet Union and the United States, helped King Hassan II to obtain his aims. Morocco also experienced considerable improvement in its global economic situation.

Present-Day Schools in Morocco

As we approach the end of the twentieth century, important changes going on all over the world, especially those within the socialist movement, have important repercussions on the Magreb. All the changes in Argelia, the end of socialism as the State's official doctrine, the abolition of the one-party system, and especially, a higher interest in its own problems, to the detriment of such external problems as the one with the Western Sahara, have enabled Morocco to improve its economy. The long-awaited end of the disputes between Morocco and Argelia resulted in the beginning of an excellent relationship between the countries. The Moroccan currency is stronger than the Algerian, and since Morocco used to buy such locally made materials from Algeria as pencils and paper, the price of these artistic materials went down considerably, thus enabling the public schools to have more materials and encourage children to study art.

A clear example could be the fact that artistic drawing became a compulsory subject for all the primary school children aged six to eleven. Art teachers could take up the use of the natural model again, because Islam scholars went beyond the words in the Koran and realized such a prohibition had only been valid for a specific period of time. When drawing, artists did not take their works as gods any more. Nevertheless, the government continued to ban naked models.

Schools began to teach in Arabic so as to expel all the possible traces colonialism could have left in the country and hence promote nationalism. Also, economic reasons existed behind the use of Arabic at school, since any foreign teacher (i.e., a French teacher) was paid twice as much as a Moroccan teacher. Obviously, the government preferred teachers to be Moroccan in order to cut down expenses. But all the big changes began in 1988. Present-day Morocco is quite different from the Morocco in the fifties, sixties, and even the seventies, both politically and economically.

Since 1983, Morocco has been restructuring its own economy, in coordination with the International Monetary Fund and the World Bank. The public sector was privatized and a lot of facilities have been allowed to promote foreign investments.

Morocco has fifty-one of the 250 most important companies in Africa, run by a generation of modern and dynamic managers, most of them trained in the Western culture. There is far more freedom of speech and more political and social improvements than previously had been the case.

Art Education
Differences between Public and Private Schools

We concentrated our study on the city of Casablanca from 1988 onward. We partly based our study on the research that Amin El Bekay did at the private school Omar el Faroq. The basic differences between public and private schools in Morocco are social and economic. Not all the schools in the country have art education since not all the country enjoys the same social or economic situation.

There are several differences between such southern cities as Casablanca, which is an important industrial and economic area, Marrakech, a large holiday resort, and such northern cities as Tanger, Ceuta, or Melilla, where, for instance, six-year-old children already sell smuggled tobacco in the streets. Even in Casablanca, a city with a population of over six million people and more than fifteen quarters, shows strong social differences. There is no doubt that art education can be within the reach of only a few students, namely the rich, who make up less than 40 percent of the city's total school population. Art education is seen as a luxury good, especially if we take into consideration that public school students, who are usually from the most neglected social classes, cannot even afford to buy text books, because their families usually have four or five children. In these cases, they usually buy second-hand books. If, on top of that, we also add the fact that the children usually have to bring their own materials to art class, this makes things even more difficult, if not impossible.

As we pointed out before, the rich are the only people in society who can afford all these extra expenses and hence educate their children's sensitivity, imagination, and creativity, and even visit the European and American art museums on their trips abroad. These favoured social classes are clearly influenced by Western civilization and European education. Nevertheless, the children of the rich do not usually become artists, since they think art is just a complement to their own culture. Most artists are born to the less privileged classes, as their art education usually comes from their closest cultural scene, as well as from necessity.

All the public schools where art education is available teach, among other subjects, drawing based on handwriting or free drawing. Handwriting teaches children aged eight to eleven how to write and draw properly, since there are at least five different types of handwriting. By analyzing the shape of the different letters, the children learn about the letter's dynamics—its gesture, line, and composition. They also learn to differentiate between all the different types of lines: straight, curve, spiral, and so on.

Moreover, crafts also provide children with manual abilities together with the development of their visual perception of shapes and colors. When doing a free drawing, any six- to eleven-year-old child will try to develop imagination and creativity by drawing things from their own world, such as houses, trees, fruit, other children, and the sun.

The differences between Moroccan public and private schooling in regard to art education is illustrated by the different conditions and programs aimed at six- to eleven-year-old children:

1. Private schools have qualified art teachers and more time is devoted to the subject (approx. four to six hours per week).
2. Private school teachers have more comprehensive training than public school teachers.
3. Programs and cultural activities are far more promoted in private schools than in public schools; for instance, visits are organized to the local craftmanship museums.
4. In the private schools, students' interests and needs are of great importance.
5. Both private and public schools teach the art of handwriting to children, linking this activity to drawing itself. Regarding modelling, private school students make mud figures, masks, small buildings, and several color-based creative works.

In contrast to the private schools, public schools for six to eleven year olds have no qualified art teachers. Art lessons for these children are taught by the French or Arabic language teachers. Children over the age of twelve have a qualified art teacher. All the qualified art teachers are trained at the Pedagogy and Fine Arts Faculties. Unfortunately, there are far more teachers than jobs. This is a sector of high unemployment.

Public schools do not devote much time to art education, merely two hours per week, while private schools teach up to six hours a week. In the public schools, children are simply taught to differentiate different shapes, such as warm and cool colors. They also do manual crafts in cardboard, wood, mud, and cut-up figures. "Male" and "female" manual crafts are differentiated. For example, girls do artistic embroidery, sew drawings on clothes, taking traditional cultural symbols as their source of inspiration.

Public schools lack rooms specially fitted for the subject, which is taught in the same room as the other subjects. Private schools do have special rooms fitted with all the necessary equipment such as sinks, shelves, and so on.

Public schools organize such activities as visits to local craftmanship museums, mural paintings, or roundtables with local artists. The students in private schools usually visit High Schools of Art. The murals children paint usually show everyday scenes, children at school, views, slim figures. They are usually done on the occasion of any political holiday, such as King Hassan II's anniversary on the throne, or Independence Day. Contests are also organized, awarding the most creative drawings.

The aesthetics in these children's works is mainly ornamental. It is based on symetry, equilibrium, harmony, and color, which are recurrent references in their own culture, particularly Islamic art. Individualism does not exist among children, whether they attend public or private schools. Islam teaches them that collectivism must be an essential value in their lives. Islam is against individualism and people from Morocco tend to be open, giving much importance to such values as friendship or the family.

Private and public school teachers both follow the same criteria when assessing six- to eleven-year-old children's works. At those ages, teachers just check whether children did the work.

On the whole, the type of education taught in Morocco is directive. The main reason for children to do art is to make children enjoy and express themselves, always following the teacher's instructions (e.g., "from eleven to twelve you'll be doing free drawing" or "you can color this figure as you please with the crayons I'll give you"). Another reason is to show the parents all the work their children did in class.

In short, art education in private schools is to stimulate children's activity, to link manual activity with visual perception, to develop children's creative skills, and help children enjoy themselves. In contrast, art education in public schools is to allow children to do something different so that they can relax and enjoy themselves.

Youth Centres and Art Education

Although the present chapter focuses on art education of children aged six to eleven in private and public schools in Casablanca, we thought it might be worth including the important role youth centres have played on the Moroccan people's art education. The youth centres were created by the government shortly after the colonization in order to protect Morocco's autonomous culture. These centres were located in the poorest parts of the cities.

The importance of these youth centres lies in the fact that people from the most neglected social classes were artistically educated there. The centres were subsidized by the government, town councils, and several companies. No subscription fees were required, and both the materials and the use of the facilities were free of cost. They also organized cultural trips at little or no cost.

All the activities at these centres were run by a group of qualified, volunteer instructors. The instructors were in charge of organizing and leading the different cultural activities such as drawing, painting, manual crafts, theatre, cinema, trips, games, conferences, contests, and lessons on the history of art. The activities were done at weekends (on Saturdays and on Sunday mornings).

The youth centres were created in 1956 and most of them belonged to the independent party in Morocco. They aimed at preserving Moroccan culture and traditions, as well as the country's history. Moreover, the centres were intended to protect the young from the colonialist influence and train them to preserve and develop their own culture (including their language, i.e., Arabic-Moroccan) and make people aware of the dangers of colonialism.

They also emphasized diversity in all the cultural activities organized to attract as many children and adolescents as possible. Cultural exchanges between young people from different regions in Morocco were one of their activities, as well as art and craftmanship exhibitions, excursions, and the like. They also promoted caring about the protection of the environment and animal rights. Care and attention was also provided to the poor and neglected people in Morocco so as to help them fight illiteracy.

Youth centres were very important from 1956 to 1990, providing art education in Morocco for about thirty years, making the most of the scarce means available. Now, they are almost nonexistent since their role was taken over at the begining of the eighties by the public schools.

Conclusion
The Global Consumer

Currently, Morocco is taking part in the development of a cultural and economic macrosystem, which has possibly European origins and American vitality. It is crossing all the space and time borders and becoming universal. However, people want to keep their language and traditions, preserving their identity as a country and promoting nationalism. The world is turning into a common market where people, regardless of their place of residence, want the same things in life.

The art six- to eleven-year-old children do in schools in Morocco is quite similar to that of Spanish children, French children, or children anywhere in the world. The important thing is to stimulate the children's sensitivity, so that they are able to "read" images and adapt to a technical and consumer society.

Distances are becoming shorter and shorter in our world. New worldwide lifestyles are continuously emerging due to the use of telecommunication and the mass media, which provide the right frame for the international markets to be established. At the same time, ethnic aspects and nationalisms are being favoured by governments all over the world. For instance, Morocco has become mainly monolingual, emphasizing the Arabic language, as opposed to the recent policy of teaching both French and Arabic in school. Similarly, Catalan schooling is highly promoted in Catalonia, Spain. Hence, we could conclude by stating that if our world can become a common and homogeneous market, and can also be described with such adjectives as *international* or *universal*, we could also say that human beings should not reject their own traditions just for someone else's convenience. Similarities make us human, but differences provide us with character and individualism.

Note

The information about the social and political context in Morocco from 1961 to 1988 was taken from the works of Domingo del Pino (1990) and Gilles Perrault (1991).

III

Professionalization

Science, Policy, and Practice in the Formation of the Field

The processes of professionalization have shaped the field of art education. The chapters in this section illustrate the ways in which these processes establish perimeters for practice, whether the practice is teaching, administering, organizing, researching, or theorizing. Professionalization has had such an influence across geographic borders that the boundaries of the field seem at times more important to art educators than the boundaries of a country. At the same time, art educational ideas always become translated in the context of practice and those contexts have contained a variety of reasons for professionalization.

David Thistlewood's chapter contains a socioeconomic and political analysis of the professional development of British art education. British art education has historically anticipated national economic needs and the effects of national crises. The author argues that changes in nineteenth-century art education, prompted by industrial standards and competition, and early twentieth-century politics influenced the professionalization of art education in

Britain. This professionalization, and specifically Herbert Read's work in developing the Society for Education Through Art, were instrumental in a profound revision of art education throughout the British Empire.

Andrea Kárpáti and Emil Gaul discuss the shift in Hungarian art education from the early twentieth-century Child Study movement, which was a cross-national, scientific effort resulting in the rejection of Prussian pedagogy, to the use of art education in a Communist regime, to a return to an international, professional perspective of art education. The authors argue that this later shift, from a centralized curriculum toward national guidelines and attainment targets that support alternative conceptions of child art, is an important innovation that has roots in the Child Study era.

The chapter by Luis Errazuriz contains a historical account of arguments used to justify art instruction in Chilean schools in the context of national change. An important aspect of these arguments is that they have been heavily influenced by professional conceptions of education and social science from outside the country, particularly North America and Europe. Errázuriz illustrates the ways in which the translation of these arguments have had both positive and negative influences on the Chilean professional field.

9

David Thistlewood

From Imperialism
to Internationalism

*Policy Making in
British Art Education,
1853–1944,
with Special Reference
to the Work of Herbert Read*

I t is conventional to analyze the history of British art education with reference to vague relationships with industry and changes in socioeconomic and political conditions, but with special attention to disciplines perceived to be *inherent* either in art itself or in a gradually liberalizing conception of education. According to this view, prior to the 1944 Education Act (which revised British art education thoroughly) there had been almost a century of *intrinsic* stability but also a steady and consistent decline in relevance to modern industry and social life. There is normally held to have been a crisis, evident when practices that had served the interests of art could no longer resist external pressures for modernization. This conventional view recognizes the 1944 act as stabilizing the curriculum once more and to such good effect that it would not require fundamental revision for a further half century. Thus the main general premises governing historical study in this field are that, for about a century after 1850, British art education was shaped by internal disputes as to its art intrinsic characteristics, that these were gradually resolved by disputation between internal factional interests, and that as a result there was achieved an intimate matching of educational principles and the main sociocultural requirements of the second half of the twentieth century.

However, it is possible that this field will sustain alternative analyses, particularly if socioeconomic and political factors are regarded as having been *instrumental* as well as incidental. What follows is merely hypothetical because it lacks scholarly attention commensurate to that received by the conventional history, but it may be suggested that art education has consistently been tuned to the *anticipated* needs of industry and international trade and—closely related—the retrospectively perceived effects of major crises such as wars. It is at any rate worthwhile transposing the usual causes and effects in order to see whether a convincing correlation may exist. It is certainly legitimate to consider the early stages in this light, for when systematic education in art began in Britain—with the 1853 curriculum devised by Henry Cole and Richard Redgrave—it was openly acknowledged that beneficial improvement of industrial art was among the desired goals. However, it is usually observed that these two legislators were prompted by a prevailing poverty of standards and a patriotic desire to compete industrially with French achievement—plausible but unexplained objectives that a new historical analysis might seek to substantiate. What then were the industrial and economic conditions of the time, and why did they require a profound, root-and-branch revision of art education throughout the whole of the British Empire?

The Strategic Importance of Art Education within an Imperial Economy

Before the mid-nineteenth century the great cycles of international trade had been determined by agricultural factors. Harvests failed, causing outflows of capital to pay for grain imports, consequent domestic deflation and, occasionally, collapse of credit and banking crises. Alternatively, harvests were abundant, producing surpluses, which gave rise to peaks of economic activity within this cyclic process. So long as agriculture ruled the economy, there was little reason for the landed establishment to provide its future workforce with more than rudimentary education, and none at all in respect of art—considered until now the preserve of the leisured classes. The great depression of the 1840s was the last in which (in Britain) agricultural failure played a major role, though it was exacerbated by simultaneous collapses of the domestic railway building boom and of foreign markets for textiles, the first great industrial export. To those capable of reading the runes, this latter phenomenon indicated the likely consequences of a sudden collapse in overseas demand for British manufactured goods, an increasingly important engine of the economy. The production of industrial goods was not subject to vagaries of nature but perhaps susceptible to equally dramatic changes of taste. Art education policy thereafter may be interpreted as maintaining good taste in the manufacturing workforce at home and in the consuming classes throughout the Empire, ensuring the perfect matching of supply and demand. The economic boom of the mid-Victorian period was the result: capital was exported in order to impose development on regions of the Empire, stimulating demand for British manufactured goods—the taste for which had been induced by Imperial education, notably in art.

It is of course possible that the initiators of the Empirewide curriculum were entirely motivated by higher principles. All the outward justification for their National System of Instruction spoke of academic values, particularly as exemplified in drawing. Unlike conceptions of drawing today, theirs was a highly systematized and regulated diet of creditable skills—predominantly copyist, effected through controlled shading and rendering of cast shadows—applied to a taxonomy of ciphers and patterns (later, historic ornament and sculpted objects) authorized by the Schools Circulation Department of the South Kensington (renamed the Victoria and Albert) Museum. As Stuart Macdonald (1970) has shown, in Victorian times this was virtually a cradle-to-grave system, in that pupils were first exposed to it in elementary school, the most able progressing to Stage Two in their local art schools, many becoming uncertified teachers who would return to continue the system's implementation at elementary level. Higher qualifications were attainable in over twenty-three stages (many with several distinct parts) for progressively fewer individuals.

The Victorian system thus presented a strong semblance of coherence, theoretically linking the earliest achievements of the five year old and the ultimate achievements of the senior academic within a carefully staged progression dedicated to gradually intensifying knowledge of historic ornamentation and the graphic skills that would give proof of such command. The great idea was that the vast number of individuals who would work in manufacturing would learn to be predisposed toward the patterning and ornamentation specified by the few of exquisitely developed taste who would be society's designers. In addition, an appreciation of the characteristic patterning and ornamentation would be cultivated throughout possessed territories abroad. Thus there was a totally self-contained socioeconomic system, in which development capital funded the education of taste abroad, creating demands for the goods stimulated by the education of manual and reproductive skills at home.

The system was defended not in terms of economic, but meritocratic, integrity: the nation required of all its citizens proficiency in drawing to match those of reading, writing, and arithmetic. As in these other fields, normal everyday discourse demanded basic command (familiarity with pattern making, reading plans, interpreting drawn manufacturing instructions, communicating with fellow craft workers), while the nurturing of the culture at large depended on refined command (measured by virtuoso success in the arena of the international exposition). There was presented an unbroken connection between the common and the refined, the theoretical possibility of advancement within the system, and a strong sense of a meritocracy in operation.

This was largely fictional, as in fact the total field of art education was fractured fundamentally. Topographical sketching, landscape watercolor painting, portraiture, studio composition, devotion to exotic historic subject matter, and nonauthorized (for example, arabesque) ornamentation—in other words, the predilections of the dilettante, the amateur, and the connoisseur—had no presence within the system's cultural purview. Yet these were taught in private institutions catering to upper-class needs. The national system had the virtue of enabling the child from an industrial background eventually to taste the success of completing Stage Twenty-Three, but the excellence so required would not have merited inclusion in the Royal Academy Summer Exhibition, the temple of success of the leisured artist class and its attendant professionals. And the system was fractured still further: every school leaver who seemed incapable of passing on to younger children knowledge of the first two stages came up against a glass barrier to advancement. Their drawing education thus (in)complete, they entered industry. Because industries were highly localized (for example, pottery in the midlands, heavy manufacturing in the north), and because of the strong industrial representation on school boards, there was an effective preselection for industrial futures and practically no potential for the sort of career self-determination that the lofty ideals of meritocracy suggested.

Responses to New Economic Circumstances
The Professionalization of Art Education

The *curricular* features of the Victorian system survived into the twentieth century—at least in the art schools. In 1895 the grip of the system was loosened in elementary schools with the introduction of an alternative curriculum privileging freearm drawing, and the 1913 Education Act transferred administration of the higher stages to the Board of Education, in the process of which they were rationalized into much less than a lifetime's devotion. But because so many senior figures had been conditioned to strive for them, principles of academic, copyist drawing remained tacit determinants of promotion in the academic world and the inspectorship. As such they continued to constitute a more or less hidden—in some quarters openly espoused—agenda of the criteria of excellence. The system thus became academized although its original purpose was now past. New markets—particularly in North and South America—could not be exploited in the Victorian way. But why did freearm drawing become suddenly significant? The default explanation is that it constituted a reaction against what went before. There is another—however faint—possibility, connected with the fact that, in the late nineteenth century, European nations were becoming militarized to an unprecedented extent. Topological drawing—necessary for sketching out the lay of the land—had always been an essential component of the education of the officer corps. But now that lower ranks were increasingly becoming responsible for such tasks as surveying terrain and calculating range and angle for bombardiering, it was necessary to disseminate a previously elite attribute (associated with the recreational skills of the upper classes) more widely throughout the population.

This may be a frivolous association of art and warfare. However, there is a much more serious case to be made for art education in Britain having been revised fundamentally because of the consequences of World War I. The Education Act of 1913 was followed, unusually quickly, by another Education Act of 1918. This signals a major revision of need, of which—it is not unreasonable to suggest—the Great War for Civilization, 1914–1918 was the cause. While permitting the continuation of curricular reforms throughout elementary education, the new act ensured that working-class children entering appropriate trades and industries would revisit the most successful principles of the Victorian system in highly concentrated postschool courses in evening classes and in daytime release from employment. This is the main reason why the system persisted well into the twentieth century in the art schools, and it was necessary because of the massive damage to peacetime manufacturing capability suffered in the war. In this war (unlike World War II, when large-scale conscription was fully operational) recruitment to active service was conducted on a voluntary, though patriotically irresistible, basis. Recruitment campaigns were conducted in localities and factories, with the result that whole townships of young men, and complete workforces, were enlisted into the same company. When, as often occurred in this war, whole companies suffered virtual obliteration, blanket losses would be visited on entire communities and industries. In one day's fighting on the Somme, most of London's bricklayers would perish, on another the

clothing manufacturing operatives of Bradford or Leeds. The 1920s wit-
nessed frantic efforts to reconstruct such industries, and a suitably mod-
ified and highly concentrated form of Victorian-like instruction was the
chief recourse.

The women who had run the mills and essential services in wartime
naturally aspired to working outside the home in peacetime, but after the
emergency there returned a strong sense as to their proper employment,
with the teaching of young children considered an appropriate field. This
suited the national need—women's large-scale entry into teaching art at
elementary level, for example, released the maximum number of "more
capable" males for senior appointments in art schools and, more significantly, industrial design and manufacturing. This caused a serious fracturing of art education, with the more liberal reforms of post-Victorian
legislation, including freearm drawing and expressive painting, becoming
associated with "women's values" and the revived principles of institutionalized design continuing to occupy the majority of men. This fracturing
became institutionalized in two separate professional organizations,
respectively, the Art Teachers' Guild (ATG) and the National Society of Art
Masters (NSAM), the sectional interests of which ruled art education in
Britain until another world war gave rise to reconciliation.

From 1918 until the late 1930s, then, the introduction of progressive
values into the early stages of art education and the protraction of the Victorian system into the later stages constituted an equilibrium of sorts. In
spite of decentralized authority in matters of curriculum, with responsibility for subject content now resting with individual head teachers, the main-
tenance of standards was effectively in the hands of the NSAM so far as
later stages were concerned, and—to a much lesser degree—the ATG in
respect to early education. The NSAM was dedicated to the preservation of
drawing as an *academic discipline*, and possession of its certificates (the
successors to South Kensington certification) indicated a teacher's competence both in classical draughtsmanship and in design allied to the industrial arts. The interests of the ATG centered on the specific educational
needs of young children; but, largely confined to infant application, they
were thus of little threat to a system of drawing education that began seriously when pupils were old enough to apply intellectual rigor to their work.
These were the two main fractional interests in art education, and within
the greater field of art they bore little comparison to the other two principal fractions of "salon" and "experimental" art. The main alignment in the
field, such as it was, was loosely between avant-garde creativity and the
child art principles to which the ATG was committed, a connection cele-
brated in the writings of Roger Fry (1917, 1919, 1924, 1933). There was a
normal distinction between the higher discipline of teaching drawing and
design and the lower discipline of teaching art. The former was associated

with national economic purposes and aspired to academic respectability; the latter evoked play and rather modest learning. The former had historic justification for calling itself Art (with a capital A) and a sense of belonging to traditions of Classical scholarship. The latter had a Romantic outlook that, along with such things as simple dress, vegetarianism, and a belief in the spiritual value of craftwork, had been a by-product of the English Arts and Crafts movement.

The aims of the NSAM encouraged its members to pursue high levels of technical accomplishment as measured by its own examination system—the true descendant of the Victorian system of achievement recognition, in which the most demanding exercises required months of unremitting attention to copying, shading, and rendering prescribed images (Macdonald, 1970, pp. 143–252). The ATG, on the other hand, was much more concerned with tactical approaches necessary for encouraging an essential creativity—an originating activity—in children not specifically destined for an aesthetic way of life. The ATG's referents therefore included theories of child-centered creativity, and it became its prime purpose to propagate the ideas of such as Ebenezer Cooke and Franz Cizek, whose arguments centered on the proposition that art was an aspect of human development, the absence of which impaired mental growth and social fitness. Before the 1930s such beliefs were regarded as peripheral to the main educational tasks of teaching drawing and design, and their attendant practices were considered at best *preparatory* to this mission.

As noted, the values embedded in the NSAM—what may be termed the "classic thesis" of twentieth-century British art education—were embedded also in government policy. They comprised an emphasis on drawing (both conventional and observational) and design (the realization of artifacts through practical involvement with materials), the twin features of a specifically modern, industrially strategic education. The 1918 act enabled local government to provide extensive postschool continuation classes for young workers entering art industries, and also to admit apprentices to half-time courses in art schools. Such trainees had special courses devoted to their crafts and industries, but their diets also included the kind of drawing fostered by the NSAM. Thus they would participate in Figure Drawing, Drawing from Nature, and Architectural and Ornamental Drawing, in which great emphasis would be placed on the received methodologies of tracing, hatching, shading, and rendering that formed the disciplinary spine of the NSAM's own standards of competence, rescued originally from the otherwise defunct South Kensington system. This linked academic drawing to the perceived needs of industry and thus directly to conceptions of the *national* well-being.

Concerns to develop *individual* propensities and attributes through art education could be accommodated to this scheme only if confined to the education of the young child, that is, to a stage preceding the serious purposes of strategic education. This was regarded as the ATG's province: throughout the 1920s and early 1930s this organization had persevered with a defense of free, spontaneous creativity as both obviously present in the drawings and paintings of young children, and also desirable in continuation beyond adolescence—that is, beyond the stage in an individual's development when unstructured creativity was deemed normally to cease. Marion Richardson (1948) was the champion of this proposal, and her work with young, adolescent, and teenage pupils was regarded as proof that inherent, spontaneous, creative aptitudes could be protracted beyond their stage of supposed decline. Her approach was based on stimulating the pupil's imagination with unconventional teaching, evoking vivid mental images through verbal discourse and cultivation of pictorial memory (Macdonald, 1970, pp. 320–54). (*Intrinsic* analysis of art education tends to assume that this form of art education was a major stimulus for the imaginations of children of otherwise drab circumstances, though this is to overlook the growing importance of the radio and the cinema in this regard.) Richardson enjoyed the support of Fry, who compared the work of her children to that of expressionist avant-garde artists. Such comparisons dignified child art as being in some sense a natural or proper form of creativity, lost in conventional education, and regained only with the greatest difficulty by those few adult artists sufficiently motivated to eliminate intellectual processes from their art making. This emphasis on individualism, especially in the 1930s when it emerged as an equally well-argued alternative to the conventional, may be regarded as the *romantic antithesis* of twentieth-century art education.

There were intermittent attempts to amalgamate the two fractional interests within a single organization, but the politics of trades unionism kept them apart until 1984. However, in 1938 the demands of the popular membership required the ATG to combine with a much smaller society of mainly male membership, the New Society of Art Teachers (NSAT). They formed a joint committee and assumed a single umbrella title—the Society for Education in Art (SEA). The intervention of World War II postponed full amalgamation until 1946, but in the meantime the joint committee ensured irreversible progress toward objectives that would actually characterize art education for most of the remaining years of the century. And it was a significant feature of this joint committee that it was constituted overwhelmingly of women. Because many NSAT members entered the armed forces and most ATG members did not, officials drawn from the latter were the ones who ran the joint committee during the war. Because many NSAM members also were conscripted, the SEA joint committee survived the war as the most authoritative and thoroughly informed body on matters of education in art. ATG values therefore prevailed not only in the fledgling SEA but also in the 1944 Education Act so far as art was concerned. This was more than a theoretical success: while the men had been absent the joint committee had diverted substantial funding—previously granted to establish a national center for research into academic excellence—toward a number of small projects. These were reported in a monthly journal developed expressly to report piecemeal research rather than the great field of strategic investigation previously proposed. In other words, the opportunity had been seized to sideline a subject-centered enterprise in favor of developing, and lobbying government for, a logic of individualism.

This logic of individualism positively determined the provisions for art within the 1944 act, leaving the NSAM to its own consistent devotion to art as academic skill. For the next forty years it would pursue this interest through two changes of identity, becoming the National Society for Art Education (NSAE) in 1944 and the National Society for Education in Art and Design (NSEAD) in 1984, when amalgamation with the SEA was at last effected. Latterly, the two dominant interests of the original fractions have become synthesized in Britain's post-1988 National Curriculum in Art, in which individual and subject-centered principles are evenly distributed and integrated throughout the whole range of general education. However, an important ramification of the SEA-inspired 1944 act merits examination for several reasons: because it offers sharp contrast to the after effects of World War I, because it had international consequences, and because it marked a defining moment of British art education in the twentieth century.

Whereas the priority of the dominant art educational association in 1918 (NSAM) had been to collaborate with government in the attempted reconstruction of prewar manufacturing capability, the reaction of the dominant association in 1944 (SEA) was to militate against this by encouraging individual-centered education and ensuring, as far as possible, that a logic of internationalism would be conveyed in the process. Herbert Read is the principal figure here. He was patron of its journal from 1939, chairman of its External Consultants from 1940, and president from 1947 until his death in 1968. His book *Education through Art* (Read, 1943) was its almost biblical text, and this work both exported British principles throughout the world and exerted formative influence in the International Society for Education through Art (INSEA), formed under the auspices of UNESCO in 1954.

Herbert Read's Logic of Individualism
in Support of an Internationalist Vision

Read's interest in child art was at first peripheral to his interpretation of the significance of the avant garde. In an early engagement of the subject he suggested (Read, 1933, pp. 46–47) that more could be learned of the essential nature of art from its origins in the primitive and its continued rehearsal in childhood imagery than from its intellectual elaboration in great periods of culture—an elaboration conventionalized in formal education. Children, he wrote, do not distinguish between the ideal (the conventionalized) and the *real*. Child art was to be regarded as an intensification of children's elementary perceptions of the reality of the world around them, which he considered also a paramount purpose of the avant garde. In this discussion there is no evidence that Read supported the notion of a necessary *continuity* of child and mature creativity. Their common feature he recognized as play, which in the adult realm was confined to special individuals who have special faculties—not of feeling or of thought, but of expression, of objectification. In other words, authentic creativity in adults is confined to individuals of particular, prelogical disposition. This was not, for the time being, to countenance the possibility that all members of the adult community might aspire equally to creative fulfillment.

Instead Read at first seemed to endorse the legitimacy of one kind of educational provision for children who would become artists and another for future artisans and all the rest: society certainly required the guidance of disinterested visionaries, but there had to be safeguards against a proliferation of visionaries too great to be supported by productive labor. Read argued this case in *Art and Society* (1937), maintaining that a consequent responsibility of art teachers would be to distinguish between the education of positive, creative capabilities in the few who would be initiators, and the encouragement of taste, discrimination, and appreciation in the many who would be consumers. This view accommodated the Freudian conception of the artist as a potential neurotic who had chanced upon ways of evading this fate by expressing what would have been repressed fantasy in plastic form.

One of the most original features of Read's philosophy in its perfected state was the extension of this principle to embrace everyone. The artist is no longer to be regarded as unusual in his or her potential neurosis: modern humanity *in general* suffers this propensity. In *Education through Art* (Read, 1943) published only six years after *Art and Society*, everyone—that is, every child—is said to be a potential neurotic capable of being saved from this prospect if early, largely inborn, creative abilities are not repressed by conventional education. Everyone is an artist of some kind whose special abilities, even if almost insignificant, must be encouraged as contributing to an infinite richness of collective life. Read's newly expressed view of an essential *continuity* of child and adult creativity in everyone represented a *synthesis* of the two opposed models of twentieth-century art education that had predominated until this point.

What prompted this change of outlook was Read's direct (more than theoretical) encounter with the work of the very young. He had been invited to advise the British Council on a collection of children's art for wartime exhibition overseas, and in the course of this he had come across an image, drawn by a five-year-old girl, which she called *Snake around the World and a Boat* (Read, 1943, p. 187; Read 1948, pp. 44–45). He was deeply moved, he said, upon immediately recognizing this image as a mandala, an ancient symbol of psychic unity, universally found in prehistoric and primitive art and in all the principal cultures of history. The child, of course, could not attach meaning to what she had done; but Read, aware for some time of what until now had been merely an interesting hypothesis of Carl Gustav Jung's, was shocked to find phenomenal evidence of archetypal imagery. He then discovered an astonishing consistency in children's art of symbols Jung had associated with community stability, and he also found them replete in the paintings and sculptures of the adult avant garde.

The most significant of these images, to Read, was the mandala, invariably a unified shape, perhaps in the form of a flower or some other fourfold arrangement, with a distinct center, the appearance of an unfolding, and a gathering perimeter. Especially in Eastern philosophy, though also for example in Christian iconography, these images had been held to symbolize collective thought and mutual belonging. Other archetypes that gave Read shocks of recognition were the tendency to fabricate a dark shadow from aspects of a personality opposed to those personified in the self and the tendency to protest against isolation, individuation, and independence by creating mother images, earth forms, and other symbols of dependence.

All of these—a fixing upon abstract unities; a collation of personality traits in externalized forms; the celebration of maternity; an acknowledgment of belonging to the land—all of these projections beyond self, Read thought, were fundamentally anarchistic. Manifest in the work of the avant garde, their purpose was to guide the collective unconscious into normal patterns of aspiration and behavior and away from those sinister alternatives (mass hysteria, nationalistic pride, dumb subservience to the state) to which the unnatural mode of modern life had left people prone. This remedial function, however, would wither into obsolescence if the self-same imagery, evident in child art generally, could be protracted into adulthood for everyone.

Read's encounter with the archetypal content of child art demanded explication. It was this research, conducted at the University of London in 1941–1942, that resulted in his definitive work *Education through Art*, the central premises of which were "that the general purpose of education is to foster the growth of what is individual in each human being, at the same time harmonizing the individuality thus educed with the organic unity of the social group to which the individual belongs" (Read, 1943, p. 8). The organic principle, signifying normal, unhampered development of individual creativity, and a corresponding development of society through collective creative enterprise, was thus adopted as both generator and evaluative principle.

Published just in time to affect the 1944 Education Act, this book provided art education with a rationale, a defiance, and an optimistic program. It comprised definitions of authenticity in art and art making; offered explanations of the materializing of images from the imagination; compared typologies discernible in the literature of psychology and in the study of children's drawings and paintings; and proposed that the *variety* evident within such typologies supported the principle that everyone could be regarded as a special kind of artist. Art was defined as respecting an organic principle, which could be illuminated by scientific analogy, thus driving art into the very core of the curriculum. Good form is perceptible in all manner of natural organisms at microscopic, normal, and macroscopic scales, and exhibits such attributes as structural order, elegance, harmony, economy, and dynamic equilibrium—as revealed to Read by the scientific philosophy of D'Arcy Wentworth Thompson (Thompson, 1942; Read, 1943, pp. 18–19).

Objectified in art making, such properties evince balance, symmetry, and rhythm, thus suggesting the comparability of growth in nature and composition in art. But for Read their applicability was not confined to objective art (that is, an art of purely formal relationships). The subjective also respects these principles to the degree that it is *externalized* (objectified) feeling, intuition, or emotion; and, Read speculated, the subjective may also tend to formal relationships even when *internalized*, for fantasy and dreaming may be instigated by pathological complexes akin to force systems, and be subject to intrinsic dramatic unities and patterns of organization (Read, 1943, p. 32).

He therefore maintained that a comparability of nature and art extends across the whole range of creative faculties that produce and appreciate art. He was particularly interested in the idea of an impulse-driven emergence of imagery from the subconscious into conscious attention by the reflex coordination of mental, physical, and perceptual faculties. Conjoining Freudian and Jungian philosophy, he wrote of the calling-up of images—images with primordial significance—from hidden depths of the mind. This formed theoretical connections between the artist's command of eidetic visualization (mental evocation or recall of images in vivid detail) and an archetypal significance (deep-seated social and cultural symbolism) that could be divined in the images so evoked. It also associated sociocultural symbolism with modes of creativity that rejected conventional, long-implemented methods of art education, concerned as they were with replication of *given* realities rather than evocation of the *new*.

Ultimately, however, *Education through Art* was received as proof that a number of distinct types of child artist could be identified in education, and a varied diet offered them, would both strengthen their natural affinities and credit their unique achievements. In his study of children's images Read discovered eight distinct categories, all transcending age or stage development. He suggested they corresponded to the four composite categories of mature creativity—realism: thinking; superrealism: feeling; expressionism: sensation; and constructivism: intuition—if each of these were considered in both introverted and extroverted modes (Read, 1943, p. 145). By this means Read constructed a coordinate system that would account for the characteristics of all apparent tendencies in child art. Moreover, this categoric division related directly to tendencies perceptible in the works of mature avant gardes. The pursuit of authentic avant-garde creativity, Read had long maintained, was so emotionally and nervously demanding that it was the conscious choice of very few. In the adult's realm it was an *obsessional* activity, while paradoxically in the child's realm it manifested the effortlessness of inherited reflex behavior. This suggested a normality of creative identification shared between all children and those adults who would strive to regain prelogical sensibility. It also suggested a fundamental abnormality in what had been considered normal in conventional education, namely the intervention of logical, intellect-dependent education at around the age of ten. If education were to go with the grain of the biological imperative, ways needed to be found of encouraging the perfection and protraction of prelogical creative states.

Read did not offer a curriculum but a theoretical defense of the genuine and true. His claims for genuineness and truth were based on the overwhelming evidence of characteristics revealed in his study of child art. But they were founded also in speculative extrapolation of a kind that was most welcome during World War II, in the period of reconstruction (when they were recognized in the 1944 act), and in succeeding decades dominated by Cold War politics. This extrapolation focused on the apparent fact that authentic creativity was an inherent human necessity. The question was why was it so necessary as to be universally present (though in eight complementary modes) in all children, and potentially present in the citizens they were to become?

Read discovered the answer in social psychology, at the same time confirming his predilection for anarchism and his recognition of profundity in Jung's conception of the archetype. The biological necessity has two aspects—to call up imagery from the subconscious and to externalize it in communicable form—the second of which is served by the originating activity and is therefore the more important. He argued that this is not an outpouring for its own sake, nor is it evidence of children conversing with, and confirming, their own individual subconscious experience: it is essentially "an overture demanding response from others" (Read, 1943, p. 164, quoting Suttie, 1935). It is thus to be regarded as an integrating activity, "a spontaneous reaching-out to the external world, at first tentative, but capable of becoming the main factor in the adjustment of the individual to society" (pp. 164–65). This not only establishes art—an authentic, nonintellectualized art—as of profound significance in education, it downgrades all other subjects in the curriculum that are intended to develop *individuation*, or rather maintains that they too may serve *integration* if taught with artistic focus. This may confidently be regarded as the great idea of the SEA wartime joint committee, profoundly elaborated beyond its strict disciplinary context.

When published, this philosophy gave new meaning to the work of many thousands of art teachers. Instead of merely assisting technical expertise, recreational skill, and consumer discrimination, their role would be to take command of the larger curriculum and help innate creative abilities survive in an uncongenial world for the sake of individual well-being, as well as for the health of a collective social harmony. The potential for success was evident in Read's observation that children quite naturally give forth imagery that maintains contact with the deepest levels of social experience and with times when social cohesion was the normal order.

A corollary, which armed the art teachers and explains the enormous, immediate, and continued success of his book, was that defects of modern life—injustice, immorality, harsh competition, even war—had roots in prevailing systems of education and, specifically, in an emphasizing of intellectual development to the exclusion of everything else, visited upon children from around the age of ten. Because of this the infant—with inborn access to ancient, collective experience—became a rootless ten year old and a center of self-interest. What the authorities considered to be liberal education was nothing more than systematic repression, the elimination of which would give rise to recovery of individual creative fulfillment, mutual communication, and collective social health. It may be significant that the only quarter in which Read's philosophical anarchism was not welcomed was the realm of U.S. federal authority—his collected papers, destined for preservation in an American University archive in the late 1960s, were denied importation clearance and went instead to Victoria, British Columbia.

Education through Art was translated into over thirty languages and is still regarded as a seminal text in countries as diverse as Egypt, Brazil, and Japan. Its message was reinforced in other books and pamphlets— *The Education of Free Men* (Read, 1944); *Culture and Education in a World Order* (Read, 1948); *The Grass Roots of Art* (Read, 1955); and *Redemption of the Robot* (Read, 1970). In the first of these he acknowledged his belonging to a tradition first given authoritative shape by Plato, simplified Platonic theory for popular consumption, sketched out a strategy for building an authentic communal culture by perfecting parent-child, teacher-child, and individual-group relationships, and argued against the curbing of schools' freedom to determine curricula appropriate to localized circumstances.

It was also within Read's scope to influence directly national and supranational institutions. As president of the SEA he had a platform for addressing UNESCO. He was extremely welcoming of policies expressed at UNESCO's launching conference in 1946—policies devoted to the cultivation of worldwide understanding through education, and the elimination of international conflict at the point of its normal origination, mutual ignorance—but he was nevertheless critical of an automatic reliance on conventional modes of education, and a perceived confusion of culture with learning, education with propaganda. He argued (Read, 1948) that UNESCO's desired moral revolution could not be secured by arguments addressed to minds corrupted with individuated intellectualization: a moral revolution required the total reorientation of the human personality, which could only be secured by integrative education. On the basis of such representation, Read, with others, succeeded in establishing INSEA as an executive arm of UNESCO.

The most compelling argument he proposed to UNESCO was that art provides the best prospect of an international medium of cultural exchange and understanding, for the comparable internationalism of science is always to be confounded by national interests. While almost all other enterprises are intended to address the removal of barriers—of sovereignty, custom, language, or trade—the visual arts know no such barriers. They constitute "a language of symbols that communicates a meaning without hindrance from country to country across the centuries" (Read, 1970, pp. 233–54). This posthumously published assertion has continued to be the cornerstone of INSEA philosophy until the present day. But it has required of officialdom a remarkable investment in faith, for what Read proposed was not a means of transforming states of mind by propaganda. Education through art is in effect a reverse propaganda: it begins with the felt truth, which is then expressed as symbol—the feeling finds its equivalent in a plastic image (Read, 1955, pp. 88–89). Images originate in collective experience and create correspondences in shared realities: the social bond is rehearsed and reinforced.

This remains a devastating critique of the international system of art education that had formed the basis of the British provision since 1853, the spurious integration of which was here replaced with authentic attempts to unite differing creative personalities within a system of diagnostic coordinates, more importantly to unite fractures formerly expressed as conventional, refined, and avant garde and, more importantly still, to unite the interests of diverse cultures. Read's definitive work is today as relevant as it was in the immediate postwar years, and it remains a useful barometric tool for gauging the main issues and currents of British art education since the onset of its universal provision. It also offers evidence of the success of the child-centered faction of British art education, for without Read's interpretation of the SEA case the conventional predication of industrial and commercial values would not have been usurped.

10

Andrea Kárpáti
Emil Gaul

The Child Study
Movement and Its
Effects on Hungarian
Art Education

A s in most of Central Europe, Hungarian art education was
originally intended for young adults (Kárpáti & Gaul, 1994,
1997; Kárpáti, 1995). Apprentices of several trades had to
learn the profession of draughtsmanship. The first teaching plans and
manuals published between 1777–1879 reflected the *technocratic* paradigm. The know-how of making simple plans for furniture and objects,
ornament design, and technical drawing had to be acquired to furnish
future carpenters, jewelry makers, or weavers with basic skills necessary
for practicing their trade. When collecting and cultivating fine arts
became a fashion of the new bourgeois class, art education was introduced in selected secondary grammar schools as a primarily theoretical
discipline: one that taught about classical—Greek, Roman, and Renaissance—styles and genres in order for the student to better appreciate the
classically based contemporary trends: romanticism and classicism. Art
classes served purposes of religious and moral education. The etchings

that reproduced famous paintings represented scenes from the Bible, mythological figures, and heroes of Hungarian past. Needless to say, nothing was to be "discovered" in these dignified images—"interpretation" could lead to blasphemy. Children had to recite what teachers taught them through the "Prussian questioning method," which contained statements ending in "isn't it?" or "doesn't he?"

The *artistic* paradigm of drawing education outlined above, manifested in curricula around 1871, was very popular among painters and sculptors who, after graduation from the Academy of Munich, Vienna, or Paris, had to make a living by teaching art classes. Another class of experts, however, qualified to take the post of the "art instructor" in Hungarian schools at the turn of the century were engineers and technicians, distant relatives of the drawing masters of the nineteenth century. Thus, education based on the moral value and cultural significance of the arts was cultivated parallel to the *scientific* model of teaching, its exact opposite. The manuals published from 1879 well into the 1940s were dedicated to the laws of geometric drawing and included rigorous and lengthy drills of manual dexterity. According to many drawing masters, developing skills of perception meant the analysis of charts, signs, and floor plans. These two paradigms had one thing in common: *neither reflected an interest in the inborn drawing potentials of the child*—in fact, they considered natural capabilities handicaps to overcome.

Hungarian art education arrived at the gate of the twentieth century, which was to be named by Ellen Key and thousands of like-minded psychologists the "Age of the Child," with firm intentions to teach as many conventions of the artistic or technical use of adult visual language as possible in the most efficient way: copying and completing schemes. According to the Hungarian humorist, Frigyes Karinthy, who attended a real, Prussian-style "gymnasium" at the turn of the century, nothing was more boring than a drawing lesson. He tells that those of his schoolmates who had some talent in drawing amused themselves with sketching caricatures of the art teacher who, after detecting a viciously characteristic portrait of himself, went mad and punished the offender with an overload of geometric study sheets to complete.

Just a few years later this same pedagogue could probably experience the shock of his lifetime: scribbles of toddlers, classroom doodles of adolescents, unfinished sketches of scenes with apparently no classical model, and wildly colorful paintings of naive and evidently untrained hands exhibited all around the country with the annoying label: "child art." The high-ranking Ministry of Education official, László Nagy, a distinguished developmental psychologist who opened these exhibitions, declared that drawing drills and imitation of ancient masters were ruled out. It was the teacher who was supposed to learn from the child. The new paradigm that confronted all the boredom—and efficiency—of Hungarian art education clearly had nothing to do with the still very conservative art tastes of the first years of our century. It was based on a new conception of the child as a source of inspiration and creative energy. *The visual output of children— as well as their mental imagery, gestures, and intellectual traits, was to be studied rather than influenced.*

The Central European Child Study Movement in Art Education

As the most important Hungarian educational reformer of the first decades of the twentieth century, László Nagy became acquainted with new conceptions of the visual language of children through the mediation of the German language—the "lingua latina" of the Central European educational community. He read C. Ricci and J. Sully in German. He strongly supported Ricci's argument about the "inborn sensitivity for beauty" of the child that must be further refined by education, but he did not share the Italian psychologist's views on the nonartistic, experimental nature of children's drawings. Nagy was the first influential Hungarian art educator who believed in the aesthetic value of child art and decided to elevate it to the ranks of high culture. He adopted the methods of Ricci, Sully, and Kerschensteiner for collecting, describing, and classifying the visual output of children as evidence for the development of manual dexterity and ability to depict more and more accurate and complex images.

Nagy found the models he needed in the works of John Dewey and Ellen Key and decided to reform Hungarian education according to their principles. John Dewey, leading ideologist of the instrumentalist tradition in the reform pedagogy movement, emphasized the importance of direct experiences and planned school life so that children could derive both social and material laws and principles on the basis of their own experiences. In aesthetic education, Dewey pointed out the importance of art criticism— regular and active encounters with works of art and their reproductions— both for aesthetic enjoyment and artistic learning. Nagy introduced "art appreciation" as a part of the curriculum of the subject "drawing" and exhibited child art in the major art hall of the country in Budapest.

Ellen Key described the school of the future—a sunny, open space without classrooms—as an island where the beauty of art and nature should mingle to cultivate free-spirited minds. In his speeches and didactic works, Nagy often quoted her ideas about the importance of being surrounded with works of art, both originals and copies, and carefully designed environments that teach about art more convincingly than occasional museum visits can. The model of a school that empowers the child and entitles her to free thinking and creative problem solving was very important for Nagy, who considered the task of his life to expand public education and bring quality schooling to the masses.

László Nagy was able to become acquainted with the work of the psychologists and educators mentioned above only indirectly—through their translated writings—as school systems in the Central European area were rather slow to adopt the ideas of the reform pedagogy movement. His direct sources of inspiration were Franz Cizek, organizer of the famous child art exhibition in Vienna, "The Child as Artist" (*Das Kind als Künstler*), in 1898, and Carl Götze, founder of the Teachers Association for the Promotion of Artistic Education in Hamburg, whose work he could closely witness.[1] Both were artists and art educators who became fascinated by the visual creativity of children through the observation of spontaneous drawings.

Cizek was a tenant in the home of a carpenter with many children who followed the work of the "artist in residence" with great interest. Cizek gave them huge sheets of wrapping paper and invited them to draw on the floor of his studio. Pleased with the freshness and original imagery of these untaught images, Cizek encouraged parents to send him works of children done at home and convinced several art teachers not to teach but to let children draw and then to send him packages of "unschooled art" for exhibitions. He was of course also interested in already detected child prodigies and exhibited their work—mostly studies of academic nature that were only found excellent because of the age of the creator.

Carl Götze was more of a scientist than an artist. He looked at the scribbles in the hope of seeing the mind of children. His deep interest in the new science of the Germanic world psychology led him to believe that visual utterances are reliable indicators of mental development and states of mind as words, gestures, and mimic.

> In the way children depict the world, a distinct developmental sequence may be followed, gradually reaching higher and higher levels of depiction, from the production of subjective images through some kind of symbolic expression up to the true-to-life depiction of results of observations. (*Die Kunst . . .* , 1901, p. 88)

László Nagy decided to follow both models to reveal the artistic excellence of talented children and search for developmental characteristics of child art. He was not trained in art but trained himself in the study of children's visual language. He wrote the first comprehensive book on child art in Hungarian (Nagy, 1905), in which he introduced this concept into Hungarian educational literature. Before this time, spontaneous creations of children were not studied or even collected as they were considered imperfect representational or decorative efforts. In fact, the word *creation* was never used in professional literature on art education, as desirable art-related activities involved depiction, copying, transformation, coloring, enlarging, or reducing.

Another concept Nagy introduced in Hungary was the idea of developmental stages in drawing. He described what the child was able to do on her own and outlined how far education could and should lead her. Authors whose views are quoted in the book include Lewinstein, Kerschensteiner, and, above all, representatives of the Child Study movement. Under the inspiration of Dewey, László Nagy initiated the establishment of Child Study departments at teacher training institutions where psychologists, doctors, and educators considered the complexities of the child's body and soul.[2] These departments were to organize child art exhibitions on a yearly basis between 1907 and 1921.

The First Hungarian Child-Centered Art Curriculum and Its Consequences for Hungarian Art Education

László Nagy introduced a new model in art education with his Basic Curriculum of 1905: the *expressive paradigm*.[3] Its aims, objectives, teaching methods, and contents were in use practically until the preparatory years for World War II, when art education became a vehicle for political propaganda.

Nagy was able to put his research into practice during his work on the elementary school curriculum (Nagy, 1921).[4] The curriculum that this document was to replace emphasized the geometrical aspects of drawing education and had clearly practical aims: the education of the craftsman. In contrast, the new curriculum was intended to include modeling in clay and nature studies—two new areas that brought the work of the child closer to that of the artist. The development of taste was another goal that became increasingly important in the era of diverse styles and trends. At the beginning of the twentieth century, the issue of good and bad taste was a matter of dispute and a major concern for art educators. Child art exhibitions, peculiarly, helped the acceptance of modern art trends and contributed to the understanding of pictorial creation to a great extent.

Mention must be made of the reaction of art teachers to the ideas of Nagy and his followers. The Association of Hungarian Art Teachers, established in 1896, raised a protest against innovations of the proposed curriculum. They found "the idea of child art adventurous," lacking all scientific verification and emphasized the dangers of "subjective drawing" and the merits of "objective" exercises; that is, tasks based on geometric models or gypsum heads of Greek deities. Still, many of the ideas in the curriculum were incorporated in the next central educational documents.

For example, areas of study for the discipline "drawing" were taken fundamentally from Nagy: (a) drawing directly from nature, (b) drawing from memory, (c) drawing from imagination, (d) technical drawing, and (e) pattern design and decorative drawing (Kôrösi, 1930).

Another important effect of Nagy and his "age of enlightenment" in Hungarian art education was the study of research and practice in a wide variety of countries. Hungarian art educators joined their professional international organization, the "International Society of Art Education" (predecessor of the contemporary International Society for Education Through Art, founded in 1954 with Hungary as a founding member). In 1929, a comprehensive book entitled *Art Education All Over the World: Models Based on Educational Goals and Objectives*, by Károly Hollós, member of the National Council for Public Education, was published. The ideas represented in the book were taken basically from the Prague Art Education Conference of the above-mentioned society that was held in 1928 (Hollós, 1929). Here is how the author summarizes the most important educational models that were presented during the meeting. (Countries whose art education system is analyzed in detail to illustrate the problem mentioned appear parenthetically.)

1. The teaching of drawing through copying decorative patterns and works of great artists (Japan).
2. Nature studies and drawing from life (Hungary, Denmark, France, Spain, and other states of South America, Romania, England, and Switzerland).
3. Drawing from imagination (Italy, United States, Germany).
4. "Child-centered," playful art education.
5. Teaching drawing through individual experimentation (Poland, Latvia, Russia, Estonia, Canada, Czechoslovakia).
6. New methods for teaching the depiction of space.
7. A unity of all the above-mentioned goals and methods (Sweden, Hungary).
8. Child art as a mirror of the soul: the psychological perception of children's drawings.

In another book, Kôrösi (1930) opened a window on the world for Hungarian art educators by symbolizing the break from the traditional, academic methodology of "drawing." Its title is *Artistic Education*, but a more accurate translation of the Hungarian title and the contents of the book would be the term introduced by Herbert Read two decades later, *Education through Art*. The book, modestly subtitled "A compilation based on the works of German, French, and English authors," began with the description of the biology and psychology of vision, a body of knowledge that would next appear in manuals of the 1970s in this country. The second chapter gave a brief overview of child art development. Then, different drawing and painting styles (among them, Impressionism and Expressionism) were discussed and their use in art education demonstrated. In the second part of the book, interdisciplinary uses of the visual language are outlined in great detail. The sophistication and modernity of theories are astonishing, but the last chapter that gives practical hints for the teacher on how to build up her program leaves no doubt in the reader that Prussian methods drills, copying exercises, and academic studies were alive and well.[5]

Traditional and innovative ideas and methods coexisted more or less peacefully in the Child Study era. Art educators had a very active—though quite conservative—professional association, regular communication with colleagues all over the world, a benevolent educational leadership that included an influential art-loving person, László Nagy, and, last but not least, an increasing number of art classes in the successive curricula. Both the educational practice and research done in the area of child art development of this age influenced the mentality of Hungarian art teachers for decades to come. They were suppressed after World War II, revealed in the early eighties, and cherished today as important parts of our educational heritage.

"The Visual Talent of the Child" Exhibitions and Hungarian Art and Design Education in the Prewar Period

From 1902–1905, Nagy conducted extensive research on the verbal and graphic development of children and produced a fascinating collection of scribbles and drawings of twins collected from the first year of life till age six. The young creators' comments about their work were recorded on the back of the drawings by the children's parents and nannies. Thus, interpretation of communicative aspects—that is, identification of characters and their moods, signs, and symbols—could be much more accurate. (For an iconographical analysis of the collection, see Kárpáti, 1985). Nagy made a distinction between *conscientious* and *instinctive* drawing (the first determined by education and the visual culture of the environment, the second by the developmental phase, abilities, and emotional status of the child), but emphasized the need for harmonizing the two visual languages.

Nagy (1905) explained his theory of child art in *Chapters from the Psychology of Children's Drawings*, one of the earliest comprehensive studies on the mental and visual traits of child art. In his preface, he attributes the work as an example of the Child Study movement that focuses on the child as an individual and draws conclusions about general characteristics of given age groups on the basis of case studies. Nagy considered the *national character* an extremely important influential factor and called for the establishment of a Hungarian archive for child art.[6]

Nagy worked with "instinctive" drawings only. He used this phrase not to indicate the spontaneous drawing activity, but images that were not taught, copied, or influenced in any other way by an adult. Giving a theme or topic was for him not only appropriate but also a necessary precondition for obtaining pictures that may be classified and typologized. For an educational policy maker such as Nagy, it was important to look at social factors, as well as educational and mental ones, so he analysed background variables, such as the natural and social environment of the child. By "natural" he actually meant the landscape that surrounds the young creator (lowlands or hills, village or city.) The description of social surroundings included not only the age and profession but also the religion, ethnic group, eventual folk customs and habits, as well as other cultural traits of the parents. The stages he distinguished were:

1. The stage of *shapeless drawing* (2–3 years of age): scribbles are produced and differentiated; the emergence of the basic images: the circle, the triangle, the spiral, and the wavy line.
2. The stage of *imaginative drawing* (3–10 years of age): the age of *artistic illusions*—a term he admittedly borrows from the German psychologist Lange—when the child enjoys producing unique, aesthetically pleasing images that lack accurate proportions and are expressions of fantasy. *Schemes*—repetitive patterns—are produced that will be used to represent a variety of different contents. Experimentation with the illusionist depiction of space will increase with age.
3. The stage of *naturalistic* drawing: the child is less inclined to draw from imagination and *does not play but experiments with the medium*. Visual memory improves and the need for technical skills will be felt more and more intensively. Young people of this age are less inclined to draw and are mostly displeased with their pictures. (Nagy, 1905, pp. 23–48)

After a detailed, richly illustrated description of these stages, Nagy wrote a chapter that was rather unusual in professional education literature of his times: "Child Art as an Art Form and as a Language." In this chapter on the didactics of art education, he outlined differences between pedagogical approaches aimed at talent development and those intending to teach the elements of visual language.

The major research achievement of László Nagy in the field of the study of child art is perhaps his focus on the visual language of adolescents—a group neglected or considered to be on the same level as untrained adults whose skills need to be developed as their childlike naiveté has vanished. He argued in *Didactics Based on the Psychology of the Child* (Nagy, 1921) that the art of adolescents is especially interesting because this is the age when individuality begins to manifest itself in the visual language. He was probably one of the first art education researchers to come up with a typology of creator types. He identified and described four major groups: (a) the creative artist, (b) the planner-creator, (c) the "true-to-life" drawer, and (d) the copier (Nagy, 1921).

The father of the concept of child art in Hungary did not seem to exaggerate the importance of artistic excellence. Nagy did not consider the true-to-life drawer or the copier a failure, neither did he insist on awakening the artist in every child. He only suggested that different types of children exist who draw differently and they all have to be taught according to their inclinations and interests. He invited teachers to explore the potentials of all creative types and to try to teach missing skills whenever necessary. With the formulation of the "planner-creator" type he is the first to suggest that art and design education should not be considered worlds apart—technology can and should be as "artistic" as art is "technical."

The pattern designing "draughtsmen culture " was soon replaced by another influence in art education: the *slöjd* model of Swedish education. "Slöjd" means manual dexterity in Danish and Swedish. The teaching program, which was based on folk arts and crafts, found enthusiastic followers in Hungary.

Slöjd made its appearance in Hungary as a part of the curriculum for handicrafts in 1905 and was dominant until as late as 1946. Elements of slöjd may still be traced in Hungarian experimental design education today.[7] The basic ideology was that handicrafts may provide a creative and, at the same time, economically rewarding activity for the children of the poor. The teaching method employed was group work in a studio atmosphere and individual instruction in a trade, mostly carpentry. Often household utensils were designed, produced, and decorated. Education was supposed to be stimulating, offering a wide variety of activities children could engage in on their own, with no adult help. Objects were intended to draw on folk art heritage and students were to develop a taste for simplicity of decoration, clarity of design, and utility of form. Because Hungarian technology/handicraft education originated in this flexible and artistic method based on folk traditions, it was possible to finally establish an interrelated structure requiring cooperation between art and technology education in the new National Core Curriculum to be discussed later.

Communist Art Education
Based on Soviet Models in the 1950s

"The epoch of personality cult" or the most rigid era of the Communist regime that ruled Hungary between 1949 and 1988 lasted from roughly

1950 until 1961, the period of the XXII Congress of the Soviet Communist Party that decided to ease central control of several spheres of life, including art and education. Till the early sixties, the arts and art education, often termed as important agents of political indoctrination, experienced a period of total control. To quote the title of an article from the professional journal of Hungarian art educators: "Art Education of Our Times Serves Ideological Education."[8] This position paper sharply criticizes the educational system of "the past" (educational systems before 1945 in general), where ideologies and tastes of "the rich" were forced on masses of "the poor."

A review of the issues of the professional journal established in 1920 reveals that before World War II, articles on foreign methods of art teaching were only mildly critical. They mostly carried outlines of those aspects that were worth considering for adaptation. In the 1950s, however, most articles that mentioned names of "Western" educational practices were highly critical, even ironic and ridiculing at times, and emphasized only negative features of methods and publications from abroad. The most important foreign model was, of course, the Soviet Union. In a content analysis of all the issues of this journal from 1920 until 1988, we found that, in the decade of the personality cult, practically all articles (94 percent) contained at least one mention of either Soviet art or education.[9]

Art education had to serve, once again, primarily practical functions: it had to prepare for "the successful realization of communism" (later, more modestly, of socialism). At this time, the central Soviet art education curriculum included the teaching of realistic representation of everyday household and school utensils and social events as seen on reproductions of the so-called social realist paintings (in order to be able to "create and understand beauty"). Political events such as Liberation Day or May 1 demonstrations were also obligatory in order to "strengthen the spirit of unity with the Party." *Social realism* is a much discussed term in art criticism applied to works done in the Soviet Union in the period from 1921 to the 1960s. (In 1921, at the annual congress of the Communist Party, nonrepresentational and even nonrealistic figurative art was condemned and, as a consequence, leading artists like Malevic, Mayakovsky, or Chagall banned from public exhibition and forced to exile.) In art criticism classes, works done later than 1900, like expressionism and cubism, were totally eliminated and only a few "state artists" were allowed to appear in school textbooks. This situation remained basically the same until the late sixties, even in Hungary where censorship was the mildest from among the so-called Communist camp.

In 1994, we started collecting videotaped interviews for our Child Art Archive at the Hungarian Academy of Crafts and Design with retired art educators, most of them in their eighties. When asked about their experiences with "social realist" art as taught at school, we found that art educators who were trained at the rather traditional Budapest Academy of Fine Arts could quite easily relate to the new "style." They received a thorough training in Classicist representational art, did a lot of copying work and thus found the stylistic requirements of social realism not totally alien to their own aesthetic ideals. Themes, of course, were found ridiculous by most of them—idyllic or heroic interpretations of the life of factory workers could not be taken seriously—but they could identify with the requirements for realism in style and thought that topics are inferior to the main aim of artistic creation: representation of visual qualities of reality.

Students, however, did not appreciate the skills they could acquire through axonometry drawings or genre paintings. The discipline lost its traditional popularity as transmitter of "high culture" that middle-class families considered an important quality of the erudite person. Memories of those who were at school in the fifties and sixties had an extremely harmful influence on the future of the discipline. When asking for financial means and increased teaching time to reform the discipline in the 1970s, art educators at many national educational conferences and discussion forums had to encounter decision makers who had the worst possible memories of their own art education. As a consequence, state support for art education decreased considerably.

The Reintegration of Hungarian Art Education into the European Socioeconomic, Artistic, and Educational Community in the 1970s

The Hungarian sixties marked not just an easing of communist dictatorship but also the renaissance of modern art in this country. The Spring Salon of 1957 was organized a few months after the oppression of the autumn revolution of 1956 and the realization that political management had to find less dogmatic ways of governance in the realm of culture. It offered, however, relatively few novelties. Several outcast artists were allowed to exhibit again but their mild, Post-Impressionistic works forecast no sudden appearance of the Hungarian avant garde. That avant garde would be manifest at the Studio of Young Artists Exhibition of 1966, the year of the first Hungarian happening, the year when "flat exhibitions" were started for a few hundred friends of friends: a form that was to communicate up-to-date styles and trends for the coming decades.

Political authorities exercising the ruling power over culture and education had established three categories: works could be either *supported*, *tolerated*, or *rejected*. In public, however, these categories were not declared and their contents were never openly explained. Still, everyone knew they existed (they even had a nickname: the three Ts, as all three categories begin with the letter t in our language), but no one could foretell for certain "how far one could go" to fall within the first two categories.

By the early 1980s, central censorship for visual arts was as good as nonexistent. With the easing of travel restrictions in the 1970s,[10] young artists soon became aware of styles and trends of Western art. By the early 1980s, Hungarian visual arts fully integrated into the world of art and became inseparable—and, more often than not, became unrecognizable as to their country of origin, cosmopolitan representatives of artistic excellence. In terms of styles, almost everything could go: more and more works belonged to the "tolerated" category, and, surprisingly for the artists themselves, leading figures of the avant garde were elevated to the position of national classic and were invited to exhibit in major art halls—although neither their style nor their attitudes toward communism changed a bit.

By the late 1980s, the two major institutions of art teacher training were directed by progressive artists who, a decade before, could not aspire to more than the leadership of an art circle in a hidden house of culture or a museum accessible to the children of a handful of intellectuals. Outstanding painters of European acclaim, Imre Bak at the Hungarian Academy of Crafts and Design and Árpád Szabados at the Hungarian Academy of Fine Arts, could now train dozens of artist-teachers each year according to aesthetic and moral ideals that were not long ago considered dangerous even for the casual visitor to an art exhibition.[11]

From the Expressive toward the Communication Paradigm
The Hungarian National Core Curriculum and the Legacy of the Child Study Movement

In Hungary, in 1990, the educational administration broke away entirely from the practice of extreme centralization and began to create the conditions of a balanced curricular regulation similar to that found in many European countries. For example, as part of this process, a national core curriculum was elaborated and a public examination system was created. The national core curriculum should ensure a common basic level of education, compulsory for every school. Beyond the core curriculum, schools are free to decide how they want that core and local curriculum taught (Báthory, 1992).

As earlier sections of this chapter explained, central regulation of the artistic and educational community had been liberalized as early as the late 1960s and modernized in the 1980s. Thus, transition from centralized to decentralized regulations was rather smooth in all spheres of life in

Hungary. One of the first actions of the new Ministry of Education was to abolish central curricula and, at the same time, begin work on the National Core Curriculum. It describes the teaching content for two levels of the primary school. The *foundation level* encompasses four junior grades (1–4, ages 6–12) and two senior grades (5–6, ages 11–12). The *intermediate level* involves grades 7–10 (ages 13–16). Compulsory education in Hungary was expanded from eight to ten years. It is presumed that the majority of the students will continue studies in secondary education in grammar schools or vocational training schools. The aims of this form of educational program were to (a) legitimize schools with a variety of pedagogical and philosophical outlooks, (b) prescribe areas of culture rather than compulsory subjects, and (c) break down requirements according to school grades (Szebenyi, 1992).

In art education, the central curriculum with a fine arts focus was finally replaced by alternative guidelines. "Visual communication" and "environmental culture," as the new areas of study were called, involved the acquisition of new art and design techniques and instructional methods, as well as a novel approach to teaching about the history of arts. The optional disciplines, at least one of which has to be taught, are represented in figure 10.1.

When teaching art criticism in "visual communication," not just fine arts but also photography, video, computer art, multimedia, and many

FIGURE 10.1
"Visual Culture" Disciplines in the Hungarian Core Curriculum

Discipline	Description	Remarks
Fine arts	Painting, drawing, sculpture, architecture; practice and theory/history	Fine arts focus, emphasis on craftsmanship, history taught for improving practice
Design	Crafts, folk art, industrial design, environmental planning; practice and theory/history	Marginally included in previous curricula as handicrafts or human technology
Visual communication	Photography, "art video," computer graphics, media; aesthetics and practice	No such subject in previous curricula

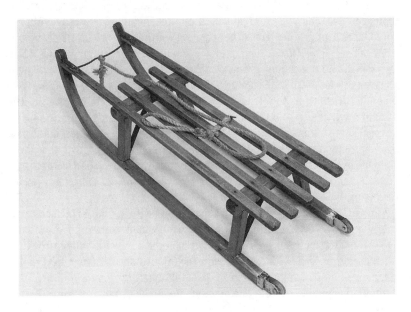

FIGURE 10.2

The rigid and theoretical art education practices of the 1990s have been refreshed by the renewal of folk tradition, and by a yearly nationwide competition for 9- to 18-year-old children.

a. This wheeled sled *(above)*, by 9-year-old prize winner Tibor Gémes of Kelebia (1988), was designed for pulling on streets cleared of snow.

b. This wire model *(at left)* is a developed version of a walking assistance frame designed by Andrea Fábián and Anikó Mazsárik, both age 13, of Budapest (1988).

genres of applied graphic arts had to be tackled. "Environmental education" meant the inclusion of architecture, folk arts and crafts, applied art forms and design in the program of art appreciation (see figure 10.2). The new document encourages design and crafts activities and emphasizes the importance of modern media, which are areas traditionally neglected in Hungarian art education. These new challenges found art teachers—who were used to constant supervision, retraining, and a prescriptive, central curriculum—totally unprepared.

The future of Hungarian art education at present depends on its innovation potentials—exactly as in the age of the Child Study movement. Basic research in visual skills as well as projects developing new methods of assessment are there to help teachers make the right choices. As in the age of László Nagy, researchers and teachers work in teams again. Case studies on the visual culture of the still neglected group—adolescents—are being prepared. Another Child Study era is ahead—hopefully with more immediate consequences for education.

Notes

The authors wish to express their gratitude and sincere appreciation to Professor Jörg Funhoff of the Academy of the Arts in Berlin, Germany, who shared his extensive research on the history of German and Austrian art education with the staff and students of the Hungarian Academy of Crafts and Design during his visits and generously shared information and visual materials of his collection of child art. This chapter is dedicated to him.

1. The German name of the association in Hamburg was "Lehrervereinigung für die *Pflege der künstlerischen Bildung.*" They organized the first child art exhibition in Germany in the exhibition hall of the Sezesion (the Jugendstil movement) in Berlin in the same year as Cizek, in 1898—"Art in the Life of the Child" (*Die Kunst im Leben des Kindes*)—and published a richly illustrated catalogue with the same title.

2. In his times, there was no psychology taught at colleges and theory of education and didactics were disciplines isolated from areas of biological study of children. The idea of the "complex" department for teacher training is reviewed in our time and efforts are made to realise it at Eötvös Loránd University, Budapest.

3. Paradigms that shaped curicula in Hungarian art education in the course of the first one hundred years of its history (1878–1980s) will be analysed in detail in a future paper by the authors.

4. Nagy, László (1921): *Didaktika gyermekfejlôdési alapon* (Didactics Based on the Development of the Child) (Budapest). Included in this work is a curriculum sketch for the eight–year Hungarian primary school that offers different methods and contents for different developmental stages of child art.

5. Schemes to be used for drawing lessons continue to be published. These booklets give thematic suggestions, model exercises for drawing, painting, calligraphy, design, and handicrafts, and describe how the work of students should be assessed. Cf.: Tirpák, 1927.

6. Unfortunately this study collection was established only recently at the Hungarian Academy of Crafts and Design, so tens of thousands of works collected by the Hungarian Society for the Study of the Child for exhibitions and research purposes diminished during and after World War II.

7. The first slöjd publications in Hungary include: Fogarassy, Ödön (1933): *Slöjd: Patterns for Handicraft Education*. Szeged: publisher unknown, Orel, Géza (1933): *The Slöjd: Proliferation of the Workshop Method in Hungary*. Budapest: publisher unknown.

8. Antal Juhász (1959): *Rajztanításunk a világnézeti nevelés szolgálatában* (Our Art Education Serves Ideological Education) *Rajztanítás* 1959/3, pp. 20–24.

9. "Rajztanítás"—*Tartalom és célok*. "Journal of Art Education": Contents and Purposes, the unpublished manuscript. Hungarian Academy of Crafts and Design, Institute for Teacher Training, Budapest, 1994.

10. From the late sixties, group tourism was allowed to Western countries once every three years. From 1976, however, individual tourism became possible. A very small amount of hard currency and tickets for train or plane could be purchased once every three years to be utilised for a tourist trip with a maximum of thirty days. There were special passports for Eastern European and for Western countries—the latter were validated for the individual trips only and could not be used otherwise. In 1988, the introduction of the "world passport"—valid for five years to all countries with necessary visas—marked the end of forty years of travel restrictions. As currency exchange possibilities are constantly being improved, travelling to the West from Hungary is at present a financial question "only."

11. The same changes of official attitudes were observable, with some time lapses, in the countryside: the Master of Arts School, the postgraduate training institution for artists, designers, and art teachers of the Janus Pannonius University of Pécs elected a prominent avant-garde painter as its director: Ilona Keserû. László Beke, the critic who devoted decades of his career to the study of progressive contemporary art—and, as a consequence, was banned from all organs of publication—was appointed head of the Department of Modern Art at the Hungarian National Gallery in the early 1980s and won the competition for the centrally issued art history textbook of the Ministry of Education (Beke, 1986).

11

Luis Errázuriz

Rationales for
Art Education
in Chilean Schools

A rt was systematically introduced into the school curriculum of Chile in 1860 as line drawing. At this time, twelve- and thirteen-year-old boys were taught art in the last two courses of primary education. Line drawing focused mainly on the practice of copying as a rigorous process of imitation of geometrical forms.

The predominant purpose of the subject was practical and utilitarian. It was to prepare human resources capable of supporting the economic development of the nation through industrial expansion. Another important purpose was to help to fulfill the aims of other subjects, like mathematics, geography, and calligraphy. Throughout the history of Chilean art education, these early goals have always been present, despite their progressively diminishing relevance during this century.

Since the beginning of the twentieth century, particularly since the syllabus for primary education of 1910, a broader view of the teaching of art was adopted. In fact, the conception of drawing as mere copying from a two-dimensional form was considered to be just one aspect of the subject, because natural and intuitive drawing had been introduced. The teaching of history of art became part of the syllabus for secondary schools for the first time in 1912 and it focused on European art movements. The teaching of modeling was introduced in the program for primary education of 1928, which provided opportunities to explore new materials and other means of artistic expression.

The view of drawing as a means of expression began to be contemplated with significant purpose with the introduction of the syllabus for primary education from 1931. Consequently, the teaching of drawing was understood more commonly as a way to develop children's capacity to give expression to their feelings, emotions, and ideas, than for development of their technical abilities.

A broadening of the concept of art occurred in the primary school curriculum of 1949, with the introduction of more systematic and varied art activities, like painting, music, drama, and the appreciation of art. This broadening was deliberately reflected in the change of the subject's name, from Drawing, as it had hitherto been known, to Fine Arts, as it became known in 1949.

Since the 1950s, the purpose of developing the creative capacity of children was spelled out in the syllabuses for both primary and secondary education. This aim has increased in importance until the present day, when it is considered the main function of art in the curriculum. During the 1960s, the teaching of design arose as one of the main objectives in the art curriculum for secondary education. This trend is still present with the intention of supporting the industrial development of the country.

Since 1967, fine arts became optional for the last two courses of secondary education, with the result that its long history as a compulsory subject was broken. In addition, a new legislation in 1980 put the subject of fine art as optional for the last two courses of primary education, interrupting its position at those levels for the first time since 1860. The consequences of this legislation became worse in secondary schools, where at present fine art is considered an elective subject for the first level and has virtually disappeared from the second level.

The aims of the subject changed throughout this century by progressively introducing other purposes, such as increasing the capacity for visual perception (1912), refining the senses and providing spontaneous ways of expression (1931), and stimulating the creation of beauty with or without a useful purpose (1949), and the art curriculum was enriched by incorporating other new lines of study like modeling, painting, architecture, history of art, design, and so on. However, although several attempts have been made to raise the teaching of history of art and aesthetic appreciation to a more prominent position in the art curriculum, particularly in the syllabuses of 1933 and 1935, the great emphasis has always been on the technicalities of making objects, mainly concerned with drawing and painting.

A deeper picture of the history of art education in Chile shows the direct influence of European and North American pedagogical ideas and reveals the tension between foreign dependence and self-sufficiency. It is obvious that a continuing need to justify art in Chilean schools, according to the arguments used in North America and in some European countries, has existed. However, it is no less true that the foreign way has often been under criticism due to its adverse consequences. For instance, in 1891, Romulo Peña a prominent art teacher, criticized the excessive emphasis given in his area to the instrumental and practical uses of drawing in the schools of some European countries.

Examining this tension and the arguments used by different authors to justify art education in Chilean schools is the focus of this chapter, with a double purpose: (a) to offer a more complex view of the historical synthesis presented in the previous paragraphs and (b) to emphasize the ways in which different political, social, and educational influences have affected the historical development of art education in Chile.

Six Voices, Arguments, and Periods in Chilean Art Education

The selection of the six authors discussed in this section was based on the following criteria: (a) each of them has written in support of the need for teaching art; (b) nearly all of them were art teachers who made significant contributions to Chilean art education, either through their work in the Ministry of Education or in universities or schools; and (c) nearly all of them have studied art education abroad. Of course, other art teachers, such as Ramon Luis Ortuzar and Armando Lira, also satisfy some of the criteria mentioned above. However, in order to attempt a balanced illustration of rationales in various historical periods, I have preferred to focus on the following authors: Romulo Peña, Juan Francisco González, Alberto Mandujano, Luisa Salinas, Enrique Gerias, and Dora Aguila.

These authors also have another feature in common. Although their views and the amount of material available for this study vary (for example, work by Alberto Mandujano and Enrique Gerias was very available, while material was scarce for Luisa Salinas and Juan Francisco González), they tend to use a similar logic to structure their thoughts. This logic may be summed up as follows: description and/or criticism of the situation of art education in their era, illustration of the need to promote art in the school curriculum, and suggestions to improve the status of the subject. The information collected from these writings did not necessarily reflect what was happening in schools in each period. This is mainly due to the fact that there is nearly always a gap between research, new educational ideas, and their introduction in schools.

Drawing for Industrial Development versus Drawing for the Education of Children
Romulo Peña

In 1891, from Dresden, Germany, Romulo Peña informed the Chilean Ministry of Education about his studies in the Royal Seminary of Teachers, by submitting an annual report mainly concerned with the importance of the teaching of drawing. He was one of the first art teachers who attempted to justify the subject in the school curriculum of Chile. Early in his report Peña explained that, in Chile, drawing was almost completely unknown as a school subject and showed concern that it had not been given the attention it received in European countries.

After criticizing the scant recognition given to drawing in Chilean schools, Peña attempted to justify its teaching in two areas, which he called "practical importance" and "pedagogical importance." With regard to the area of Practical Importance, he rather dogmatically described the various uses of drawing in society and suggested that anywhere people looked, and in all the objects around them, they unavoidably found the need for drawing. Hence according to him, nobody could deny its relevance or hesitate to acknowledge its practical utility. From the viewpoint of practical importance, the most recurrent argument to justify drawing in the curriculum was concerned with the development of craft and industrial expansion. This was mainly due to the fact that the Chilean economy at that time was almost entirely based on mineral and agricultural products. Therefore, Chile needed to create its own industry in order to produce basic products, which otherwise had to be bought on the foreign market. Thus, from the practical point of view, the main justification for drawing was based on the need to prepare human resources to contribute to the economic development of the country.

However, the arguments pointed out by Peña to explain the pedagogical importance are rather different and some of them may even appear contradictory:

1. Children can exercise their eye and hand through drawing to develop skills and accuracy.
2. Drawing has an important role in developing the intellectual faculties of children.
3. Drawing provides opportunities to inculcate in children habits of order, precision, and cleanliness, because these are necessary requirements to draw any image.

4. Inventive drawing is the most suitable artistic activity to develop the intellectual faculties of children and encourage their creative abilities.

Peña also gave special attention to what he called the "cultivation of taste." To support this idea and to explain its importance, Peña referred to the thought of two French educators, Raverson and Rousselot, who suggested that the role of art in education was not only to prepare children for manual activities (useful in a future profession or work), but also to provide them with artistic culture, which they could enjoy and employ for a better use of their spare time.

One of the most interesting contributions of this Chilean art teacher was to criticize the excessive emphasis given in his era to the instrumental and practical uses of drawing in schools. In order to understand the relevance of this criticism, we have to bear in mind that one of the main features of this period, in Europe as well as in North America, was to consider drawing merely as a useful tool for industrial development. Reacting against this tendency, Peña wrote:

> The English and German influence in education has mutilated the essential aims of the teaching of art, because they have placed too much emphasis on only material and practical objectives and have destroyed the actual educational purpose of drawing. (as cited in Errázuriz, 1985, pp. 40–41)

According to Peña, the actual educational purpose of drawing lay chiefly in its artistic dimension and in its contribution to intellectual and moral development:

> The teaching of the arts in Primary schools should only be focused on the development of the aesthetic feelings, the intellectual and physical faculties of the child, but it should not be degraded to the point of it being used only as a lucrative purpose in the long run. (as cited in Errázuriz, 1985, p. 41)

The way used by Peña to justify art may be summed up by saying that, although he recognized a "practical importance" of the subject to help the economic development of the country, his main justification focused on the "pedagogical importance." It would seem that Peña was aware that he could not strategically avoid the practical argument in order to persuade the Ministry of Education. However, at the same time he emphasized the pedagogical aims, so much so, that the respective justifications may appear contradictory.

Education through Art for the Development
of Visual Perception and Expression
Juan Francisco González

Juan Francisco González was one of the most important and prolific artists in Chile's history. As a painter he spent part of his life traveling through Europe and living in France.

In 1906, González gave a presentation in the Honor Assembly Hall of the Chilean University, entitled *The Teaching of Drawing*. This address was mainly to illustrate the need for art in education, particularly in relation to drawing. It was also to suggest a new approach to art teaching chiefly based on the idea of the subject as a means of expression and for the development of visual perception.

The first part of this address was devoted to explaining the need for change in the national curriculum. According to González, in Chilean schools, too much emphasis had been given to theoretical teaching, despite the increasing demand for more practical education, which was required to impel the progress of the country. The concept of progress was associated with industrial development, which was seen as the key to achieving economic growth, and González showed concern about having to compete with international neighbors.

After referring to the kind of curriculum needed for the country to progress, González justified why "artistic drawing" should play an essential role in "practical education." It is interesting to note that from the very beginning he called the subject "artistic drawing," in order to make a clear distinction from geometrical and linear drawing, which had already been practiced in Chilean schools for nearly two decades as a compulsory subject. In doing so, he clearly wanted to emphasize the aesthetic dimension of drawing because, in his opinion, a misconception existed about the role of drawing in education as just being tedious work, rather than having cultural significance.

In order to illustrate the importance of artistic drawing, González pointed out the function that art has played in various civilizations (Egyptian, Greek, Roman, etc.). This historical argument was chiefly based on the idea that art had performed an essential role in preserving the legacy of these civilizations. He argued that this artistic heritage should be a central component of the teaching of drawing, not only for its great significance to intellectual life, but also for its contribution to industrial development.

González described the relevance of the role of art in industrial progress by illustrating the close relationship between the areas of art and industry. In his opinion, industrial products were directly derived from the great arts, that is to say from painting, sculpture, and architecture. For example, painting has been influential in the textile industry and as a source of inspiration in aspects concerned with color production. Sculpture originated from areas of production involving carving, wood, metal, clay, and so forth. Architecture, through its styles, generated the production of furniture.

One of the most notable contributions of this presentation was the stress placed on a need to develop children's visual perception by means of "education through art." By the development of visual perception, González referred to the refinement of vision in order to enable children to "see intelligently" and thus foster a new faculty, to perceive with sensitivity the aesthetic dimension around them. González argued that only education through art could prepare children to appreciate what they see.

With regards to the concept of education through art, which was used several times in the presentation, it should be stressed that this was, as far as I am aware, the first time that such a term was employed by a Chilean author in a document. Art is considered, in itself, to be a powerful source of education and therefore its value in the curriculum goes beyond the development of certain skills to satisfy merely instrumental purposes.

Paradoxically, González's ideas about education through art which, in a broad sense, may be considered very similar to Herbert Read's, are almost completely unknown among Chilean art teachers. In my opinion, this is largely because no written history of Chilean art education exists, and therefore, no diffusion of ideas of our thinkers in the field.

Another important idea suggested by this Chilean artist was to perceive drawing as a means of expression instead of a system of copying. In order to explain this idea, first of all, he attacked the teaching system currently in force, by pointing out that its only achievement was to weary the children in doing meticulous and tedious work, which was a waste of time and nonsense in relation to the actual purpose of drawing.

According to González, seen from the above perspective, the subject of drawing has a wide scope in education in order to cultivate the spirit of youth, develop their capacity for observation and cultural interest. Moreover, because there is no other subject aimed at achieving these purposes, they must be fulfilled through the teaching of drawing.

The end of the presentation was devoted to emphasizing the need to educate children through art, by showing the importance this kind of education had achieved in Europe and North America. According to González, the Chileans had very little contact with the arts and therefore it was necessary to create "good taste" and an artistic cultural tradition in the country, for the benefit of the arts and industry.

In summing up, the "historical argument" together with "foreign influence" constitutes the central ground of justification used by González to support the teaching of art in schools. His advanced concept of education through art to develop visual perception, as well as his understanding of drawing as expression, shows that this Chilean artist is not only important as a painter, but also as a significant pioneer in the field of art education.

Aesthetic Education for the Cultivation of Taste and Moral Instruction
Alberto Mandujano

Between 1912 and 1913, Alberto Mandujano wrote several articles in Brussels and Paris to be published in the Chilean *Journal of Primary Instruction*—for example, "Characteristics of the New Tendencies of the Modern Method of Drawing," "Drawing and Craft in Primary Schools," and "Art in Schools."

Like Peña and González, Mandujano pointed out in his earlier writings some of the main problems of Chilean art education. For instance, in "Characteristics of the New Method of Drawing," he denounced the teaching of drawing in Chile as being thirty years behind the methods used in European countries and North America. However, in contrast to the Chilean writers discussed above, Mandujano attempted a more specific way to justify art in the curriculum. He illustrated the aims of the subject by considering them in the following areas:

1. *Natural drawing.* This was regarded as the most important activity to the general purpose of education, because it taught students to discern, compare, and appreciate the beauty of nature and develop aesthetic taste.
2. *Decorative and ornamental drawing.* This activity was to create and transform shapes derived from nature. After natural drawing, this was considered an important exercise because it provided children with a graphic means to reveal their thoughts, taste, and mentality, as well as to develop their initiative, inventiveness, and spontaneity.
3. *Memory and imaginative drawing.* This was to illustrate the contents of various subjects, following a reading, a class of geography, natural history, etc. This exercise was used to assess children's memory and imagination.
4. *Geometrical and mathematical drawing.* This was considered mainly necessary to prepare children to be skillful craftsmen and to help them in their learning of other subjects.
5. *Knowledge of colors.* As a general view, experimentation with colors belonged to the innate pleasure of children and therefore constituted a powerful factor to develop their cultural, aesthetic taste.

The main arguments used by Mandujano to support the role of art in schools were based on a need for aesthetic education. He suggested that children have a natural sense of beauty, which is expressed through their drawings, plays, and songs, as well as through their interest in flowers and admiration of the natural world. He believed that if this natural sense was not cultivated from the beginning, it would progressively atrophy.

Mandujano argued that aesthetic education should form part of the whole curriculum and be closely associated with moral education. From his viewpoint of moral education, aesthetic feelings constituted a powerful means of improvement of the person because it acts against "rude instincts and passions." Furthermore, Mandujano believed that aesthetic emotions are particularly necessary for the working class, both as a catharsis to relieve hard work and for a refinement of their habits and passions.

Mandujano also placed special emphasis on the "education of taste," which he saw as one of the key aims of aesthetic education. According to Mandujano, the schools' architecture, its decoration and nature, plays an important role in what he terms "the education of taste," in as much as these are kept in an orderly way and very clean. On the other hand, classrooms were to be decorated with works of "good taste": prints, plaster figures, flower pots, and the like, which he believed must be arranged in order and symmetry. Also, all the subjects through their teaching must influence the education of taste and the aesthetic culture of children.

The chief argument used by Mandujano to support the teaching of art in schools may be summarized as follows: Art, through natural drawing and the other forms of drawing, develops children's cultural life, imagination, sensitivity, and memory. In contrast, aesthetic education, which is seen as part of general education and particularly tied to art, is closely associated with the development of taste and moral education, both chiefly understood as instruction on standards of behavior. In contrast to Peña and González, Mandujano scarcely refers to the "industrial development" to justify art in the curriculum.

Art Education for Children's Self-Expression
Luisa Salinas

In 1928, thirty-seven years after Peña's visit, Luisa Salinas was commissioned to study in the Pedagogical Institute of Dresden in order to apprise the modern methods of teaching art in German schools and hence to propose new ideas to be introduced in Chilean art education. As well as Dresden, Salinas visited schools in Berlin, Hamburg, and Vienna, where she was studying the new Austrian system to teach art in schools.

The experience of this Chilean art teacher in the countries mentioned, was described in two articles published in the *Journal of Pedagogical*

Instruction. Salinas regarded art education as an important means to develop the aesthetic capacity of children, but for rather different reasons than Mandujano. While Mandujano conceived of aesthetic education as mainly for moral instruction, Salinas considered it chiefly as a means for children's enjoyment. Thus, without denying the instrumental purposes claimed for art education in her era—that is, to inculcate habits of order and good behavior—Salinas placed the major emphasis on a recognition of child art.

Consequently, one of the most distinctive features of Salinas's approach to art education was her attempt to understand the function of the subject from the children's perspective, as if art was one of the few areas of the curriculum that belongs to them and therefore should not be governed by adult values:

1. At the beginning, children must draw in schools as if they were playing and the teacher must be able to play with them.
2. Children must do in art class what they want to do and choose materials with complete freedom.
3. Children's creations must be carried out within an environment of happiness and without the teacher's interference, because the artistic means of expression are *"the best sign of their intellectual level of development and the only external manifestation of their internal life"* (as cited in Errázuriz, 1985, p. 193).

Of course, these ideas were mainly based on the new development of art education in Germany and Austria, which Salinas viewed as liberating children from influences that prohibit them from expressing feelings and imagination and instead it activated "spiritual forces in order to create and prepare productive men" (as cited in Errázuriz, 1985, p. 197).

Although Salinas justifies art chiefly as a means of children's self-expression, she also considers the subject as a means of helping to teach other areas of the curriculum. She illustrates this point by saying that drawing is closely related to a great part of the school subjects and one of its principal functions should be to animate their teaching through sensitive visual images.

In my opinion, one of the major contributions of Salinas was, on the one hand, to point out that drawing must be the patrimony of all individuals and, on the other, to stress the needs to nationalize our art, by introducing the study of Chilean artistic indigenous culture in our schools. She argues: "Aboriginal and primitive 'Araucanos' leave us a good and beautiful production of decorative motives in their ceramics. This source must be studied and practiced in schools in order to nationalize our art" (as cited in Errázuriz, 1985, p. 191).

In summing up, the main argument used by this art educator to justify the subject in the curriculum is based on the notion that, in art, children can develop their capacity of self-expression and enjoy aesthetic experience. Hence, drawing, modeling, and painting are mainly seen as "creative expressions" to communicate children's interior life and learning by exercising their intellectual and practical faculties. Salinas also believed that the practice of the above aims, together with the use of art to teach other areas of the curriculum, encourages the education of creative and productive men.

Art Education for Intellectual and Spiritual Fulfillment
Enrique Gerias

Gerias was perhaps the most persistent and determined art teacher to defend art education in Chilean schools. There is a good deal of evidence of this fact in several articles he wrote during the 1940s, where the main issue is nearly always concerned with the marginal status given to art and consequently the need to vindicate the subject in the curriculum.

His main criticism is focused on the curriculum framework. According to Gerias, the Chilean educational system has been submitted for quite a long time to the European "encyclopedic" notion of education, which was brought into the country in the nineteenth century and at the beginning of the twentieth. Moreover, he believed that as a consequence of this foreign "intellectualist" view of the curriculum, the individual had been disintegrated because too much emphasis has been laid on the "god of reason" to the detriment of children's spiritual needs.

The principal argument presented against the above educational idea is that school, through the curriculum plan, had taught children to undervalue the artistic areas, due to the fact that art was considered to be a "technical subject" and, as such, less important than the "scientific" and "humanistic" areas. In order to bring out the significance of this criticism, it is necessary to remember that during the 1940s the Chilean school curriculum was divided into three areas: scientific, humanistic, and technical. Gerias argued that the main implication of this discriminatory treatment toward art is that our society had grown up with a low esteem for artistic and aesthetic knowledge, because generation after generation had learned to undervalue artistic activities in schools.

Following this argument, he attempted to justify art education by explaining its importance chiefly from the cultural and intellectual viewpoint. For instance, he used the "historical argument" to illustrate that in other cultures and eras, such as those of Greece and the Italian

Renaissance, art played a much more prominent role in the society as a whole and therefore in the life not only of the aristocracy and upper classes, but also the great majority. However, according to Gerias, the twentieth century, which has been dominated by mechanical power, positivism, and historical materialism, has neglected the place of art in society, thus impoverishing the quality of our spiritual life. Consequently, he suggested that there was a need to return to the spiritual values by advocating art in schools, because these are the institutions where the new generation will be introduced to knowledge.

Although Gerias did not study abroad, as the other Chilean art teachers did, he used what I have called the "foreign argument" in order to contrast the status given to art in Chilean schools with the position achieved by the subject in the developed countries and particularly North America. According to Gerias, drawing and aesthetic education enjoyed a better status in other countries than in Chilean schools, mainly because these were regarded as part of the intellectual area. Hence, his principal foundation to justify the teaching of art (as equally important as the teaching of other areas), was based on what we might call the "cognitive argument." His view regarding the cognitive importance of art in relation to other subjects is expressed in the following:

> To define Leonardo superior to Cervantes or vice versa, will be a mistake. Now then: the first one is studied in a subject [art] which is underestimated by the authorities and children and the second in the principal subject of the school [Spanish]. This difference certainly creates in children a conflict of categories towards culture, which is necessary to remedy as soon as possible. (Gerias, as cited in Errázuriz, 1985)

In summing up, perhaps the most significant innovation made by Gerias in art educational thought, concerning the justification of art in Chilean schools, was to underline the contribution of the subject to children's intellectual development and point out the need for a balanced curriculum in which artistic and aesthetic appreciation should be seriously considered in order to educate the new generations culturally and spiritually.

Art Education for Cultural Identity and the Development of Creativity
Dora Aguila

Among the Chilean art teachers who have attempted to justify art in schools, Dora Aguila is perhaps the one who offers the broadest view about the various functions of art education. Her thought has been mainly influenced by two books in the field, already mentioned: Read's *Education through Art* and Lowenfeld's *Creative and Mental Growth*. Another important source of influence was certainly a master course she attended in 1977 at the University of Wales in Great Britain.

The chief source of information about Aguila's view is her argument used to illustrate man's constant need to be involved in art. According to Aguila, this need is closely associated with the unique capacity of human beings to project feelings and ideas through symbolic forms. She believed that art has permanent, essential, and instrinsic value. In fact, Aguila very early in her dissertation wanted to underline the key role art has played in previous civilizations in order to make a contrast with its status in our contemporary society. This contrast becomes clear when she, like Gerias, denounces the neglect of art in education as a result of being considered appropriate only for talented students.

In general terms, the main argument presented to justify art in schools, is based on the idea that children should be educated in a balanced educational system, aimed to develop them as whole human beings. Hence, art education is associated with a wide range of educational aims and thus is seen as a necessary component of this view of education.

It appears that Aguila was trying to suggest that when the subject is neglected in the curriculum, various areas of children's development are also disregarded; not only because art is involved in the development of a broad spectrum of aims, but also due to the fact that some of these aims may only be achieved through art. Art is presented as an essential component both for the understanding of the human beings' experience and the recognition of cultural identity. Perhaps the need for this, already pointed out by Salinas in 1928 and restated in 1977 by Aguila, may be more clearly understood in the Chilean context, if we bear in mind the strong foreign influence and thus cultural dependence Chile has experienced throughout its educational history.

The aim of promoting cultural identity by means of art education may be considered one of the most significant contributions made by Aguila in her attempt to clarify the function of art in Chilean schools.

Too often educational systems are mere copies of those devised in other countries and it is an essential task of educators to redefine and remodel their own educational programs in the light of their countries' aims and their actual social economic and cultural conditions. The demand for recognition of cultural identity is both a prerogative and responsibility for every country. The role that education and art can play in this cultural identification and growth is of considerable significance. (Aguila, as cited in Errázuriz, 1985)

In summing up, although Aguila recognizes various functions of art in schools (for example, promoting children's sensitivity and self-fulfillment within aesthetic experience, providing a means of expressing and communicating feelings and emotions, and understanding of symbols and images, etc.), according to the conclusions of her dissertation, it seems clear that she tends to emphasize the fostering of cultural identity and the development of the creative capacity. With regard to the latter, the main premise is that creativity is a central element in art as well as a common capacity of all individuals and therefore should be encouraged through education.

Summary and Conclusions

The purpose of this chapter has been to illustrate how art in Chilean schools has been justified for nearly a century. The main arguments made by the authors discussed above may be summarized as follows:

1. *The Industrial Rationale.* Art is regarded as a useful and indispensable subject to help the industrial development and hence the economic prosperity of the country. This argument was particularly strong during the nineteenth century and at the beginning of the twentieth century.
2. *The Historical Rationale.* Since art has enjoyed a permanent and high position throughout history, it should not be neglected in the education of the contemporary society. This is one of the few aims constantly used to justify art in schools.
3. *The Foreign Rationale.* The status of art is important in the education of the developed countries so it should improve its position in Chilean schools. This statement is closely related to the industrial argument and was very influential during the nineteenth century and the early twentieth century.
4. *The Moral Rationale.* The teaching of art contributes to children's moral education through the refinement of their spiritual and emotional life. This rationale was mostly argued until the nineteen forties, although it still tends to be considered relevant.
5. *The Expressive Rationale.* Children can project through art their feelings, emotions, and whole interior world, which otherwise cannot be communicated. This argument began to be known as self-expression during the nineteen thirties and since then has evolved toward a more balanced approach.
6. *The Cognitive Rational.* Art encourages children's intellectual development and thus it should be more seriously regarded in schools. This view has been mentioned since very early times but its main development began during the nineteen forties.

7. *The Creative Rationale.* Schools should develop children's creative capacity and the role of art is of vital importance in its development. Since the nineteen fifties this idea has become the main argument to justify the subject.

Throughout this study, two major areas of conflict or controversy may be recognized:

1. *Foreign Dependence versus Independence.* It is quite obvious that there has been a permanent need to justify art in Chilean schools according to the arguments used in North America and in some European countries. However, it is not less true that the "foreign way" has often been under criticism due to its adverse consequences. Hence, it would seem that a more independent way of justification has progressively emerged, but without denying the foreign influence.
2. *Classic Justification versus Romantic Justification.* Here I am referring to Lawton's concept of education in order to exemplify two different kinds of justification. In fact, while the industrial and moral arguments may be classified as "classic Justifications," the expressive and creative arguments may be regarded as "romantic."

Finally, with regard to the historical account of justification presented in this chapter, I would like briefly to underline some positive aspects and also mention others that may be considered negative.

Among the positive aspects, some criticisms of the art teachers concerning foreign influence seem interesting (Peña and Gerias). Consequently, it is also appropriate to point out the significance of the view that referred to the need for cultural identity (Salinas and Aguila). The visionary contribution of González, who in 1906 pointed out the need to develop children's visual perception by means of education through art, deserves special mention.

Some of the aspects that may be considered negative are the meaning of certain justifications and aims. This tendency is clear, for instance, in the deficiency of conceptual analysis. In fact, concepts such as creativity, sensitivity, feelings, expression and are very often used in a rather loose sense and without clarifying their scope in the context of art education.

Kerry Freedman
Fernando Hernández

Conclusion

A Sociological Framework for International Art Education

As Elliot Eisner (1994) has stated, "The issues raised in the debate about what values should guide schools—what aims are really central, what is marginal, and what has no proper place within school's purview—are of fundamental importance" (p. 15). The chapters in this book focus on these issues. They illustrate the importance of studying the cultural contexts of a school subject in order to understand the meaning of these issues. Without such an understanding—of the social, political, and economic mileux in which curriculum is theorized and enacted—aspects of a school subject would make little sense. The forms of curriculum, even the existence of the school subject, have been in relation to influences from outside, as well as inside, schools.

The case studies presented here illustrate the point in relation to art education. For example, the emphasis on industrial design in various countries at different times was consistent with the staggered development of industrialism; the shift in Sweden to a focus on visual literacy responded to an environment of increasing mass media influence; and the emphasis on therapeutic art education followed from concerns about population change, effects of world war, and economic stress. The middle and late twentieth-century focus on the structure of professional disciplines may not have occurred without the emergence of those particular disciplinary communities in the nineteenth and early twentieth century and the emphasis on international competition that followed the development of a global political economy after World War II.

These histories, then, tell us why we theorize, write policy, and develop curriculum as we do. They also shed light on the ways in which art education is practiced. Although the chapters differ in their amount of focus on classrooms and instruction, they all illustrate how milieu influences and is played out through the various practices that make up the professional field. These practices include the debate that has occurred within and without educational institutions. The case studies can be analyzed in relation to two levels of debate. The first involves ideas in and about art education (including their dynamics and educational contexts); the second concerns the relationship of these ideas to the curriculum process.

Art Education
A Reflection of Leading Ideas and Values

According to historian Lawrence Cremin (1961), progressive education in the United States was the translation of American progressivism in schooling. He argued that it was a broadening of schooling to improve life as a whole (health, work, family, community), an application of new scientific principles (particularly from psychology), the enactment of the hopes of a generation before that all children would be educated (resulting in an increasingly varied population of school children), and finally, the democratization of culture.

Art education has had a similar role in that it has represented the leading ideas of its times. Often, these have been progressive ideas; occasionally, the ideas have been conservative. Art in school has been used to promote national agendas, support social ideals, and apply scientific principles. Internationally, art, children, and education have all been at the center of hopes for the future.

The case studies presented here illustrate the ways in which these ideas have been internationally circulated. They have often taken circuitous routes. For example, Japanese art education was influenced by Europe in the late nineteenth century (Isokaki, this volume) and influenced the United States in the early twentieth century, such as through the work of Arthur Wesley Dow.

The influence of Europe has been substantial in the international establishment of art in public schools. The first wave of European influence is found in the work of Rousseau, Pestalozzi, and Froebel, who helped to give shape to the idea of drawing and the manipulation of objects by children as a necessary part of education. The second wave came from Germany, Austria, France, England, Scandinavia, and the Netherlands, which established art in school for industrial purposes and character development. The third wave focused on studies of artistic development as part of Child Study in, for example, Germany, Hungary, and the United States. The fourth wave was reflected in the work of progressive educators who sought to promote the art of children and establish a common goal for fine art and education. The fifth wave, which involved moving ever closer to fine art, followed the shift of the center of the European fine art community and Bruner's seminal work on discipline-based education. We are now in a sixth wave, one of expansion to include all visual culture, which is grounded in global, socioecological concerns and what it means to live in increasingly image-based, technological environments.

Although art education is often characterized as a bastion of individualism in school, several of the chapters illustrate the ways in which theory and practice are appropriated internationally and the official reasons given for the appropriation. Arguments concerning the leadership position of a country in the world have also been used to reform the field. These arguments are less concerned with the advancement of individuals than of nations and are socially, politically, and economically motivated.

Curriculum as a Collage of Time and Place

Clifford's (1988) conception of ethnographic studies of culture can help us to understand the social problem of curriculum. He speaks of culture as a collage of many cultural identities that are selected and translated on a continuing basis. Far from being a unified whole, any particular culture is a combination of others, with its resulting contradictions and incongruities. The curriculum forms of social production (theorizing, development, research, and implementation) have similar collage-like qualities. Curriculum is made of multiple contributions, from various sources, with competing interests.

Bourdieu's (1965, 1985) conception of intellectual fields sheds light on the relationship of these case studies to each other as we consider the collage-like qualities of curriculum. He argues that each field has an internal logic and its own peculiarities. These histories demonstrate that a peculiarity of the intellectual field of a school subject is that it is less of an integrated whole than an agreed-on set of contested sites (Foucault, 1966/1970). These sites expand and contract as new debates and practices emerge and old ones are revisited. The case studies illustrate the peculiarities of these debates and practices, while reflecting the internal logic of the field, as well as the *habitus* related to our cultural production (Bourdieu, 1993).

One of the messages we can take from these case studies is that art educators have been influenced by visual culture of various sorts as they have created curriculum. The impact of professional fine arts communities has been long standing and international. Efland's (1976) discussion of the "school art style" explains something of the tenuous relationship between artistic and educational priorities since the nineteenth century. However, the chapters here illustrate that although a distance exists between the professional fine art and art education communities, changes in art and art practices, now and in the past, have influenced curriculum. Influence has not only been felt as a result of fine art. Commercial design, popular culture, and mass media technology have also had an impact to varying degrees. Consider the attention to mass media in art education as a good illustration of differences of influence between countries: the focus on mass media, which has been prevalent in Sweden (Lovgren & Karlsson, this volume), has been given little attention in the United States where television watching is a major past time.

The case studies also bring to light some of the many important contributions made by people who became art educators such as Franz Cizek, Ellen Key, Viktor Lowenfeld, László Nagy, Herbert Read, and Walter Smith as they and their ideas crossed national boundaries. Our common goals join those of us in the present to these past members of the professional community. As the goals connect us to the past, they and the community extend us into the future.

Professional educators who were not art educators per se have also influenced the field. For example, progressive educators, such as John Dewey, who have had a major role in the history of educational ideas generally, played a part in art education. European Child Study psychologists have had an important impact, in part because they believed that art was a vital form of children's communication and worthy of investigation.

However, art educators did not come by their ideas only through a line of individuals in the school subject, general education, and the visual arts. They were influenced by their milieu at large. In a sense, curriculum has been shaped by the structure of time and place.

One important aspect of the influence of time and place has to do with the socioeconomic conditions of countries and individual policy makers, including the process of their education. Economic industrial development has instigated many efforts at educational reform. In several of the chapters, the opportunity for international travel, for the purpose of education or work in another country, has had an impact. For example, in Chile, the shift of ideas from one country to another sometimes occurred while the person responsible was away from home, in another country (Errázuriz, this volume).

At times, art has been considered of great value in the schools. At other times, the value of the arts has been ignored or disavowed. However, the cases here, through the struggles to maintain art in school by so many people in so many places, illustrate its importance. Art has survived in schools all over the world through periods of war, economic depression, political upheaval, and social crisis. It has been used as a humanizing influence, to convince, for vocational preparation, to promote creativity, and so on. It has been valued as a liberating force and shunned for the same reason, not only by authoritarian political regimes, such as in Hungary (Kárpáti & Gaul, this volume) and Spain (Hernández, this volume), but by, for example, late nineteenth-century Victorians who sought to protect children from the power of art.

We can further analyze the case studies as having three themes of curriculum that define the cultural history terrain of a school subject. The first theme is *the professionalization and internationalization of a field*. The second theme involves *state politics and the resilience of national identities* in the context of this internationalization. The third theme concerns the focus on *cultural ideals and the construction of self* reflected in curriculum policies and practices.

The Professionalization and Internationalization of a School Subject

Professional ideas sometimes grow up simultaneously in various places as a result of professional patterns and directions determined from outside the field. Professional patterns, part of what Bourdieu calls "habitus," direct us to think and act in certain ways that are consistent with our training, our professional community, and so on. These, in turn, are part of the social and historical structure that acts as a medium for actions, while at the same time constraining them (Giddens, 1987). For example, this structure enables art education to be considered an important part of a liberal education, while simultaneously making it seem unnecessary in the context of "rational" industrialism (Freedman, 1995).

However, a key aspect of the internationalization of a school subject is the transportation of old ideas to new contexts and their transformation in the move. This process is particularly potent when new national contexts are ready for those ideas. That is, the professional patterns that have emerged in the new contexts are in some way consistent with those in the context from which the ideas came. In the process of the reinterpretation of ideas that influence art education as they move from one country to another, previous contexts are lost or shifted to the background. At times, for example, curriculum contents or structures are consciously rejected because they are thought to be irrelevant to the new environment. At other times, however, it is the translation of ideas as they move from place to place that enables change to occur.

The case studies in this book suggest that when a country seeks educational change, professionals often go outside their national borders, to the professional community at large, for new theories and practices. When this search for new ideas begins, a cross-fertilization occurs. The professional community, which exists at a different level than a nation state, becomes, in a sense, a place for the generation of transformational ideas. In such a place, people and ideas cross boundaries, heroes are established, and international events, such as Cizek's traveling show of children's art, gain currency.

The ideas that have influenced the field have changed over time as well as place. The shifts in time are exemplified even in the ideas that seem to have remained the same, for example, from the attitude of Rousseau concerning the differences in education for males and females to the change of Froebel's "Kindergartener" title (from the women who taught children to the label for the children). Even the meaning of expression when referring to art, including children's art, has changed over time.

Part of the process of professionalization in art education involved the movement from a focus on skills to concepts. This occurred for several reasons, such as the development of new technologies that made certain skills less important; the newly developing culture of images; museum education to make fine art increasingly accessible; greater attention to issues of equity in general education; and the shift from behavioral to cognitive psychology. However, the movement from a focus on skills to concepts was also part of a change in consciousness of art educators as they increasingly embraced fine art and education as professional communities.

The developing professionalism in general education involved the growth of professional organizations. In many countries, professional education associations, including art education associations, emerged at about the same time. Particularly after World War II, a number of international associations of educators were established.

The establishment of the International Society for Education through Art (INSEA) is one example of this postwar process. Following World War II, the United Nations established its Educational, Scientific, and Cultural Organization (UNESCO) to promote international cooperation in the enrichment of children's lives. In the summer of 1951, a UNESCO seminar on the "Teaching of the Visual Arts in General Education" was held in Bristol, England. Thirty-six representatives from various countries attended the seminar to discuss ways of improving international communications through visual arts education. The possibility of such a purpose for art education had only developed as a result of changes in international relations, although art educators had been influencing each other across national borders for a long time.

Perhaps the most important idea to emerge from the Bristol seminar was that of forming an international group built on a foundation of Herbert

Read's argument for education through art (Thistlewood, this volume). Since at least the 1920s, art educators in several countries had related the avant garde (itself a cultural construction) to conceptions of pre-cultural freedom, regarding the production of art as a humanizing force and a natural deterrent to destructive social forces that would otherwise damage children. This perspective of art education reflected the hopes of Americans in the post–World War period that art could be used to promote the development of what they considered to be a natural, democratic personality in children (Freedman, 1987). However, the members of the Bristol group were particularly sympathetic to Herbert Read's portrayal of the even more extensive possibilities of education *through* art, which had antecedents in the work of Ellen Key and others, that involved putting art at the center of schooling.

The following year, Edwin Ziegfeld, then Head of the Department of Fine and Industrial Arts, Teachers College, Columbia University, was named head of the UNESCO planning commission to develop a proposal for establishing an international society for art education. The planning commission drafted a constitution and a program of activities with the help of UNESCO to coordinate the development of the constitution. The Constitution Assembly of the Society was held in Paris in 1954. The constitution was adopted and Ziegfeld was elected president of the organization.

The establishment of INSEA was one step in the professionalization and internationalization of art education. However, internationalism, and even professionalism, have taken on new meanings as global interconnections increase in number and complexity. Now, for example, "national" curriculum guidelines for art education look remarkably similar across countries, international programs (such as the International Baccalaureate) provide leadership in curriculum development and student assessment, and computer networks enable students to easily access people and art from around the world.

State Politics and National Identities

Art education has been influenced by political initiatives, social priorities, and cultural crises. It has reflected mainstream cultures, as well as the interests of particular people. The field goes across national, societal, and institutional boundaries. However, it has never lost its ties to national cultures. Although connections have been made as ideas, people, and texts crossed international boundaries, the fermentation of those ideas, the conversations of those people, and the readings of those texts in the context of national culture is extremely important.

Art education is a site of contested ideas, while housing areas of concensus. These agreements and disagreements may be conceptualized as levels. At one level, art educators generally agree that art is a vital part of life and that the overall purpose of the profession is to improve people's lives by helping them learn about art.

At a second level, discourse is created to support this general agreement. However, as it emerges, it is interpreted, negotiated, and changed, and contradictions (or dualisms) and multiple meanings become apparent in, for example, the ways in which language is used. The authors of the chapters in this book often use similar language, but with subtle differences. This is the case, in part, because the cross-fertilization of discourse across cultures results in different translations within different contexts. The discourse was not simply borrowed and transported unchanged; rather, it is appropriated and, in the process, transformed.

At a third level, policies and practices function to reflect and reify different ways in which art educators, and those who influence the field from without, such as state legislators, believe that art will improve students lives. Theoretical "camps" emerge and individual and group differences in teaching and research become apparent. Debates concerning approaches to curriculum, lesson content, and instructional strategies occur, which then work back on the purposes and discourse of art education.

Several of the chapters in this book illustrate the importance of people from outside the field, but within a country, on curriculum. Cultural policy makers, such as government officials, act on the field in ways that reflect national politics and economies. At times, these actions have lessened the impact of art education or moved in a direction unsupported by professionals in the field. At other times, however, they have promoted growth of the field, as in the case of Morocco (Pintó & El Bekay, this volume).

Such support or neglect from state bodies illustrates the uneasy place of art in contemporary life. However, art continues to have an important position in the creation and maintenence of national identity, as it has for centuries. In many cultures, it is a representation of political power and authority. Countries that have art in schools appear to the world as sophisticated, enlightened, and prosperous.

The importance of politics and national identity in relation to art education is illustrated by the current attention to discipline-based art education in the United States. Jerome Bruner's (1960) text, *The Process of Education*, in which he made an argument for discipline-based education, was an American response to a particular social, political, and economic situation that included the advance of progressive education (interpreted as a reduction of standards), an increasingly competitive global market, and a cold war with the Soviet Union. Art educators in the United States gave attention to discipline-based approaches to curriculum following a focus on disciplines in other school subjects, and later, as a result of support from the Getty Foundation.

Even when borrowing from another country, national identity is formed. For example, one of the most widely documented South Kensington educators was Walter Smith, who was appointed by the Massachusetts Board of Education in 1871 and established the major elements of the South Kensington system in that state. The work of South Kensington, and Smith in particular, also influenced Canada (Chalmers, this volume), Australia (Boughton, this volume), and other countries. The British system, which had its own international roots, reconstructed in the United States by Smith, was one of industrial drawing. However, bringing Smith to North America was not just a matter of making American art education more British. It helped to define what was to be important in education in the United States and, hence, became part of the process of creating a national identity of industrial capitalism. The eventual rejection of Smith and the South Kensington system was just as much a part of that defining process as education in the United States moved toward greater attention to conceptions of individual development.

Cultural Ideals and the Construction of Self

Educational historian Herbert Kliebard (1987) wrote of the changes in United States schooling in the 1890s:

> As cities grew, the schools were no longer direct instruments of a visible and unified community. Rather, they became an ever-more critical mediating institution between the family and a puzzling and impersonal social order, an institution through which the norms and ways of surviving in the new industrial society would be conveyed. Traditional family life was not only in decline; even when it remained stable, it was no longer deemed sufficent to initiate the young into a complex and technological world. (p. 1)

Kliebard might be talking of any industrially developing country that has taken up the challenge to sponsor a public school system to help students develop the sophistication required to live in an increasingly complex world. Part of becoming a sophisticated person, in many contemporary societies now and in the past, has involved becoming educated in the arts. To be thought of as knowledgeable in the past meant that one understood and appreciated the arts, usually the elite arts, as a vital part of culture. Knowledge of the arts was considered, simply, part of a good life.

However, the way in which art teaching in public schools has supported this aim, generally, has not been to provide students with an education in the range of complexities of visual culture, or even the complexities of the fine arts. In the past, internationally, art has been typically used in public schools to serve a very particular part of this aim:

personality development. In each of the chapters in this volume, art educators are seen to have taken over much of the responsibility for personality development in children.

In a sense, the focus on personality development in art education has been a union of social and personal goals. One aim of a culture or society, reflected in art education, has been to establish a population with certain characterisitics. Art in school has been viewed as promoting the development of personalities in students that were, for example, disciplined, creative, or democratic. An important part of the focus on personality development has been the construction of the self as a sociological being. That is, art has not only been to help students, for example, feel better about themselves, but to function well in society, be good citizens, appreciate the importance of artistic efforts by other human beings, and so on. Even in the case of the United States, where individualism was vital to arguments for art education, the individualism was a cultural condition (Freedman, this volume).

However, at times, the focus of general education and art education have seemed at odds with one another. The place of individualism in debates about art education in the United States is but one example. In this case and others, curriculum was, and still is, used to counteract the regimentation of other aspects of schooling. For example, in Brazil, at least the surface aspects of this conflict are the same (Frange, this volume). Brazilian teachers define creative personality development as "spontaneity, self-liberation, and originality" (Barbosa, 1990, p. 79).

Poststructural theorists interpret the symbolic character of discourse as playing an important part in the construction of self. From a poststructural perspective, the creation of self is based on the subject being invested with certain characteristics through symbolic representation (Lacan, 1977). The effects of images and language shape an individual's conception of him/herself. Through the use of symbols, the subject appropriates the characteristics of "the individual" and the representation becomes reified when the subject adopts the representation as a description of him/herself.

This has been a vital foundation of art education in several countries. Students are told that they can express personal meaning through art, to heal themselves through its processes, develop self-confidence through its exhibition, and understand self and others through its viewing. Curriculum is a representation of the characteristics educators hope that students will appropriate, and students develop conceptions of themselves and the arts through their interaction with that representation. They learn how to make and look at images, including images in which they themselves are reflected.

French theorist Jean-François Lyotard (e.g., 1983, 1984) has developed a new conception of the therapeutic value of art (Efland, Freedman, &

Stuhr, 1996). He explains contemporary imagery as celebrating sensuality, promoting the natural flow of desire, and intensifying feeling. In contrast to Lyotard, Baudrillard (1983) has concerns about the psychological manipulation of people by contemporary imagery. From this perspective, the psyche is bombarded with images antithetical to its nature, and therefore, detrimental. Baudrillard, Harvey (1989), and other postmodern theorists point to developments in technology, advanced levels of industrial capitalism, and totalizing mass media as initiating current social conditions.

The work of these theorists has revealed that societal shifts, which may seem on the surface unrelated, reflect cultural and psychological change. Art education has played a vital, if sometimes subtle, role in this change. As people have developed knowledge, beliefs about the purpose and place of the visual arts have been formed. The beliefs have acted on learning, reinforcing old ways of doing things and introducing new ways.

Conclusion

Histories of curriculum are stories about the translation of cultural knowledge. The stories of translation help us to understand the ways in which our current policies and practices change over place and time, soon becoming part of the past. The cultural knowledge is overlaid on an epistemology of curriculum, which is highly influenced by the sociopolitical conditions that shape knowledge as it is constructed and reconstructed by individuals and social groups. The range of influences is wide and includes popular culture, national politics, and professional goals.

One of the important messages of the chapters in this book is the vitality of both self-consciousness and mutual understanding in a global community. Pride in one's home is important, but what is conceptualized as "home" is changing. The dynamics of cross-cultural relationships reflected in these chapters illustrate the importance of reducing stereotypes and prejudices.

History of art education is more than a history of a single school subject. It is a story of curriculum in general. More research is required concerning historical and cultural implications of school subjects. In this research, a focus is needed on collective understandings of history, as well as on heroes. The cases here suggest reasons for going farther and deeper in such investigations to find out how and why the range of human conditions have maintained constancy and promoted change in curriculum.

References

Introduction

Altbach, P. G., Arnove, R. F., & Kelly, G. P. (1982). *Comparative education*. New York: Macmillan.

Barraclough, G. (1967). *An introduction to contemporary history*. Harmondsworth, Middlesex: Penguin Books.

Blandy, D. (1987). Art, social action, and the preparation of democratic citizens. In D. Blandy and K. G. Congdon (Eds.), *Art in a democracy*. New York: Teachers College Press.

Blandy, D., & Congdon, K. G. (Eds.). (1987). *Art in a democracy*. New York: Teachers College Press.

Boughton, D., Eisner, E. W., & Ligtvoet, J. (Eds.). (1996). *Evaluating and assessing the visual arts in education: International perspectives*. New York: Teachers College Press.

Braudel, F. (1980). *On history*. Chicago: University of Chicago Press. Trans. by Sarah Matthews. (First published in 1969.)

Burke, P. (Ed.). (1991). *New perspectives on historical writing*. University Park: University of Pennsylvania Press.

Clifford, J. (1988). *The predicament of culture: Twentieth-century ethnography, literature, and art*. Cambridge, Mass.: Harvard University Press.

Collins, G. (1987). Masculine bias and the relationship between art and democracy. In D. Blandy and K. G. Congdon (Eds.), *Art in a democracy*. New York: Teachers College Press, pp. 14–26.

Collins, G., & Sandell, R. (1984). *Women, art, and art education*. Reston, Va.: National Art Education Association.

Duncum, P. (1982). The origins of self-expression: A case of self-deception. *Art Education, 35* (5), 32–35.

Efland, A. (1990). *A history of art education: Intellectual and social currents in teaching the visual arts*. New York: Teachers College Press.

Eisner, E. W. (1985). *The educational imagination: On the design and evaluation of educational programs* (2d ed.). New York: Macmillan.

Foner, E. (Ed.). (1990). *The new American history*. Philadelphia, Pa.: Temple University Press.

Foucault, M. (1970). *The order of things: An archaeology of the human sciences*. New York: Vintage Books. (First published in 1966.)

Freedman, K. (1987a). Art education as social production: Culture, society, and politics in the formation of curriculum. In T. S. Popkewitz (Ed.), *The formation of school subjects: The struggle for creating an American institution*. New York: Falmer.

———. (1987b). Art education and changing political agendas: An analysis of curriculum concerns of the 1940s and 1950s. *Studies in Art Education, 29* (1), 17–29.

———. (1989a). Dilemmas of equity in art education: Ideologies of individualism and cultural capital. In W. G. Secada (Ed.), *Equity in education*. New York: Falmer.

———. (1989b). The philanthropic vision: The Owatonna Art Education Project as an example of "private" interests in public schooling. *Studies in Art Education, 31* (1), 15–26.

———. (1994). Teaching gender and visual culture in art classrooms. *Studies in Art Education, 35* (3), 135–47.

Frisch, M. H. (1993). The face on the cutting room floor: The place of practice in changing approaches to historical analysis. In P. Karsten & J. Modell (Eds.), *Theory, method, and practice in social and cultural history*. New York: New York University Press, pp. 181–98.

Gardner, H., Winner, E., & Kircher, M. (1975). Children's conceptions of the arts. *Journal of Aesthetic Education, 9* (3), 60–77.

Giddens, A. (1987). *Social theory and modern sociology*. Stanford, Calif.: Stanford University Press.

Graff, G. (1987). *Professing literature: An institutional history*. Chicago: University of Chicago Press.

Hernández, F. (1993). Ambigüetés de l'education artistique en Espange. *INSEA News, 1*, 20–21.

———. (1994a). La historia de la Educación Artística: Recuperar la memoria para comprender y transformar el presente. *I Jornades sobre Història de l'Educació Artística*. Barcelona: Facultat de Belles Arts, pp. 1–16.

——. (1994b). Para una cronología de la Educación Artística en España. *I Jornades sobre Història de l'Educació Artística*. Barcelona: Facultat de Belles Arts, pp. 215–65.

——. (1994c). Nombres. *Boletín de las Artes Visuales, 1*, 4. Barcelona: Facultat de Belles Arts.

——. (1995). La trayectoria de la Educación Artística en España. *Revista de Arte e Eduçao, 1*, 55–72.

Hernández, F., & Planella, M. (1996). *II Jornades sobre Història de l'Educació Artística*. Barcelona: Facultat de Belles Arts.

Hernández, F., & Trafí, L. (1994). *I Jornades sobre Història de l'Educació Artística*. Barcelona: Facultat de Belles Arts.

Hunt, L. (Ed.). (1989). *The new cultural history*. Berkeley: University of California Press.

Karsten, P., & Modell, J. (Eds.). (1993). *Theory, method, and practice in social and cultural history*. New York: New York University Press.

Korzenik, D. (1985). *Drawn to art: A nineteenth-century American dream*. Hanover, N.H.: University Press of New England.

Lowenfeld, V. (1947). *Creative and mental growth*. New York: Macmillan.

——. (1957). *Creative and mental growth* (3d ed.). New York: Macmillan.

Lowenfeld, V., & Brittain, W. L. (1964). *Creative and mental growth* (4th ed.). New York: Macmillan.

May, W. (1994). The tie that binds: Reconstructing ourselves in institutional contexts. *Studies in Art Education, 35* (3), 135–47.

Parsons, M. J. (1987). *How we understand art: A cognitive developmental account of aesthetic experience*. Cambridge: Cambridge University Press.

Popkewitz, T. S. (Ed.). (1987). *The formation of school subjects: The struggle for creating an American institution*. London: Falmer Press.

Preziosi, D. (1989). *Rethinking art history: Meditations on a coy science*. New Haven, Conn.: Yale University Press.

Rees, A. L., & Borzello, F. (1986). *The new art history*. Atlantic Highlands, N.J.: Humanities Press International.

Soucy, D., & Stankiewicz, M. A. (1990). *Framing the past: Essays on art education*. Reston, Va.: National Art Education Association.

Starn, R. (1989). Seeing culture in a room for a Renaissance prince. In L. Hunt (Ed.), *The new cultural history*. Berkeley: University of California Press, pp. 205–32.

Stuhr, P. (1994). Multicultural art education and social reconstruction. *Studies in Art Education, 35* (3), 171–78.

Thistlewood, D. (Ed.). (1992). *Studies in the history of art and design education.* London: Longman Press.

Wilson, B., & Wilson, M. (1977). An iconoclastic view of the imagery sources of the drawing of young people. *Art Education, 30* (1), 5–11.

1. Artistic, Cultural, and Political Structures Determining the Educational Direction of the First Japanese Schoolbook on Art in 1871

Isozaki Y. (1979a). Rhinoceros and the iconographical history. *Bulletin of Fukushima University.*

——. (1979b). What Western-style painters of Japan learned from Dutch books and illustrations in National Isolation. *Bulletin of Fukushima University,* p. 40.

——. (1979c). Shiba Kokan and Jan and Caspar Luykens's Het Menselijk Bedrijf. *Bulletin of Fukushima University,* pp. 42–43.

——. (1980). Aeudoo Denzen. *The Catalog of Aodo Denzen Exhibition,* pp. 10–11.

Moxon, J. (1670). Practical perspective: Or, perspective made easy.

2. Australian Visual Arts Education

Aland, J. (1992). *Art and design education in South Australian schools, from the early 1880s to the 1920s: The influence of South Kensington and Harry Pelling Gill.* Unpublished master's thesis, University of Canberra.

Barbosa, A. M. (1984). Walter Smith's influence in Brazil and the efforts by Brazilian liberals to overcome the concept of art as an elitist activity. *Journal of Art and Design Education, 3* (2), 233–46.

Boughton, D. G. (1986). How do we prepare art teachers for a multi-cultural society? *Journal of Multi-cultural and Cross Cultural Research in Art Education, 4* (1), 94–99.

——. (1987). Australian art education: Past present and future. *Canadian Review of Art Education, 15* (1), 49–56.

——. (1989). The changing face of Australian art education: New horizons or sub-colonial politics? *Studies in Art Education, 30* (4), 197–211.

———. (1992). Will the national arts curriculum be stillborn or resuscitated through research? *Australian Art Education, 16* (1), 37–44.

Chalmers, F. G. (1985a). South Kensington and the colonies: David Blair of New Zealand and Canada. *Studies in Art Education, 26* (2), 69–74.

———. (1985b). South Kensington and the colonies II: The influence of Walter Smith in Canada. In B. Wilson & H. Hoffa (Eds.), *The history of art education: Proceedings from the Penn State Conference.* Reston, Va.: National Art Education Association, pp. 108–12.

———. (1990). South Kensington in the farthest colony. In D. Soucy & M. A. Stankiewicz (Eds.), *Framing the past: Essays on art education.* Reston, Va.: National Art Education, pp. 71–85.

Crowell International. (1990). *The concise encyclopaedia of Australia & New Zealand.* Sydney: Horwitz Graham.

Curthoys, A. (1982). Good Christians and useful workers: Aborigines, church and state in NSW: 1880–1883. In Sydney Labour History Group (Ed.), *What rough beast? The state and social order in Australian history.* Sydney: Allen & Unwin.

Dawkins, J. (1987). *Higher education: A policy discussion paper.* Canberra: Australian Government Publishing Service.

———. (1988). *Strengthening Australia's schools: A consideration of the focus and content of schooling.* Government Green Paper. Canberra: Australian Government Publicity Service.

Efland, A., Freedman, K., & Stuhr, P. (1996). *Postmodern art education: An approach to curriculum.* Reston, Va.: National Art Education Association.

Emery, L., & Hammond, G. (1992). *Brief for National Curriculum Statement and Profile in the Arts.* University of Melbourne, Institute of Education, School of Visual and Performing Arts Education. (Brief submitted to the Arts Steering Committee of CURASS, June 18.)

Executive Summary. (1984). Review of the Commonwealth Multicultural Education Program: Report to the Commonwealth Schools Commission. Canberra: ACT.

Grassby, A. (1978). Australia's cultural revolution: The effect of multicultural society on the arts. In J. Condous, J. Howlett, & J. Skull (Eds.), *INSEA Arts in cultural diversity.* Sydney: Holt, Rinehart, & Winston, pp. 161–65.

Grundy, S. (1994). The national curriculum debate in Australia: Discordant discourses. *South Australian Educational Leader, 5* (3), 1–7.

Hammond, G. (1981). Art education ideologies: Current emphases in Australia. *Journal of the Institute of Art Education, 5* (3), 83–84.

Harris, M. (1923). Art and the child. *South Australian Education Gazette* (July 14), 174–76.

Harris, S. (1994). Pay the rent: Mabo and the big picture of Aboriginal education. *Social Alternatives, 13* (3&4), 20–22.

Hillson, M (1987). Walter Smith: An indirect connection with Australia. *Journal of the Institute of Art Education, 11* (3), 46–54.

Loton, B. (1991). Declaration of Goals for Australia's Schools. Canberra: ACT, National Industry Education Forum.

MacDonald, S. (1970). *The history and philosophy of art education.* London: University of London Press.

Mandelson, L. (1985). From drawing to art in Australian state schools. *Journal of the Institute of Art Education, 9* (1), 35–45.

Neale, M. (1993). Yiribana: An introduction to the Aboriginal and Torres Strait Islander Collection, Art Gallery of New South Wales. Sydney: Art Gallery of New South Wales.

NIEF (National Industry Education Forum). (1992). *Improving Australia's schools: Building the foundation for a better Australia.* Deakin: ACT, Australian Chamber of Commerce.

Pearson, N. (1994). A troubling inheritance. *Race and Class: A Journal for Black and Third World Liberation, 35* (4), 1–9.

Poynton, P. (1994). Mabo: Now you see it now you don't. *Race and Class: A Journal for Black and Third World Liberation, 35* (4), 41–56.

Roberts, M., Jones, R., & Smith, M. A. (1990). Artifacts in strata: Optical dating at Death Adder Gorge Northern Territory indicates human occupation between 53,000 and 60,000 years ago. *Australian Archaeology, 37,* 58–59.

Rogers, T. (1994). Art and Aboriginal cultures. *Australian Art Education, 17* (2), 12–20.

South Australian Aboriginal Education Consultative Committee. (1983). *Rationale, aims and objectives for Aboriginal education in South Australia.* Adelaide, S.A.: Education Department of South Australia.

Thomas, D. (1988). Traditional Aboriginal art. In Daniel Thomas (Ed.), *Creating Australia: 200 Years of Art 1788–1988,* Art Gallery of South Australia. Sydney: International Cultural Corporation of Australia & Art Gallery Board of South Australia, pp. 12–31.

Wolfe, P. (1994). Nation and miscegenation: Discursive continuity in the post-Mabo era. *Social Analysis, 36,* 93–152.

Young, M. (1985). *A history of art and design education in South Australia.* Unpublished masters thesis, Flinders University, Adelaide.

3. Teaching Drawing in Nineteenth-Century Canada—Why?

Art Journal. (1857). Department of Science and Art: Distribution of medals at Manchester. *Art Journal*, 353.

Ashwin, C. (1981). *Drawing and education in German-speaking Europe 1800–1900*. Ann Arbor, Mich.: UMI Research Press.

Blair, D. (1903). *Canadian drawing series*. Toronto: CoppClark.

Braidwood, T. (1853). *Schools of design in America*. Circular. Philadelphia, Pa.: Archives of the Franklin Institute.

Casselman, A. C. (1894). *The high school drawing course*. Toronto: Canada Publishing.

Chalmers, F. G. (1993). Who is to do this great work for Canada? South Kensington in Ontario. *Journal of Art and Design Education, 12* (2), 161–78.

Chief Superintendent of Education. (1860). *Annual report of the normal, model, grammar and common schools in Upper Canada*. Quebec and Toronto: Legislative Assembly.

Conseil des Arts et Manufactures et le Conseil de l'Instruction Publique. (1878). *Manuel de dessin industriel a l'usage maitres d'écoles primaires d'apres la méthode de Walter Smith*. Montreal: Duvernay Freres and Dansereau.

Currie, M. (1990). Origines historiques de l'utilisation de manuels d'enseignement du dessin au Canada au XIXe siecle. Étude du contenu de deux manuels de L. O'Brien, J. H. McFaul et Wm. Revell (1885) et d'un manuel de J. H. McFaul (1892). Unpublished paper, Concordia University, Montreal.

Dawson, J. W. (1851). *Report of the schools of Nova Scotia for the year 1850*. Halifax: Richard Nugent.

Efland, A. (1983). School art and its social origins. *Studies in Art Education, 24* (3), 149–57.

———. (1985). Art and education for women in nineteenth-century Boston. *Studies in Art Education, 26* (3), 133–40.

Grace, J. G. (1870). On art training: An address delivered at a meeting of art workmen February 15th, 1870. London: John Bumpus.

Inglis, K. S. (1963). *Churches and the working classes in Victorian England*. London and Toronto: Routledge and Kegan Paul and the University of Toronto Press.

Latta, S. J. (1900). *Hints on drawing designed for self-instruction*. Toronto: Educational Publishing.

MacDonald, S. (1970). *The history and philosophy of art education.* New York: American Elsevier.

McFaul, J. H. (1892). *The public school drawing course.* Toronto: Canada Publishing.

Minihan, J. (1977). *The nationalization of culture.* London: Hamish Hamilton.

Normal School of Nova Scotia. (n.d.). *Industrial drawing from blackboard and object.* Course for the Normal School of Nova Scotia arranged by Walter Smith (two workbooks). Truro, N.S.: Normal School of Nova Scotia.

O'Brien, L. R. (1879). Art education—A plea for the artisan. *Rose Belford's Canadian Monthly and National Review* (May), 584–91.

O'Brien, L. R., McFaul, J. H., & Revell, W. (1885). *The Canadian drawing course.* Toronto: Canada Publishing.

Public Schools Report. (1875). *British Columbia Public Schools Report.* Victoria, B.C.: Queen's Printer.

Public Schools Report. (1889). *British Columbia Public Schools Report.* Victoria, B.C.: Queen's Printer.

Royal Commission on Elementary Education Acts. (1888). *Foreign returns.* London: Her Majesty's Stationery Office.

Scott, C. H. (1922). Importance of drawing in the public schools. *The B.C. Teacher* (September), 14–15.

St-Théotiste, C.N.D., Soeur. (1878). *Definitions geometriques appliquees au dessin lineaire.* Montreal: Congrégation de Notre-Dame.

Selby and Company. (1895). *The progressive drawing course.* Toronto: Selby.

Smith, W. (1860). *The importance of a knowledge of drawing to working men.* Lecture delivered in the mechanics' institution, Keighley, November 24, 1859. London and Leeds: Hamilton Adams and Charles Goodall.

——. (1878). *Teachers' manual for freehand drawing in intermediate schools.* St. John, N.B.: J. and A. McMillan; and Toronto: A. Miller.

——. (1883a). *Technical education and industrial drawing in public schools*: Reports and notes of addresses delivered at Montreal and Quebec. Montreal: Council of Arts and Manufactures.

——. (1883b). *Teachers' manual for freehand drawing in primary schools.* Toronto and Winnipeg: W. J. Gage.

——. (1884). *Teachers' manual for freehand drawing in primary schools.* Montreal: Gazette Printing.

Soucy, D. (1986). Religion and the development of art education in Nova Scotia. *Arts and Learning, 4,* 36–43.

Southey, R. (1930). The life of Wesley. In M. Weber (Ed.), *The Protestant ethic and the spirit of capitalism.* New York: C. Scribner.

Templé, E. M. (1886). *Méthode nationale de dessin.* Cours preparatoire. Guide du maitre contenant une note explicative pour chaque modele et illustré de nombreuses vignettes. Montreal: E. M. Templé.

————. (1891). *National method of drawing.* (S. C. Stevenson, trans.). Approved by the Council of Arts and Manufactures and Council of Public Instruction of the Province of Quebec. Preparatory Course. Teacher's Manual. Montreal: E. M. Templé.

Thistlewood, D. (1986). Social significance in British art education 1850–1950. *Journal of Aesthetic Education, 20* (1), 71–83.

Tyrwhitt, R. St. J. (1868). *Handbook of practical art.* Oxford: Clarendon.

Vossnack, E. (1879). *Drawing in public, high and normal schools.* A letter from Emil Vossnack, C.E., Lecturer of Mechanical Engineering, Naval Architecture, and Instrumental Drawing of the Technological Institute of Halifax to the Council of Public Instruction for the Province of Nova Scotia, and the School Commissioners of the City of Halifax. Halifax: John Burgoyne, Daily Reporter and Times Office.

4. Framing the Empty Space

Adsuar, J. (1899). *La enseñanza del dibujo en las Escuelas Primarias y Normales de España.* Madrid: Librería de Hernando y Compañía.

Arañó, J. C. (1986). *La enseñanza de las Bellas Artes en España. Facultad de Bellas Artes.* Unpublished doctoral dissertation, Universidad Complutense, Madrid.

————. (1989). La enseñanza de las Bellas Artes como forma de ideología cultura. *Arte, Individuo y Sociedad, 2,* 9–30.

————. (1992). Art education in Spain: 150 years of cultural ideology. *The history of education: Proceedings from the second Penn State conference.* Reston, Va.: National Art Education Association.

Artola, M. (1976). *La burguesía revolucionaria (1808–1874).* Madrid: Alianza.

Barcelona's Town Hall. (1931). *Program for handicraft and home teaching.* Barcelona: Town Hall.

Blanco, A. (1919). *El dibujo libre y espontáneo de los niños y su relación con la inteligencia.* Madrid: J. Cosano.

Cabezas, L. (1984). *Tratadistas y tratados españoles de perspectiva: Desde sus orígenes hasta la geometría descriptiva de Gaspar Monje (1526–1803).* Unpublished doctoral dissertation, Universidad de Barcelona.

Calvo Serraller, F. (1973). Las academias artísticas en España. In N. Pevsner (Ed.), *Las academias de arte.* Madrid: Cátedra (1982).

Cassià Costal, C. (1931). Informe. L'escola actual no és pas educativa. Un gran defecte d'ella. *Seminari de Pedagogia.* Arxiu Artur Martorell. Barcelona: Institut Municipal d'Educació.

Cousinet, R. (1912). El nuevo método de enseñanza del dibujo. *Revista de Educación, 5* (May), 15.

Cuenca, A. (n.d.). *La enseñanza del dibujo en las Escuelas de Magisterio, 1839–1986.* Unpublished doctoral dissertation, Universidad Complutense, Madrid.

Diputació de Barcelona. (1914). *Program of the 1914 Summer School.* Barcelona: Diputació of Barcelona.

Domínguez Perela, E. (1990). Introducción al problema de las conductas estéticas durante el franquismo (1939–1960). *Arte, Indiviudo y Sociedad, 3,* 17–98.

Ferrer, F. (1912). *La escuela moderna: Póstuma explicación y alcance de la enseñanza racionalista.* Barcelona: Elzeviriana.

———. (1913). *The origins and ideals of the modern school.* New York: G. P. Putnam's Sons.

Freedman, K. (1987). Art education as social production: Culture, society, and politics in the formation of curriculum. In T. S. Popkewitz (Ed.), *The formation of school subjects.* New York: Falmer Press.

Galí, A. (1982). Història de les institucions i del moviment cultural de Catalunya, 1900–1936. *Ensenyament tècnico-artístic: Moviment artístic, 62* (5).

Gay, J., Pascual, A., & Guillet, R. (1973). *Sociedad Catalana y Reforma Escolar. La continuidad de una institución.* Barcelona: Laia.

Hernández, F. (1994a). La historia de la Educación Artística: Recuperar la memoria para comprender y transformar el presente. *I Jornades sobre Història de l'Educació Artística.* Barcelona: Facultat de Belles Arts, pp. 1–16.

———. (1994b). Para una cronología de la Educación Artística en España. *I Jornades sobre Història de l'Educació Artística.* Barcelona: Facultat de Belles Arts, pp. 215–65.

———. (1994c). Nombres. *Boletín de las Artes Visuales, 1,* Barcelona: Facultat de Belles Arts.

———. (1995). La trayectoria de la Educación Artística en España. *Revista de Arte e Eduçao, 1,* 55–72.

Hernández, F., & Planella, M. (1996). *II Jornades sobre Història de l'Educació Artística.* Barcelona: Facultat de Belles Arts.

Hernández, F., & Trafí, L. (1994). *I Jornades sobre Història de l'Educació Artística*. Barcelona: Facultat de Belles Arts.

Krause, K. (1883). *Compendio de estética*. Madrid: Victoriano Suárez. (Original German edition, 1837.)

Jiménez, A. (1987). La Institución Libre de Enseñanza y su ambiente, II. *Período parauniversitario*/1. Madrid: Taurus.

Llorente, A. (1995). *Arte e ideología en el franquismo*. Madrid: Visor.

Martinez Cuadrado, M. (1974). *La burguesía conservadora (1874–1931)*. Madrid: Alianza Editorial.

Masip, R. (1995). *El pintor Fracesc d'Assis Galí. Nova visió pedagògica de l'ensenyament artístistic*. Unpublished doctoral disseetation, University of Barcelona.

Masriera, V. (1917). *Manual de Pedagogía del Dibujo*. Madrid: A. Alcoy.

Monés, J. (1994). L'educació artística i les classes populars. Els cas català (1990–1939). *I Jornades sobre Història de l'Educació Artística*. Barcelona: Facultat de Belles Arts, pp. 17–50.

Oliver, B. (1923). Resum crític de l'art educateur per D. Parodi a Revue Pedagogique. *Butlletí dels Mestres*, 62.

Perez Sanchez, A. (1986). *Historia del Dibujo en España: De la edad media a Goya*. Madrid: Cátedra.

Pi i Suñyer, C. (1923). *Per la cultura obrera: L'acció de les nostres escoles professionals*. Barcelona: Agrupació d'alumnes i ex-alumnes de l'Escola Municipal d'Arts del Districte VIII.

Porral, R. (1991). *La enseñanza institucionalizada de las artes en Galicia: 1886–1986*. Unpublished doctoral dissertation, Universidad Complutense, Madrid.

Replinger, M. (1989). *El pensamiento artístico en las revistas románticas españolas (1835–1855): El programa de restauración de las artes*. Unpublished doctoral dissertation, University Complutense, Madrid.

Rodríguez Perela, E. (1990). Introducción al problema de las conductas estéticas durante el franquismo. *Arte, Individuo y Sociedad*, 3, 17–98.

Ruiz Ortega, M. (1986). *Primera experiencia pedagógica en la Escuela Gratuita de Diseño de la Junta Particular de Comercio de Barcelona (1775–1808)* (Como nuevo organismo de enseñanza dentro del marco de la reforma educativa ilustrada). Unpublished doctoral dissertation, Universitat de Barcelona.

Solà, P. (1976). *Las escuelas racionalistas en Cataluña*. Barcelona: Tusquets.

Vall Alberti, J. (1933). L'educació estètica dels infants. *Butlletí dels Mestres*, 162–65.

5. The Importance of Modern Art and Art Education in the Creation of a National Culture

Barnes, A. C. (1925). *The art in painting.* New York: Harcourt Brace.

———. (1928). *The art in painting* (2d ed.). New York: Harcourt Brace.

Beck, R. H. (1959). Progressive education and American progressivism: Margaret Naumburg. *Teachers College Record, 60* (4), 198–208.

Cane, F. (1926). Art in the life of the child. *Progressive Education, 3* (2), 154–70.

Cremin, L. (1961). *The transformation of the schools.* New York: Knopf.

D'Amico, V. (1942). *Creative teaching in art.* Scranton, Pa.: International Textbook.

Dewey, J. (1931). *Art as experience.* New York.

Diggins, J. P. (1992). *The rise and fall of the American left.* New York: W. W. Norton.

Duncum, P. (1982). The origins of self-expression: A case of self-deception. *Art Education, 35* (5), 32–35.

Efland, A. D. (1990). *A history of art education: Intellectual and social currents in teaching the visual arts.* New York: Teachers College Press.

Faulkner, R., Ziegfeld, E., & Hill, G. (1941). *Art today: An introduction to the fine and functional arts.* New York: Henry Holt.

Freedman, K. (1987). Art education and changing political agendas: An analysis of curriculum concerns of the 1940s and 1950s. *Studies in Art Education, 29* (1), 17–29.

———. (1989a). The philanthropic vision: The Owatonna Art Education Project as an example of "private" interests in public schooling. *Studies in Art Education, 31* (1), 15–26.

———. (1989b). Dilemmas of equity in art education: Ideologies of individualism and cultural capital. In W. G. Secada (Ed.), *Equity in education.* London: Falmer, pp. 103–17.

Graham, E. G. (1935). Teaching art in the primary school. In W. E. Rusk (Ed.), *Methods of teaching the fine arts.* Chapel Hill: University of North Carolina Press, pp. 3–12.

Greenberg, C. (1940). Towards a newer Laocoon. *Partisan Review, 7* (Fall), 296–310.

Guilbaut, S. (1983). *How New York stole the idea of modern art: Abstract Expressionism, freedom, and the cold* war (A. Goldhammer, trans.). Chicago: University of Chicago Press.

Haney, J. P. (1914–1915). *Art in the high schools of New York City.* New York: Department of Education.

Karier, C. J. (1986). *Scientists of the mind: Intellectual founders of modern psychology.* Urbana: University of Illinois Press.

Kliebard, H. M. (1987). The struggle for the American curriculum. New York: Routledge & Kegan Paul.

Lowenfeld, V. (1947). *Creative and mental growth.* New York: Macmillan.

Lynes, R. (1973). *Good old modern: The Museum of Modern Art.* New York: Atheneum.

Macdonald, S. (1970). *History and philosophy of art education.* New York: American Elsevier.

Naumburg, M. (1928). *The child and the world.* New York: Harcourt, Brace.

Pearson, R. M. (1925). *How to see modern pictures.* New York: Dial Press.

——. (1941). *The new art education.* New York: Harper & Brothers.

Ravitch, D. (1988). *The great school wars: A history of New York City public schools* (2d ed.). New York: Basic Books.

Rousmaniere, K. (1994). Losing patience and staying professional: Women teachers and the problem of discipline in New York City schools in the 1920s. *History of Education Quarterly, 34* (1), 49–68.

Rugg, H., & Schumaker, A. (1928). *The child-centered school.* Yonkers, N.Y.: World Books.

Rushing, W. J. (1995). *Native American art and the New York avant garde.* Austin: University of Texas Press.

Sargent, W. (1921). *Report on the biennial survey of education, 1916–1918.* Washington, D.C.: United States Bureau of Education.

Sarinen, A. B. (1958). *The proud possessors: The life, times, and tastes of some adventurous American art collectors.* New York: Random House.

Staff and Students of Teachers College. (1942). *Art Education Today.* New York: n.p.

——. (1943). *Art Education Today.* New York: n.p.

Thistlewood, D. J. (1990). Educating in contemporary art. In D. Soucy & M. A. Stankiewicz (Eds.), *Framing the past: Essays on art education.* Reston, Va.: National Art Education Association, pp. 167–82.

Trachtenberg, A. (1989). *Reading American photographs: Images as history, Mathew Brady to Walker Evans.* New York: Hill & Wang.

Von Blum, P. (1982). *The critical vision: A history of social and political art in the U.S.* Boston: South End Press.

Walden School pamphlet. (n.d.). Teachers College Education Archives.

Wygant, F. (1988). Dewey and Naumburg: An unresolved debate. *Canadian Review of Art Education, 15* (2), 29–40.

6. From Art Making to Visual Communication

Arvas, B. (1986). *Mer om hundra språk*. Stockholm: Moderna museet.

Bengtsson, P., Karlsson, S-G., & Eklund, S. (1970). *FB Bildkunskap 1*. Stockholm: Liber Utbildningsförlaget.

Breitholtz, N. (1962). *Barnens bildvärld, idéer och motiv*. Stockholm: Swedish Teachers Company.

Dahlberg, G., & Åsén, G. (1993). Reggio Emilia och den moderna barndomen. *Bild i Skolan, 2.*

Eisner, E. (1973–1974). Examining some myths of art education. *Studies in Art Education, 15* (3), 7–16.

Ekegren, S. (1988). *Skolplanschernas värld*. Stockholm: LTS förlag.

Hansson, H., Karlsson, S-G., & Nordström, G. Z. (1974). *Bild och form*. Gävle: Skolförlaget.

———. (1992). *Bildspråkets grunder*. Stockholm: Almqvist & Wiksell.

Hansson, H., & Qvarsell, B. (1983). *En skola för barn*. Stockholm: Liber Utbildningsförlaget.

Isling, Å. (1988). *Det pedagogiska arvet*. Stockholm: Sober förlag.

Jarenskog, J., & Svanvik, K. (1968). Gasklockan—ett miljöproblem. *Teckning, 2/68.*

Karlsson, S-G., Nordström, G. Z., & Wikell, I. (1967). Piloterna vet varför de anföll. *Teckning, 8/67.*

Key, E. (1899). *Skönhet för alla*. Stockholm: Albert Bonnier.

Larsson, L. (1970). *Vill våra barn ärva våra ljusstakar?* Stockholm: Forum.

LGR. (1962). Swedish National Curriculum.

Lovgren, S. (1992). Från klotter till bildspråk. In U. Lind (Ed.), *Tidsbilder*. Stockholm: Utbildningsradion, pp. 106–17.

Nordström, G. Z. (1967). Den tredje vågen—Den alternativa metodiken. *Teckning, 8/67.*

Nordström, G. Z., & Romilson, C. (1970). *Bilden, skolan och samhället*. Stockholm: Aldus/Bonnier.

Pettersson, S., & Åsén, G. (1989). *Bildundervisningen och det pedagogiska rummet*. Stockholm: HLS förlag.

Richardsson, G. (1990). *Svensk utbildningshistoria*. Lund: Studentlitteratur.

Rothe, R. (1937). *Den fria barnteckningen*. Stockholm: Sveriges lärarförbund.

Segerborg, H. (1916). *Teckningsundervisningen i folkskolan*. Stockholm: Nordstedt.

―――. (1910). *Åskådningsteckning*. Stockholm: Nordstedt.

Seyler, H. (1983). *Hur bonden blev lönearbetare*. *Industrisamhället och den svenska bondeklassens omvandling*. Lund: Studentlitteratur.

Sjöholm, L. G. (1961). *Att bli undervisad. Minnen och funderingar*. Stockholm: Svenska lärartidnings förlag.

Sjöholm, L. G., & Goés, A. (1916). *Handledning vid undervisningen i hembygdkunskap*. Stockholm: Nordstedt.

―――. (1936). *Handledning vid undervisning i hembygdkunskap*. Stockholm: Nordstedt.

Skolöverstyrelsen. (1980). *Läroplan för grundskolan*. Stockholm: Liber Utbildningsförlag.

Statens ungdomsråd. (1981). *Ej till salu. Rapportserien: Till varje pris-slutrapport 9*. Stockholm: Liber Utbildningsförlag.

Thomeaus, J. (1980). *Den förnekade bilden*. Stockholm: W. & W.

Wallin, K. (1993). *Flygande mattor och forskande barn*. Stockholm: HLS förlag.

Wikell, I. (1967). Lärare i miljökunskap. *Teckning, 2/67*.

7. Brazilian Connections between Fine Art and Art Teaching Since the 1920s

Arnheim, R. (1989). *Intuição e intelecto na arte*. São Paulo: Martins Fontes.

Azevedo, F. A.G. (1995). Sobre a dramaticidade no ensino de Arte: Em busca de um currículo reconstrutivista. In L. G. Pimentel (Ed.), *Som, gesto, forma e cor; dimensões da Arte e seu Ensino*. Belo Horizonte: C/ARTE.

Baddeley, O., & Fraser, V. (1954). *Drawing the line and the cultural identity in contemporary Latin America*. London: Verso.

Barbosa, A. M. T. B., & Salles, H. M. (Eds.). (1990). *Simpósio Internacional Sobre O Ensino Da Arte E Sua História*. São Paulo: MAC/Usp.

――――. (Eds.). (1991). *A imagem do ensino da arte*. São Paulo: Perspectiva; Porto Algre: Fundação Iochpe.

Benjamin, A. E. (1991). *Thinking art beyond traditional aesthetics*. London: ICA.

Brett, G. (1992). Note in the writings. In H. Oiticica, Galerie Nationale du Jeu de Paume. Paris: Projeto Hélio Oiticica; Rio de Janeiro: Witte de With, Center for Contemporary Art, Rotterdam.

Brito, R. (1985). *Neoconcretismo: Vértice e ruptura do projeto construtivo brasileiro*. Rio de Janeiro: Funarte.

Campos, H. (1992). O músico da matéria. In *Folha de São Paulo*, 5 (February), 16.

Castro, A. (1985). Manifesto Neoconcreto. In R. Brito, *Neoconcretismo: Vértice e ruptura do projeto construtivo brasileiro*. Rio de Janeiro: Funarte.

Coli, J. (1984). *O que é arte* (2d ed.). São Paulo: Brasiliense.

Duarte, J. F., Jr. (1981). *Fundamentos estéticos da educação*. São Paulo: Cortez; and Uberlândia: EDUFU.

Eisner, E. W. (1988). Structure and magic in discipline-based art education. *Journal of Art & Design Education*, 2 (7), 14–25.

Favaretto, C. (1993). Restauração e resgate da arte contemporânea. In A. M. Barbosa & A. M. T. Bastos (Eds.), *O Ensino das Artes nas Universidades*. São Paulo: EDUSP, CNPq.

Foucault, M. (1986). *As palavras e as coisas*. São Paulo: Martins Fontes.

Frange, L. B. P. (1995). *Por que se esconde a violeta?* Isto não é uma concepção de desenho, nem pós-moderna, nem tautológica. São Paulo: Annablume; and Uberlândia: EDUFU.

Freire, P. (1985). *Por uma pedagogia da pergunta*. Rio de Janeiro: Paz e Terra.

Fusari, M. F. R., & Ferraz, M. H. C. T. (1991). *Arte na educação escolar*. São Paulo: Cortez.

Guatarri, F. (1990). *As três ecologias*. Campinas: Papirus.

Gullar, F. (1978). *Etapas da arte contemporânea; do cubismo ao concretismo*. Rio de Janeiro: Civilização Brasileira.

Kujawski, G. M. (1988). *A crise do século XX*. São Paulo: Ática.

Machado, R. (1991). In A. M. T. B. Barbosa & H. M. Salles (Eds.), *A imagem do ensino da arte*. São Paulo: Perspectiva; and Porto Algre: Fundação Iochpe.

Oiticica, H. (1986). *Aspiro ao grande labirinto*. Rio de Janeiro: Rocco.

――――. (1992). Galerie Nationale du Jeu de Paume. Paris: Projeto Hélio Oiticica; and Rio de Janeiro: Witte de With, Center for Contemporary Art, Rotterdam.

Ortiz, R. (1985). *Cultura Brasileira e Identidade Nacional.* São Paulo: Brasiliense.

Paz, O. (1961). *The labirinth of solitude.* Middlesex: Penguim Books.

Pedrosa, M. (1979). *Arte, forma e personalidade.* São Paulo: Kairós.

Penna, M. (1995). Diretrizes para uma educação artística democratizante: A ênfase na linguagem e nos conteúdos. In R. Peregrino (Ed.), *Da camiseta ao museu.* João Pessoa: UFPB.

Stuhr, P. L. (1991). *Contemporary approaches to multicultural art education in the United States. INSEA News* (Columbia).

Taylor, R. (1987). *Educating for art: Critical responses and development.* Essex: Longman.

Zoladz, R. W. V. (1990). *Augusto Rodrigues: O artista e a arte poeticamente.* Rio de Janeiro: Civilização Brasileira.

9. From Imperialism to Internationalism

Fry, R. (1917). Children's drawings. *Burlington Magazine, 30* (June), pp. 225–31.

———. (1919). Teaching art. *Athenaeum, 22* (November), 204–6.

———. (1924). Children's drawings. *Burlington Magazine, 44* (January), 35–41.

———. (1933). Children's drawings at the County Hall. *New Statesman and Nation, 24* (June), 844–45.

Macdonald, S. (1970). *The history and philosophy of art education.* London: London University Press.

Read, H. (1933). *Art now.* London: Faber.

———(Ed.). (1936). *Surrealism.* London: Faber.

———. (1937). *Art and society.* London: Heinemann.

———. (1943). *Education through art.* London: Faber.

———. (1944). *The education of free men.* London: Freedom Press.

———. (1945). *Art and society* (2d ed.). London: Faber.

———. (1948). *Culture and education in a world order.* New York: Museum of Modern Art.

———. (1952). *The philosophy of modern art.* London: Faber.

———. (1955). *The grass roots of art.* London: Faber.

———. (1970). *Redemption of the robot.* London: Faber.

Richardson, M. (1948). *Art and the child.* London: London University Press.

Suttie, I. D. (1935). *The origins of love and hate*. London: London University Press.

Thompson, D. W. (1942). *On growth and form* (new edition). Cambridge: Cambridge University Press.

10. The Child Study Movement and Its Effects on Hungarian Art Education

Báthory, Z. (1992). Hungarian experiences in international student achievement surveys. *Prospects, 22* (4), 434–40.

Beke, L. (1986). *Műalkotások elemzése* (Analysis of works of art). Tankönyvkiadó: Budapest. Textbook for secondary grammar school art education, grades 1–3, age groups 15–17.

Die Kunst im Leben des Kindes. (1901). Catalogue of the exhibition. Berlin: Secession.

Götze, C. (1987). *Zur Reform des Zeichnenunterrichts. Heft 1* (On the Reform of Drawing Education. Part 1). Hamburg: Lehrervereinigung für die Pflege der künstlerischen Bildung.

Hollós, K. (1929). *Öt világrész rajzoktatása, irányelvek szerint csoportosítva* (Art education all over the world: Models based on educational goals and objectives). Budapest: Attila Press.

Kárpáti, A. (1985). Towards an iconography of children's motifs, signs and symbols. The messages of a 75-year-old visual diary. In H. Hoffa & B. Wilson (Eds.), *The history of art education*. University Park: Pennsylvania State University, pp. 185–91.

———. (1987). Based on the disciplines. Research and practice in contemporary Hungarian art education. *Canadian Review of Aesthetic Education, 15* (1), 35–40.

———. (1990). A mensagem do passado. In A. M. Barbosa-Heloisa & M. Sales (Eds.), *O ensino da arte e sua história*. São Paulo: Universidade de São Paulo, pp. 81–95.

———. (1995). Assessment of art educarion in Hungary: Historical problems in contemporary perspective. *Journal of Art and Design Education, 14* (3), 277–88.

———. (1995). Arts education in post-communist Hungary: Policies, curricula and integration. *Arts Education Policy Review, 97* (1), 11–17.

———. (1996). From post-communism to pre-capitalism—Hungary's dilemmas of changing paradigms for art and education. A keynote address of the INSEA World Congress. In M. Briére (Ed.), *Proceedings of the INSEA World Congress, Montreal, 1993*. Montreal: University of Montreal, pp. 38–46.

Kárpáti, A., & Gaul, E. (1990). Art and technology in Hungarian art education: Conflicts and compromises. *Leonardo Magazine, 23 (*2), 189–96.

——. (1994). Umweltgestaltung in Kunsteriehung und Werkunterricht in Ungarn. In K. Dörhöfer (Hrsg.), *Wohnkultur und plattenbau. beispiele aus Berlin und Budapest.* Berlin: Dietrich Reimer, pp. 139–54.

——. (1997). Episodes from the social history of Hungarian art education from an international perspective. Submitted for consideration to the *Proceedings of the Penn State History of Art Education Symposium, October 1995.* University Park: Pennsylvania State University.

Korosi, L. (1930). *A rajztanitas modszerei.* Budapest: Singer.

Közoktatási reformtervezet (Reform Plan for Public Education). (1918). Budapest: Hungarian Society for the Study of the Child.

Menzen, K. (1982). *Eine Erziehungsgeschichte der Ästhetik.* Weinheim and Basel: Beltz.

Nagy, L. (1905). *Fejezetek a gyermekrajzok lélektanából* (Chapters from the psychology of children's drawings). Budapest: Singer és Wolfner.

——. (1921). *Didaktika gyermekfejlôdési alapon* (Didactics based on the development of the child). Budapest: Ministry of Education.

Szebenyi, P. (1992). Two models of curriculum development in Hungary (1972–1992). *Educational Review, 44* (3), 285–94.

Tirpák, S. (1927). Mit rajzolunk az idén? Rajzminták a normál tanmenethez as elemi iskolák IV. osztálya számára (What do we draw this year? Models for teaching the basic curriculum in the 4th grade of elementary school). Budapest: Szent István Társulat.

11. Rationales for Art Education in Chilean Schools

Errázuriz, L. (1985). *100 años de educación artística en Chile* (One hundred years of art education in Chile). DIUC 100/83. Chile: Universidad Católica de Chile.

Conclusion

Barbosa, A. M. (1990). Art education in Brazil: Reality today and future expectations. *Visual Arts Research, 16* (2), 79–88.

Baudrillard, J. (1983). *Simulations.* New York: Semiotext(e).

Bourdieu, P. (1965). Intellectual field and creative project. *Social Science Information, 8,* 89–119.

———. (1985). The genesis of the concepts of *habitus* and of *field*. *Sociocriticism, 2,* 11–24.

———. (1993). *The field of cultural production: Essays on art and literature.* Edited by R. Johnson. New York: Columbia University Press.

Bruner, J. (1960). *The process of education.* Cambridge, Mass.: Harvard University Press.

Clifford, J. (1988). *The predicament of culture: Twentieth-century ethnography, literature, and art.* Cambridge, Mass.: Harvard University Press.

Cremin, L. A. (1961). *The transformation of the school: Progressivism in American education, 1976–1957.* New York: Vintage Books.

Efland, A. (1976). The school art style: A functional analysis. *Studies in Art Education, 17* (2), 17–43.

Efland, A., Freedman, K., & Stuhr, P. (1996). *Postmodern art education: An approach to curriculum.* Reston, Va.: National Art Education Association.

Eisner, E. W. (1994). *Cognition and curriculum, reconsidered* (2d ed.). New York: Teachers College Press.

Foucault, M. (1966/1970). *The order of things: An archaeology of the human sciences.* New York: Vintage Books.

Freedman, K. (1995). Educational change within structures of history, culture, and discourse. In R. W. Neperud (Ed.), *Context, content, and community in art education: Beyond postmodernism,* pp. 87–108. New York: Teachers College Press.

Giddens, A. (1987). *Social theory and modern sociology.* Stanford, Calif.: Stanford University Press.

Harvey, D. (1989). *The condition of postmodernity: An enquiry into the origins of cultural change.* Oxford: Basil Blackwell.

Kliebard, H. M. (1987). *The struggle for the American curriculum, 1893–1958.* New York: Routledge & Kegan Paul.

Lacan, J. (1977). *Ecrits.* New York: Norton.

Lyotard, J-F. (1983). Regles et paradoxes et appendice svelte. *Babalone 1,* 67–80. Reprinted as Rules and paradoxes and svelte appendix, trans. by B. Massumi, in *Cultural Critique,* 1986–87, *5* (Winter), 209–19.

———. (1984). *The postmodern condition: A report on knowledge.* Translated by G. Bennington & B. Massumi. Minneapolis: University of Minnesota Press.

About the Contributors

DOUGLAS BOUGHTON is a professor of art education in the School of Education at the University of South Australia in Underdale. His research interests include student assessment, program evaluation, and international education. As well as publishing widely, he is the world chief examiner in art and design for the International Baccalaureate Organization, a vice-president of the International Society for Education through Art, and has won the *Studies in Art Education* Lecture Award for excellence in research. He has recently published a co-edited book, *Evaluating and Assessing the Visual Arts in Education: International Perspectives.*

GRAEME CHALMERS is a professor of art education in the Department of Curriculum Studies at the University of British Columbia in Vancouver. He has widely published in journals and books, including authoring a recent book on multicultural art education. His research interests range from histories of art education, particularly the influence of South Kensington, to contemporary issues in art education from a sociocultural perspective. He is currently editor of *Studies in Art Education*, a past vice-president of the International Society for Education through Art, a National Art Education Association Distinguished Fellow and has received INSEA's Ziegfeld Award.

KHALID EL BEKAY is an artist and master of fine arts at the University of Barcelona. He has held several exhibitions in his native country of Morocco and in Spain, particularly in Catalonia where he now lives. He has collaborated on multicultural curriculum projects with primary school groups.

LUIS ERRÁZURIZ is a lecturer and researcher in the Aesthetic Institute of the Catholic University of Chile in Santiago. His research interests include history of art education, aesthetic education, and the relationship between art and society. He has published and presented several papers focusing on the conditions of Chilean art education.

LUCIMAR BELLO PEREIRA FRANGE is an artist and professor of art at the Federal University of Uberlândia, Minas Gerais. She has had many exhibitions of her art in her native country of Brazil and participated in international exhibitions in Japan, Spain, Chile, and Argentina. She has won several awards for her work, including a scholarship from the VITAE Foundation in 1994.

KERRY FREEDMAN is an associate professor of art education and curriculum studies in the Department of Curriculum and Instruction at the University of Minnesota in Minneapolis. Her research focuses on questions concerning student responses to visual imagery, technological influences on images and audiences, and the relationship of curriculum to culture. She has authored many journal articles, book chapters, and other publications on art education, including co-authoring the book, *Postmodern Art Education: An Approach to Curriculum*.

EMIL GAUL is director of the Institute of Education at the Hungarian Academy of Craft and Design in Budapest. He has written books and television scenarios for primary schools focusing on design education and launched nationwide student design competitions. He has taken part in several national and international projects, including the development of the *Hungarian National Core Curriculum* and the *Dutch-Hungarian Art and Design Certificate of Education*.

FERNANDO HERNÁNDEZ is an associate professor of art education on the Fine Arts Faculty of the University of Barcelona. His research focuses on questions concerning the process of understanding visual culture and the relationships between school innovations, teacher education, and new technologies, particularly multimedia. He has authored many journal articles and other publications, including co-authoring the books *Knowing the Subject is Not Enough When Teaching*; *What Does Art Education Mean?*; *Curriculum Organization through Thematic Projects*; *Encounters with Art from Anthropology*; and *Psychology and Pedagogy*.

YASUHIKO ISOZAKI is professor of history of art education in the Department of Education at Fukushima University. He has authored many journal articles and other publications on Japanese art education.

ANDREA KÁRPÁTI is an associate professor in the Department of Education at Eötvös Loránd University and deputy head of the Institute for Teacher Training at the Hungarian Academy of Crafts and Design. Her publications include books, articles, and book chapters on the development of creative and perceptive skills, teaching art criticism, and historical and international trends in art education. She is co-editor of *Expression of Anxiety in Child Art* and *Aesthetic Education in Hungary*. She is currently a vice-president of the International Society for Education through Art and has participated in several national and international projects.

STEN-GOSTA KARLSSON is on the faculty of the Department of Teacher Training at Uppsala University. His research interests include art education methods and visual communication. He has co-authored *Art and Form*; *The Foundation of Visual Literacy*; and *Space, Relation, and Rhetoric: A Project about the Theory of Images and Analysis in Postmodern Society*.

STAFFAN LOVGREN is on the faculty of the Department of Teacher Training at Uppsala University. His research interests include methods of art education, interpretation and semiotics, and new media. He has co-authored *Images of Time: Perspectives on School and Art Education Over 150 Years*; *Space, Relation, and Rhetoric: A Project about the Theory of Images and Analysis in Postmodern Society*; and numerous articles.

JORDI PINTÓ is master of fine arts at the University of Barcelona. His main area of interest is multiculturalism and art education, particularly in the schools of Catalonia where children attend from different cultural traditions.

DAVID THISTLEWOOD is professor in history of art at the University of Liverpool. His research interests include the histriography of twentieth-century Western art. He is past president of the British National Association for Education in Art and Design, former editor of the *Journal of Art and Design Education*, and current editor of the Liverpool Tate Gallery *Critical Forum Series*. He has published extensively on Herbert Read, including the biography *Herbert Read: Formlessness and Form*, and edited *American Abstract Expressionism*; *Joseph Beuys: Diverging Critiques*; *Barbara Hepworth: Reconsidered*; and *Sigmar Polke: Back to Postmodernity*.

Name Index

Subject Index